Convenient or Invasive:

The Information Age

Adam Barreras	Amit Mathur
Justin Blincoe	Jessica McKnight
Brittany Burgess	Brent McRae
Madison Buske	Brett Mencin
Matthew Collett	Kimberly Miller
Christopher Cook	Kyle Momii
Alexa Cowen	Steve Monahan
Eric Dawson	Steven Moulton
Joy Eagle	Ryan Murray
Krista Fox	Minji Park
Jacob Fuller	Sejal Patel
Kelsey Good	Travis Rabi
Mari Gottlieb	Amanda Rick
Lauren Griffin	Jarret Roberts
Lindsey Gross	Danielle Shea
Anna Kaufman	Jamie Stoll
Nicole Kennedy	Caroline Sweeney
Ji Hye Kim	Thomas Van De Bogart
Valerie Kirby	Kim Ward
Blair Krause	Ben Weinbaum
Morgan MacBaisey	Yael Wolf
Matt Macko	Drew Woodcock

Editorial Committee:
Brittany Burgess, Krista Fox, Kelsey Good, Mari Gottlieb, Anna
Kaufman, Nicole Kennedy, Matt Macko, Jessica McKnight, Steve
Monahan, Amanda Rick, Thomas Van De Bogart, Drew
Woodcock

Formatting Committee:
Sejal Patel and Brent McRae

Cover Design:
Valerie Kirby

Editors:
Kai R. Larsen
Zoya A. Voronovich

ETHICA PUBLISHING
Boulder, Colorado

i

FIRST EDITION, MAY 2007

Copyright © 2007 by Ethica Publishing

All rights reserved under International and Pan-American Copyright Conventions. Published in the United States by Ethica Publishing.

Library of Congress Cataloging-in-Publication Data
Convenient or Invasive: The Information Age/ Kai. R. Larsen
and Zoya A. Voronovich. (editors) – 1st ed.
ISBN 0-9764284-3-1
1. Social Sciences – Business Ethics
Typeface: Palantino Linotype

TABLE OF CONTENTS

ACKNOWLEDGEMENTS

The authors and editors of this book would like to express their gratitude and thanks to the

for their aid in the funding of this text, and their commitment to helping Colorado business students achieve success.

Further, we would like to thank Anne Bliss for all her help with the process of writing the book as well as her guest lecture that started us out on the right foot. Other guest-lecturers also helped with different aspects of research for the book: Carol Krismann (libraries), Jay Ballantine (Leeds School), Paul Ohm (School of Law), Gerhard Eschelbeck (CIO, Webroot).

PREFACE

A 1998 Carnegie Foundation report suggested that large research universities should improve undergraduate education through large-scale participation of undergraduates in the universities' research mission. This book is an example of putting the Carnegie suggestion into practice, and it was borne out of the belief that research universities can add unique elements to student education. As a highly ranked research university, the University of Colorado at Boulder has top-notch students with research abilities that should be tapped more often. By learning how to conduct research and by carrying it out, students improve their critical thinking abilities and develop other skills that carry over to all other aspects of their future professional life.

Three years ago, when the book *Technology and Privacy in the New Millennium* was published, it seemed unlikely that an equally pensive and interesting book on the topic of privacy would see the light of day. With the 2007 release of *Convenient or Invasive: The Information Age,* Leeds School students have once again demonstrated their ability to write and edit a major work of research in less than a semester. The writing level and the quality of the editing of this year's authors are superb, showcasing the quality of Leeds School graduating undergraduates. Some of these undergraduate students are already on par with graduating Ph.D. students. Most importantly, the students have improved greatly in both areas over the course of the semester.

After considering the content of the book, the students decided to focus the title on privacy invasion and convenience, two factors at the core of many of today's technologies. In this book, we define privacy as *an individual or entity's ability to control personal information.* Convenience is defined as *any method, opportunity, or object that simplifies a process; something that makes life easier.*

Perhaps more than anything, as the facilitator for this book, I have learned much from working with these dedicated and intelligent students. Throughout this process of helping students find the inspiration to write their own textbook, several goals have been at the forefront:

1. Expose students to cutting-edge materials
2. Challenge students intellectually
3. Involve students in actual research
4. Instill enthusiasm for scholarship

While goals 1-3 were clearly reached; only time will tell whether goal number four was reached. It is hoped that the combination of knowledge gained from researching and writing this book will combine with the increased focus on privacy in the media to develop further interest in scholarship.

In fact, just days before the chapters for this book were due in their final version, *The Wall Street Journal* broke a major story about the privacy of Wal-Mart employees and partners. In what can best be described as a truly Orwellian setup, Wal-Mart security staff routinely read employee emails on the Wal-Mart email system as well as their private email on such systems as Hotmail and GMail, monitored employee telephone and computer use as well as computer use of employees of partner organizations, while banning use of alternative modes of communication, such as personal cell-phones. Nothing in the story came as a surprise to the chapter authors of this book, as each individual chapter detailed a piece of the societal trend of giving up privacy for convenience. However, as the Wal-Mart example aptly demonstrated, often citizens and employees have no choice in whether to give up their privacy.

For anyone reading Orwell's *1984*, perhaps the biggest surprise is the technological simplicity of the government surveillance techniques. Only a few citizens could be monitored through their TVs at the same time, and behavior was modified through the fear of being monitored. Today, almost anything we do can be and is being monitored, including our online hobbies and real-life friends, the places we visit and when we visit that location (through our cell phones and GPS technology), what we talk about in the privacy of our own homes and vehicles (through the microphones on computers and onboard navigation systems), and even what we think (through monitoring of the brain's p300 responses). In the year of 1984, the general consensus was that Orwell had incorrectly predicted the technological sophistication that 36 years could bring. Today, close to 60 years after Orwell wrote his book, we are far beyond any technology Orwell imagined, and we are living with today's technology permeating our lives.

I

PERSONAL INFORMATION PRIVACY

1

Campus Invasion: Security Breaches and Their Trends in Universities Across the U.S.
Christopher Cook & Morgan MacBaisey

Introduction

As a current or alumni university student, you may or may not know how much personal information the school has on file about you. You also may not realize how vulnerable this information is to theft and hacking. How would you feel if you received a letter or e-mail stating the following?

"A new case of unauthorized computer access has been identified at the University...The potentially exposed information includes about 49,000 database entries on a server containing ancillary information used by the Registrar's Office. The information dates from June 1999 to May 2001 and from fall 2003 to summer 2005...the University is notifying individuals of potential identity theft so they may take precautions. Sensitive information that may have been accessed includes: Social Security numbers, names, permanent addresses and phone numbers" (Boulder).

Every college student across the U.S. has the potential to receive a similar letter at any point in their college career and even after graduation. Krista, a student at the University of Colorado at Boulder, was studying abroad one semester when both she and her mother, a CU alumni, received letters containing the previous information. With her daughter abroad, Krista's mother thought nothing of it. Many months later, Krista received a letter from a credit card company notifying her of potential fraudulent activity present on her account. There was worse news to come: Krista did not even have an account with the credit card company that sent her the notification. The address they had on file for her was wrong. It was actually an address on the other side of the country where Krista had never resided. At the time she received the information from the credit card company, Krista had forgotten about the letter she had received from the University of Colorado. Krista ordered credit reports to verify the damage to her credit. She subsequently noticed that there was a correlation to when her school information was stolen and when the credit card account was fraudulently set up in her name.

An interview with the University of Colorado Records Department revealed that personal student information such as telephone numbers, e-mail addresses, social security numbers (SSNs) and physical addresses are stored on file for an unlimited amount of time. Many schools also store their students' medical records. It was mentioned that no one could get this information without proper access. The truth is that this information is accessible. This being said, it is possible that you may receive a letter, like the one above, years after you graduate and have moved on with your life. One may think this information is harmless if obtained, but there is a potential for extensive identity theft as a result of a campus information security breach.

Data loss has occurred for centuries. To demonstrate the lack of privacy and security at universities and the severity thereof, consider the following incident. In the article "Social Security Numbers Exposed in CCSU Letters," "approximately 750 CCSU [Central Connecticut State University] students have received mail from the Bursar's office that revealed their SSN's in the name and address window of the envelopes" (Attrition). Surprisingly, this egregious mistake occurred on February 7, 2007. It would seem as though Universities would be more careful in protecting their databases in 2007, considering the growing prevalence of identity theft over the preceding years. This chapter will examine trends with regards to university information privacy across the U.S., student opinions and knowledge of data theft and information privacy, as well as a discussion of worst-case scenarios, and the role of the media.

Trends Across the Country

Out of the hundreds of universities in the U.S., a recorded 177 schools have had one or more instances of security breaches in the last two and half years. Information about students, faculty and alumni was illegally stolen or accidentally released. This information included everything from a person's social security number (SSN) to their semester class schedule. As an increasing number of universities with security breaches were discovered, trends began to emerge in terms of public versus private universities, the location of the schools themselves and the methods of the breaches.

A complete chronology of data breaches of universities across the country has been documented on the Privacy Rights Clearinghouse (PRC) website. The PRC details each breach by when it happened, the number of people affected, and exactly how the information was stolen.

We used the information from the PRC to examine the different trends with regards to security breaches. Our analysis used a simple random sample of 50 schools from 2005 through March 2007. The average number of people affected by each breach was 41,780. Some schools did not release the number of people affected or simply stated "tens of thousands" of people. As an example, the University of Southern California, ranked number one, with 320,000 people put at risk. At times, the number of affected individuals from any single breach can be much larger then the current student body. This is because the number of individuals affected includes past students, faculty, alumni, and even perspective students who have applied to the University.

One of the first trends found was the number of schools breached over the past two and a half years. Our research clearly indicates an increase in the total number of schools experiencing security breaches yearly. This increase is attributed to the constant advances in technology, as well as the increasing volume of personal information stored on line and web accessible files (such as online databases). Historically, a select few possessed the skills and knowledge to successfully hack and steal information. However, in recent years, the necessary skills have become more prevalent, and the essential technologies became widely available. Through the analysis and collection of secondary data, the graph below demonstrates the trend of security breaches per month.

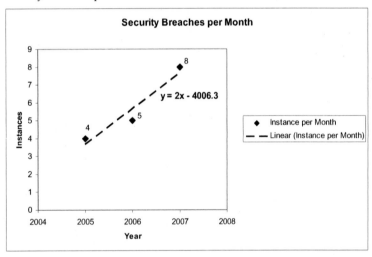

As you can see from the equation of the trend line, every year the rate is increasing by two breaches per month. From this information, we can estimate that in 10 years, the monthly security breach rate will increase to 28 separate instances of information loss per month from schools across the country. That translates into millions of people's private/personal information in the hands of the wrong people.

Hacking

People find interesting ways of getting a hold of people's information stored on university property and databases. This ranges from simply stealing a professor's laptop to actually creating programs to hack into a schools' computer system. Either way, information is being stolen and made available for a variety of negative uses, which can lead to identity theft.

Also analyzed for trends was the culprit, or who was stealing the private information. Out of the sample of 50 schools, the statistics on how the information was lost as well as who actually committed the crime is listed below.

Method of Breach

Percent of Schools Affected by Hacking	84%
Percent of School Affected by Internal Errors	16%
Culprit	
Number of Schools Affected by Insiders	20%
Number of Schools Affected by Outsiders	54%
Unknown	26%

Of the 50 schools, 84% fell victim to hacking. It is important to note that this method of breach includes, but is not limited to physical computer theft. This is not surprising due to the ease and anonymity of hacking. Looking at the culprit statistics from the sample, 54% and 20% of schools were affected by outsiders and insiders respectively. In June 2006, at the University of Texas in El Paso, "students demonstrated that the student body and faculty elections could be rigged by hacking into student information (databases) including SSN's" (Data Breaches). This illustrates the ease at which people can gain access to private information. There is significant motivation for individuals to want access to information stored on university databases. This motivation ranges from money gained through stolen identities, to popularity and power achieved by rigging elections. At the University of Texas in El Paso, 4,719 students and university personnel were put at risk for identity theft from this simple demonstration.

In another example, at the University of Colorado at Boulder, "two computers had been placed in storage during the school's move to temporary quarters in May. When they were to be retrieved August 28, they were found missing. They had been used by two faculty members and included students' names, SSNs, and grades" (Data Breaches). It does not take knowledge of computers to steal information. It is a matter of being in the right place at the right time.

There have also been occurrences of schools accidentally posting confidential student information on their website. This recently happened in March 2007 at the University of Idaho where "a data file posted to the school's Web site contained personal information including names, birthdates and SSN's of University employees" (Data Breaches). Because of the school's error, 2,700 people were put at risk for identity theft. Another recent mistake occurred at the Los Rios Community College in Northern California where "student information, including SSN's, were accessible on the Internet after the school used actual data to test a new online application process in October" (Data Breaches). At least 2,000 individuals were put at risk.

Not only are hackers getting access to people's SSN's, but in some cases they are gaining access to credit card information as well. At East Carolina University, "a programming error resulted in personal information of 65,000 individuals being exposed on the University's Web site. The data has since been removed. Included were names, addresses, SSNs, and in some cases credit card numbers" (Data Breaches). Incidents like this put university members, many times unknowingly, one step closer to having their identity stolen. Our research indicates that personal information is at risk from not only outsiders, but also the threat lies within the university itself where many would not expect.

Public versus Private

It was found that 64% of the schools breached were public Universities. We hypothesize that this is due to the greater number of students (student body and staff) at public schools. In other words, hackers have a greater pool from which to potentially steal valuable information. Private schools experienced a lesser percentage of breaches, but this does not mean the loss of information was any less detrimental to the affected individuals.

An alternative hypothesis for this result is that private schools may not be subject to the same requirements and standards as public universities. This may lead to skewed statistics. The truth may be that private schools do in fact have a higher percentage of breaches, but they are not requited to make the instance public, containing the knowledge of the breach. This is exactly the problem that needs to be addressed in public and student policy.

East Versus West

It was interesting to see that more West Coast schools were experiencing instances of information breaches. Analysis indicated that 64% of our sample was located on the West Coast—leaving only 36% of instances on the East Coast. (Note: we divided the country in half and did not include a third category for the central U.S.) When students are faced with the decision of which side of the country to attend college, many factors are taken into consideration. These may range from climate difference to the distance from home. According to our research, students may want to ask themselves one last question: "Am I willing to take on greater risk of information loss by attending a West Coast school?

Student Survey Information

By analyzing the frequency, location, and trends of security breaches across the U.S., it is apparent that data theft is rampant. Not many students have the luxury of knowing their information is actually at risk before their information is stolen. Unfortunately, students must be aware of the risk in advance to be able to take the necessary precautions for protection. It takes awareness and motivation on the part of the individual alone because in many cases, no one is going to explicitly tell someone that their information is at risk.

According to the Identity Theft Resource Center (ITRC), "college students are easy targets for identity thieves because it takes the average student longer to discover the fraud. In a recent report, almost 90% of student victims were unaware of their compromised identity for several months" (CU Identity Theft). Having access to students across the country through family, friends and online social networks, a survey of past and current university students was conducted to examine the awareness and knowledge with regards to various topics related to information safety and privacy at universities.

The survey was created using surveymonkey.com, an online data analysis company. This company allows users to create a free ten-question survey and provides the user a web link for the pseudo webpage containing the survey. This hyperlink can be sent to any individual with access to the Internet. By clicking on the link, respondents are redirected to the requested survey. Our survey contained ten questions, ranging from "yes or no" questions to individual "short-answer" responses. 75 surveys were returned by individuals for our analysis. The survey was sent to a random sample of individuals across the U.S. and allowed for generalizations to be made that encompass students attending private, public, and East / West Coast schools. This is an important aspect of the analysis because bias and area specifics wanted to be minimized. Below are a few examples of our most telling survey questions and their corresponding statistics. (Note: all surveys were anonymous.)

First, respondents were asked whether they were currently attending a university followed by how many years they have been enrolled. Out of the 75 respondents, 80% are currently enrolled in school. There are 48.6% in their fourth year, 15% had been enrolled for less than one and 15.4% had been students for more than four years.

The next question asked if they had been aware of any security breaches where their private information could have been compromised. Surprisingly, only 37% said yes. They were then presented with this question:

"Have you ever received a letter/e-mail containing information similar to the following: A new case of unauthorized computer access has been identified at Your School. The potentially exposed information includes about 49,000 database entries on a server containing ancillary information used by the Registrar's Office. The new incident creates a potential identity theft problem for former students and some current students. Sensitive information that may have been accessed includes social security numbers, names, permanent addresses and phone numbers.'"

Of the respondents, 37% (as above) said that they had received a similar notification. Interestingly, 15.1% responded, "maybe, I do not remember." Out of 75 people 12 do not even remember if their information was potentially stolen. Recall, from the section above, the average university population affected by each security breach is 41,780. Now realize that that equals a potential 6,267 individuals who do not remember if their information was compromised. This number is daunting when put into context of total security breaches per month.

Our survey indicates that 88.1% of students that received the notification did not take any of the suggested precautions detailed in the letter. Precautions include contacting the three major credit bureaus (Equifax, Transunion, and Experian) and putting an identity theft fraud alert on your file. A fraud alert stops new offers of credit to be extended for up to seven years and increases awareness on your account. However, "this is an advisory statement and has been found to be only partially effective" (Reporting). A more comprehensive and effective recourse is to get a "credit freeze in states that have passed that legislation" (Reporting). A credit freeze requires authentication from the individual to make any modification, however small, to the account. There are precautions and steps for individuals to take to limit their risk. However, many college students have a very trusting and naive attitude when it comes to the security of their private information stored with universities.

Respondents were asked to indicate which of the following personal information they think there school has on file about them. The following list was presented: social security number, telephone numbers, gender, permanent address, local address, medical records, marital status, information about your family, financial information. 98.6% said they know the school has their social security number, telephone number, gender, and permanent address on file. Only 56.2% of our respondents knew that the schools have their medical records on file. 83.6% said they had financial information, 76.7% said they had information about their family on file. Schools actually have information on students ranging from address, social security number, medical history, and in case of students that use financial aid, your financial information.

Individuals were then asked to rate on a scale of one to five, how at risk they felt their personal/private information was at their university with five being extremely vulnerable. Of the respondents, 63% answered between zero and two, indicating they felt their information was either not at risk or low risk. Furthermore, 45.2% of respondents felt that it was solely the universities' responsibility to protect their private information held by the school. Students need to realize that they no longer can put the security of their personal identity in the hand of some of the most accredited institutions in the country. Even though there is no realistic way that a student can protect information held by the university, they must realize that constant vigil must be taken to make sure that if their information is compromised, they are aware and can take remedial action. This includes checking your credit report. 54.8% of respondents said it was the responsibility of both the individual and the university to protect their information. This idea is more realistic.

The last question asked of the respondents was how they would feel if their personal information were stolen from their university by a hacker. The responses to this question varied. One individual said "I guess I wouldn't be surprised. The student database has been hacked before and it will probably get hacked again. If I knew my information had been accessed, I would review my credit reports and update as many of my credit accounts as possible." This individual was one of the respondents that have received one of the security alert letters in the past, but who have also read what to do in case of a breach. It is alarming that he/she said they would "not be surprised." Today, the majority of students are desensitized to the severity and importance of their private information. By the time they have filled out their college applications students may have potentially printed their social security number on over 20 pieces of paper. One respondent said they would be "shocked," but that there was "realistically probably nothing [he/she] could do. [And] unfortunately those things happen." There are steps these students can take to prevent and protect themselves. As our research indicates, many students are either unaware of their options or have come to accept the fact that their information will be stolen. This is the wrong attitude to move into the 21st century.

Humans tend be oblivious, or ignore the severity of any situation unless they are obviously negatively impacted. Having your information lost by the school is a direct negative impact, but as our research shows, this is not enough of a threat for many students to feel at risk. In turn, appropriate action is not taken. Until actual identity theft and financial damage occurs to more students from these security breaches, it is unlikely that we will see a change in attitude. One respondent proved this exact point. They said they would feel "frightened" if their information was stolen and that they would "have to go through and cancel credit cards and would constantly be afraid, and on the look out for identity theft in the future." Students need to be "on the lookout" for identity theft now and prevention is the only real protection.

Worst Case Scenarios

With peoples' information at risk on campuses across the country, there are many examples of worst-case scenarios where identities have been stolen. These people can not directly prove their identity was stolen due to the hacked information at their school, but there was an interesting correlation in the timing of events in all cases.

As previously mentioned, at the beginning of this chapter, Krista had her identity stolen right after her private information stored on university computers was stolen by a hacker. Her credit scores are now lower and she has had to place a security alert on all of her accounts. Krista lives in fear of future financial damage and identity theft due to a single security breach at her university.

In a similar case at the University of California at Los Angeles (UCLA), the school discovered that someone had been hacking into their schools databases for an unspecified amount of time and about 40,000 people were at risk. Although the school downplayed the threat and told potential victims that "there was no indication the information had been misused," one student at UCLA also had their identity stolen (Breach Effect 1). He said, "I can't prove my identity was stolen from this UCLA break-in, but it certainly is quite a coincidence" (Breach Effect 1).

Schools Starting to Take Notice

Due to some of these "coincidences" schools are finally realizing they have to be more vigilant in protecting student information. Many schools are no longer using SSN's as student identification numbers and, in one case at California State Fullerton, the school no longer "keeps alumni information in its student database" (Breach Effect 1).

A recent policy was adopted by the University of Minnesota after three different incidences of breaches took place. It states, "the University shall provide timely and appropriate notice to affected individuals when there has been a breach of security of private data about them" (Reporting). It goes on to define what exactly they mean by a breach in security, "a breach in security occurs when there is an unauthorized acquisition of private information maintained in any form by the University" (Reporting). This simple regulation, however minimal, allows the plaintiff to at least be notified of the breach so they can take remedial action. Before this regulation, it was not explicitly stated that a university must inform affected students of breaches. This, for now, is the best the school system has to offer. Unfortunately, it offers little in terms of protection; the focus right now is prevention and the minimization of damages.

Media's Role

When thinking about breaches in university's security and information loss, one probably does not think about how the media plays a role. The media brings light of the situation to the public, beyond just the university students. "The media frenzy surrounding each security breach has helped put consumers and merchants alike on the alert; once notified, many victims quickly get on the horn with their bank and credit-card company" (ID Theft 35). The media's role has increased over time and helps to raise awareness about the importance and volatility of private information. As seen from the survey, most students do not even realize how serious these incidents are and so the media is playing its part in prevention. By publishing or broadcasting articles and stories about breaches, the media helps to bring knowledge and awareness to students.

Conclusion

Every year, thousands of students send applications to colleges across America and trustingly place their private information in the seemingly secure hands of universities. These applications and student files contain personal information, such as SSN's and credit card information, that if obtained by the wrong people could have a devastating affect on their lives. Our research was conducted in attempts to gain knowledge and identify trends across the country with regards to university student information privacy. By conducting surveys of students and faculty, as well as studies on actual university information security breaches, it has become apparent that there are indeed countrywide trends regarding information security. It was found that West Coast schools and public institutions have a higher percentage of security breaches than East Coast and private schools. The frequency of breaches is increasing at a daunting rate of two schools per month, and the average breach affects 41,780 individuals.

Many universities are lackadaisical and relatively passive with their approaches to information security. A majority of students feel their information is safe in the hands of their university when in reality it is at risk. Many students do not feel or are unaware that there are steps they can take to reduce their risk of possible identity theft if their information is, in fact, stolen. These misconceptions must be corrected. Universities need to work with the students to find ways to better ensure the safety of personal information they store on file. With advancement in technology and the skills of hackers greatly increasing, universities need to minimize avoidable internal errors that put students at an unnecessary risk. As mentioned before, it needs to be a collaborative effort. Students need to head the breach notifications that schools send out, as well as take the preventative measures outlined. Unfortunately this is an evolving and growing problem where complete protection is not possible. Minimizing risk is the only alternative.

Works Cited

Attrition. 2007. Feb 14, 2007. <http://attrition.org>.
Boulder. 2007. University of Colorado. 14 February, 2007. <http://www.colorado.edu>.
CU Identity Theft. 2007. University of Colorado at Boulder. 13 March 2007. <http://www. colorado.edu/its/security/awareness/privacy/>.
Data Breaches. 2007. Privacy Rights Clearing House. March 2007. <http://www.privacyrights. org/ar/ChronDataBreaches.htm>.
Foust, Dean and Ryst, Sonja. 2007. ID Theft: More Hype then Harm. Business Week; July 2006 Issue 3991, p34-36. <http://businesssourcepremier.com>.
IDRC. 2007. Identity Theft Recourse Center. 13 March 2007. <http://www.idtheftcenter.org/ vg100.shtml>.
Reporting and Notifying Individuals of Security Breaches. 2007. Reporting. 13 March 2007. <http://process.umn.edu/groups/ppd/ documents/policy/securitybreach_pol.cfm#100>.
Wolfe, Daniel. Breach Effect. 2007. American Banker. January 2007, Vol. 172 Issue 9. <http://businesssourcepremier.com>.

2

Is Banking Online a Safe Alternative to the Old Fashioned Paper and Pen?

Jamie Stoll & Matthew Collett

Introduction

The newest form of identity theft is known as account hijacking, i.e. unauthorized access to a given account. Whether the successful break-in occurred from information gathered online or from personal documents that did not get shredded. Account hijacking can be accomplished in a number of ways: retrieving hard-copy documents, luring consumers into giving up usernames and passwords, loading malicious software onto public or private computers, and via the most familiar method: hacking. Regardless of method, account hijacking is the fastest growing type of consumer fraud. "In 2003, 10 million Americans discovered they were victims of identity theft with a total cost approaching $50 billion" (Putting). The ease of break-ins is partly a result of weak yet accepted security: "Our current culture, where identity is verified simply and sloppily, makes it easier for a criminal to impersonate his victim" (Schneier). Online banking has become an easy target for account hijacking, with valuable information just waiting to be stolen. How safe is online banking and what is being done to protect this personal information?

Background

Giving up privacy in order to conduct more efficient and timely financial transactions can pose a big security risk, yet many Americans still choose to do so everyday. With the click of a button, purchases made within the last day, week or even earlier can be displayed. What prevents a hacker from stealing that information or a malicious program from saving and downloading it elsewhere? Financial institutions have implemented several consumer security measures to reassure their customers of the safety of online banking. These include encrypted numbers and letters that have to be entered to gain access to a site and a lock icon indicated a trusted and secure site. Although these security measures may appear to be sufficient at first glance, they are being sabotaged and exploited by account hijackers using methods of their own.

Phishing

Phishing can come in the form of an e-mail or fake website, asking for personal information such as name, address, social security number, age and even account numbers and passwords. Once this information is obtained by the phisher, it can be used for opening new credit card accounts, obtaining car and home loans, and even buying real estate. Most, if not all, large financial institutions and electronic bill-paying services (such as PayPal) have been subject to phishing attacks (Putting). This topic is covered in greater detail in a later chapter.

Hacking

Financial institutions are frequently targeted by hackers because they contain valuable information about their customers. Fraudsters hack into financial institutions' databases or service provider systems to steal confidential customer information to use at their discretion (Putting). Many people believe that their financial institution has strict laws and policies regarding security, but, realistically, the development and implementation of most security and protection programs is the responsibility of the individual company. The federal Gramm-Leach-Bliley Act, or GLB, only provides minimal requirements to protect your financial information, and in the end these regulations are actually guidelines rather than strict rules for compliance (Is).

Hard-copy Documents or Looking Over Someone's Shoulder

Forgetting to shred physical personal documents can lead to severe consequences. There have been many reported incidents of banks, credit card companies and even retail shops throwing away documents with sensitive data without shredding them before hand. "Current and former account holders of the Circuit City credit card are being notified that their personal information was thrown out with the trash" (numbrX). Thieves also resort to "dumpster diving," where they rummage through trash to get sensitive and confidential information, which is much more labor intensive than other methods. Once they have this information they can easily steal someone's identity. Although this is a much harder way of retrieving information it does happen and people should be aware of this risk.

Using Insiders

Industry analysts and security professionals estimate that 65 to 70% of identity theft is committed by confidential information being stolen by employees or participants in transactions or services (Putting). This form of hacking is often unpredictable and actions against it are the responsibility of the company involved. It is more common than not to have security cameras, employees checking other employees, and forms to be filled out when dealing with money. Companies tend to not notice such problems until something is out of the ordinary. Then, it is simply a matter of them discovering the theft in time and promptly taking action.

Malicious Software

Malicious software programs can be put onto personal or public computers without the users' knowledge, and can be used to collect various types of personal information such as passwords, usernames, account numbers, etc. These programs are known as "spyware" and can come in several forms, from pop-up ads to unknown icons installed on your desktop. Spyware removal programs exist, but without widespread awareness of these issues this method of theft is hard to detect and prevent.

How Banks are Securing Information?

The newest ways that banks are attempting to increase information security is to require customers to identify certain preset pictures, multi-factor authentication, and electronic bank notes.

Preset Pictures

When a customer opens an account they are prompted to choose a picture that will pop-up when logging into their account online. This technology is beneficial, but could become obsolete if scammers find a way to get a copy of the preset pictures, or begin sending phishing e-mails to find out what particular picture a customer has.

Multi-Factor Authentication

Banks are now implementing multiple security measures to gain access to an online account. Some of these new and existing technologies include tokens, thumbprints, retina scans, and other data. Tokens are battery-powered devices that display a random six digit password every 60 seconds (Banks). Along with entering the token password, customers still need to enter their personal username and password. Some banks are even implementing retina scans and thumbprints to verify the customers' identity.

Electronic Bank Notes

"The blinded note numbers are 'unconditionally untraceable' that is, even if the shop and the bank collude, they cannot determine who spent which notes" (Chaum). Electronic bank notes are basically messages signed using a particular key, and then the bank would have another key in order to verify the account. Here is an example of how electronic notes would work:

> To withdraw a dollar from the bank, Alice generates a note number (each note bears a different number, akin to the serial number on a bill); she chooses a 100-digit number at random so that the chance anyone else would generate the same one is negligible. She signs the number with the private key corresponding to her "digital pseudonym" (the public key that she has previously established for use with her account). The bank verifies Alice's signature and removes it from the note number, signs the note number with its worth-one-dollar signature and debits her account. It then returns the signed note along with a digitally signed withdrawal receipt for Alice's records (Chaum).

Although this system appears to be very secure because of the randomness and security processes, electronic bank notes still pose problems of hacking. For instance, if the notes are stored in a database at the bank, they can be hacked into. In order to prevent duplication of the notes and to ensure their privacy and protection from outside hackers, a bank must implement an efficient and centralized verification system.

How Safe is Online Banking and is Personal Information Protected?

Information is being accessed and stolen so easily because the right precautions are not being taken to prevent theft. Shouldn't banks be stricter with security policies in order to protect consumers? How many customers are aware of the risks involved with online banking? Does age, gender, or a previous fraud experience affect a person's outlook regarding banking online? The following firsthand research was conducted to determine the average consumers' knowledge about online banking and the security risks involved.

Survey Research

In order to gain an insight into what online banking customers know about online security threats, an 11-question survey was conducted. The survey was administered online through facebook.com, and distributed to a senior level class at the University of Colorado as well as to the employees of respective the researchers' family members' workplaces. The questions were created to target the weaknesses and strengths of online banking. Two of the questions were rated on a ten-point scale with one being the lowest possible score a respondent can give and ten being the highest.

Table 1 reveals the quantitative results of the survey. Through analysis of the data gathered, certain conclusions were reached about how gender, age, and experience with online banking fraud can affect an individuals' knowledge and opinion of online banking.

Table 1. Survey Results

	All Respondents	Female Respondents	Male Respondents	Do Not Bank Online	Online Banking Fraud Experience
Average Age	32.5	33.5	30.4	37.8	39.1
% Male	33.3%	0%	100%	27.3%	37.5%
% Female	66.7%	100%	0%	72.7%	62.5%
% With A Bank Account	100%	100%	100%	100%	100%
% That Bank Online	79.6%	77.8%	83.3%	0%	62.5%
Average Safety Rating When Banking Online (1-Not Safe, 10-Very Safe)	7.9	7.8	8	5.7	6.2
% That Had A Personal Experience With Online Banking Fraud	14.8%	14.3%	16.7%	27.3%	100%
Average Worth Of Online Banking (1-Not Worth It, 10-Very Worth It)	7.7	7.3	8.4	5.8	5.4

Gender and Attitudes

Studying the gender of the respondents along with their respective results one can conclude that there are slight differences in how females and males feel about banking online. Males are more likely to bank online compared to females, with results showing that 83.3% of the male respondents bank online as opposed to 77.8% of the female respondents, although this difference of just over 5% is not drastic In order to understand this disparity, it is necessary to examine the questions surveyed relating to feelings toward online banking.

This result can be directly correlated to how safe the respondents feel banking online is as well as how the convenience of online banking can outweigh the risks involved. The survey findings show that when asked how safe they feel banking online is, on a scale of one to ten (one representing not safe at all, ten representing very safe), male respondents feel safer than female respondents with average scores of 8 and 7.8 respectively. When asked if the risks were worth the convenience provided by online banking, rating the risks on a scale of one to ten (one representing not worth it, ten representing very worth it), male respondents answered an average of 8.4 while female respondents answered with an average of 7.3. These statistics support the conclusion that female respondents are less likely to bank online than males. Despite the minimal quantitative difference in males and females' feelings of safety, when examining if the risks are worth the rewards of convenience, a larger disparity exists. These results suggest that as a whole, women do not value the convenience of online banking over the risks it poses in comparison to their male counterparts, who feel that the risks are worth the rewards of convenience.

Age and Use

Does age affect how people adapt to new and advancing technologies, such as online banking? The average age of survey respondents was 32.5 years old. Of those who currently do not bank online, the average age was 37.8. This statistical difference of over five years suggests that the older a person is, the less likely they are to bank online (assuming that they have a bank account, as all the respondents in the survey did). This could be caused by many factors. People can become set in their ways, and if they are used to banking in person, it can be difficult to change and adapt to the online banking process and technology. In a world of rapid technological advances, it can be difficult for a person lacking experience with such technologies to successfully acclimate to them.

The average age of the respondents surveyed who have had a personal experience with online banking fraud was 39.1 years old. This is compared to the average age of all respondents being 32.5 years of age. Since online banking fraud has and continues to affect so many people, the more time a person spends banking online, the higher chance they have of experiencing online banking fraud, which helps explain the statistical differences from above. This age disparity can also be explained by the theory that older online banking customers are unaware of the newest technological advances in online banking fraud, and are thus potentially more susceptible to falling victim to them. Either way, survey results show that the older a person is, the greater the chance they have of being exposed to some type of online banking fraud.

Personal Experiences with Banking Fraud

Of all survey respondents, nearly 15% had a prior personal experience with online banking fraud through either their own personal experience, or that of someone they know. The statistics show that if a respondent fell into this category their feelings about banking online were severely effected. Out of a highest possible score of ten, the respondents who have had a personal experience with this type of fraud gave online banking an average safety rating of 6.2, a decrease of 1.7 points from the overall average safety rating of 7.9. They also had an average answer of 5.4 when asked to rate the convenience of online banking versus the possible security risks. This score is more than a 2-point decrease from the survey average of 7.7, and is expected to be due to the individual personally experiencing the consequences of this type of fraud. Of these respondents, 62.5% of them still bank online but are becoming increasingly more careful about their private information.

Why Do Some People Not Bank Online?

According to the survey, 20.4% of respondents do not bank online but still maintain an active bank account. After further analysis of the collected data, it is clear why these individuals have made this decision. Out of a highest possible score of ten, the average rating given when asked how safe they feel while banking online was 5.7, down from the survey average of 7.9. Also, the respondents who do not bank online rated an average of 5.8 when asked to weigh the convenience of online banking to the risks involved. This is down from the 7.7 survey average. It is apparent that these respondents do not bank online due to safety and security issues, and do not feel that the convenience provided by online banking outweigh the security and privacy risks involved.

The survey conducted produced a large amount of quantitative data that was analyzed and used in making many conclusions about online banking security in the previous pages. However, the survey also contained important questions that required qualitative responses from the respondents. These responses are also extremely important to gain an understanding of the opinions of online banking customers, and how aware they are about important security issues. The following contains summaries of the answers given.

Why Do People Bank Online?

In order to understand why so many people bank online while simultaneously accepting the risk of exposing themselves to online banking fraud, it is important to recognize the advantages online banking offers to the customers. Of the people surveyed who use online banking, 100% of them answered "convenience" when asked why they bank online. The ease of online banking and the ability to make financial transactions without having to leave the comfort of home is an attractive incentive to banking customers. Online banking can also save customers money on checks that would be used to make the same transaction in person. Customers can also keep close track of their accounts to monitor if there has been any fraudulent or unusual activity. There are undeniably many positive aspects of banking online, which could make it difficult to resist these conveniences, even when considering the negative aspects.

How Do Criminals Obtain Personal Information?

It is essential to examine the respondents' awareness of the methods used to extract personal information from online accounts to pinpoint the areas where customers are more likely to fall victim to online banking fraud. Of all the answers given, the most common responses were "stealing social security numbers, sending out bogus emails in the attempt to gain personal information, and hacking into a computer". Although these are all valid ways of stealing personal information, many of the methods described in the beginning of this chapter were absent from the responses. These commonly given answers demonstrate that many of the respondents are aware of possible threats, but there are still some respondents that are completely unaware of any threat whatsoever. It is important for the safety of online banking customers that they become aware of the various ways criminals can obtain private information.

How Banks Can Increase Security

One of the last questions in the survey asked respondents "what can banks do in order to increase security with online banking". Other than technology advances, the most common responses were "to increase awareness of the types of online banking fraud, and take precautions to protect oneself". Banks could accomplish these objectives by requiring customers to read a packet of updated online banking scams and what steps to take to avoid falling victim to them. Another option would be for banks to offer free computer security software when customers sign up for online banking. This would ensure that those customers who are not aware of the importance of securing their computer will have the proper software to do so.

Weaknesses

As with any survey research there are weaknesses that need to be addressed. The primary weakness of the survey conducted arises from the small sample size of respondents that completed the survey. In order to gain data that would more strongly support the previous conclusions, a larger sample of people would have to be surveyed. Another weakness encountered was the under-representation of certain demographics. It cannot be determined if class or race concentrations would reveal different survey results, but a more diverse sample could have produced more accurate statistics to better represent the online banking community as a whole. Also, every respondent was either in college or had college degrees, which is not likely to be representative = of the customers who use online banking. These respondents may be more aware of the steps to take in order to protect themselves than others due to their education. Lastly, the survey conducted switched between quantitative responses and qualitative responses. It would be important to remain consistent during each part of the survey in order to keep respondents interested and possibly less confused.

Further Considerations

Due to time constraints, various types of research and considerations could not be investigated or addressed. First, creating a more in depth survey including such categories as race, income level, location, education level, and party affiliations would have helped gain a deeper insight into the diversity of online banking customers. With this knowledge correlations could be found among respondents to determine whether attitudes vary within these categories, as well as how those attitudes affect what precautions are taken for protection and security. It would also be beneficial to personally interview online banking professionals about the future of the industry, as well as about the biggest issues regarding online banking security. Finally, conducting actual experiments with online banking customers regarding new technologies would be valuable to the progress of online banking in the future. It would be imperative to explore these issues further in order to expand on this chapter and the issues discussed within.

Conclusion

Through extensive research and analysis, the following conclusions have been reached. For the most part, consumers are very unaware, or are not taking the time to be concerned about their security in terms of online banking. In such a technological era, it seems that people would be more aware of the dangers and risks that involve sensitive information and the Internet. What seems to be playing a role is that people have such busy lives, that they would rather sacrifice their security than take the time to make sure the right precautions are taken to protect it. It is also apparent that consumers need to be better informed regarding the security steps required to protect their private information from those trying to acquire it.

Research data concluded valuable insight into gender and age differences concerning issues involved in online banking. It is apparent that in a world where speed and time efficiency are becoming increasingly important to an individuals success, the convenience of online banking would be the only choice when trying to keep up with the competition. It is for this reason that younger people are more likely to bank online, because they have to maintain and strive for a competitive advantage when making the transition into the business world. There is no question that the emergence of online banking has increased the rate at which people conduct business today.

With identity theft costing billions of dollars, it is staggering that online banking customers are so highly unaware of the different methods criminals use to obtain private information. Banks need to take more initiative to inform their customers of the potential dangers involved with online banking fraud. They need to understand that online banking sells itself through its convenience and ease of use, and that their role should be as a guardian with respect to their customers' information. Until these security issues are resolved, criminals will continue to reap the benefits from the overall lack of knowledge and action by both banks and online banking customers.

Works Cited

Banks Try New Systems to Protect Online Users. 2 Jun. 2005. MSNBC. 5 Mar. 2007. <http://www.msnbc.msn.com/id/8071171/>.

Chaum, David. Achieving Electronic Privacy. Scientific American. Aug. 1992: 96-101.

Is Your Financial Information Safe?. Sept. 2004. Privacy Rights Clearinghouse /UCAN. Mar. 4, 2007. <http://www.privacyrights. org/fs/fs24e-FinInfo.htm>.

numbrX Security Beat. 8 September 2006. Privacy Rights Clearing House. 16 March 2007. <http://www.numbrx.net/category/banks/>.

Putting an End to Account –Hijacking Identity Theft. 14 Dec. 2004. Federal Deposit Insurance Corporation. Mar. 1, 2007. <http://www. fdic.gov/consumers/consumer/idtheftstudy/ index.html>.

Schneier, Bruce. "Solving Identity Theft." Forbes.com 22 Jan. 2007: 1.

3

FICO Scores: Uses and Misuses
Jacob Fuller and Eric Dawson

The Fair Isaac Corporation and FICO Scores

Debt is an important tool for both businesses and individuals. It can be used to leverage returns, raise capital or make purchases that would otherwise be unattainable by most. Before exchanging money for a promise to repay, lenders need to judge the creditworthiness of a borrower to accurately assess the risk involved and to determine the required rate of return on their investment. When the loan involves a corporation, ratings agencies such as Standard & Poor's or Moody's, will rank the credit risk using publicly available information. When the borrowers are individual consumers, another approach to measuring credit risk must be employed.

The Fair Isaac Corporation provides exactly this, a method for quick and accurate assessment of the credit risk of individuals. Other companies provide similar services, but the FICO score is, by far, the most popular indicator of credit risk for individual borrowers. Since consumers are not required by law to publicly announce income, expenses, cash flows or savings, it becomes much trickier to accurately predict an individual's ability to meet debt obligations. The FICO score attempts to accomplish this by using complex statistical models based on information gathered from credit reporting agencies. While there are admitted drawbacks to the methods used in calculating these scores, a

FICO score is seen by many lenders to be a critical piece of information when assessing credit risk of an individual.

This chapter is intended to gain insight as to how accurately a FICO score measures credit risk of individual borrowers. Additionally, it will address what affects any shortcomings of the score may have on borrowers, lenders and financial institutions as a whole. Do most people know what affects their credit score? If so, can a score be manipulated to reflect the most positive aspects of the borrower? While transparency in the marketplace is seen as an extremely important aspect of an efficient, competitive market, at what point does evaluating the risk of individual borrowers encroach on personal privacy?

Background on FICO Scores

Before the value of the FICO score can be analyzed, an understanding of how it is calculated needs to be attained. Since Fair Isaac's exact models are proprietary and virtually impossible to access, only a rough outline of the scoring system is available. An approximate breakdown of the components used to calculate a FICO score includes: punctuality of payment in the past (35%), the amount of debt (30%), length of credit history (15%), types of credit used (10%), and recent searches for credit and the amount of recently obtained credit (10%) (Fair Isaac). Missing loan payments will clearly have a negative affect on a FICO score, but the ways in which some of the other factors affect scores are less obvious. For example, the total amount of debt a person has is not weighted as heavily as the percentage of debt used in proportion to available credit. Also, if two people have joint loans, any delinquencies will have a negative affect on both people's FICO scores despite who was responsible. The nature of this scoring system creates an environment where the average borrower does not have a perfectly clear idea of how their activities and history affect their credit.

Nationally, FICO scores range from 300-850 and the distribution is skewed towards the higher end. Figure 1 shows this distribution. A higher FICO score indicates a lower credit risk. According to the Fair Isaac Corporation:

> By law, credit scores may not consider your race, color, religion, national origin, sex and marital status, and whether you receive public assistance or exercise any consumer right under the federal Equal Credit Opportunity Act or the Fair Credit Reporting Act (myFiCO 4).

Some other factors not included in a FICO score are age, salary, occupation, employment history, child/family support obligations and rental agreements. While many see these restrictions as a positive in terms of equal opportunity lending, it could be argued that some of the restricted factors are useful in determining credit risk (my FiCO).

Figure 1. Source – The Fair Isaac Corporation.

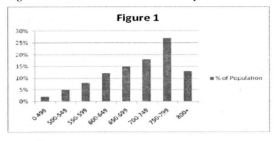

Users of FICO scores

Commercial Lenders

Almost all commercial lenders use some type of credit score before loaning money to an individual. There are many different credit scores, but the FICO score is the most widely used. When a borrower applies for credit at a bank, the lender will check the borrower's credit report and FICO score. When the score is delivered, it may also include up to five 'score reasons' which will help determine why a particular score is a certain number (myFiCO). The FICO score is intended to give a "snapshot" of the borrower's current credit risk based on their credit history. Since the FICO score does not include some important information such as income, employment, or savings, the lender will typically request verification of this information.

Institutional Investors and Securitization

The process of securitization has grown exponentially in recent history. This process involves the purchasing, repackaging, and sale of loans to investors (usually institutional) in the form of bonds. A wide variety of individual loans are securitized, including credit cards, student loans and auto loans. The largest sectors of securitized loans made to individuals are mortgage and home equity loans.

If the securitized mortgage loans meet certain requirements, they may be guaranteed by the Government National Mortgage Association (GNMA, also known as Ginnie Mae). This means that if the bonds (backed by mortgage loans) default, the United States government will pay back the interest and principal to the investor leaving no credit risk. However, if the bonds are not backed by the U.S. government, the credit risk associated with the underlying loans remains. Since there are many loans that do not meet the criteria for federal guarantees, FICO scores become essential to the assessment of credit risk when investing in these types of securities.

The dollar value of financial assets secured by mortgage loans in the U.S. exceeds $6 trillion. This is more than half of the gross domestic product (GDP) of the United States. At the same time, "recent studies show that nearly 80 % of mortgage lenders use credit scores as the primary determinant of an individual's credit risk" (Schrock 1). Since this enormous amount of debt has been issued based on FICO scores, it is clear that there may be major repercussions in the financial markets if these scores do not accurately measure credit risk.

Individual Borrowers

The borrowers for which FICO scores are given are also users of these scores. While it is required by law in some states that borrowers be allowed to access their credit reports for free at a certain frequency, the actual credit scores are not included in this report. Borrowers may buy their scores from the various companies that calculate and track them. Individuals can use this information to gain a better understanding of their own credit risk. It may help them to decide whether or not they would be able to make certain purchases or apply for lines of credit. If borrowers know their scores, they also have a better idea of how they have been managing their credit.

Another important use of FICO and other credit scores is for individuals to check on the possibility that they have been a victim of identity theft. If someone has used another person's identity to apply for loans, this information will appear in the credit report. For example, if someone uses a credit card under another's name and does not make the payments, a delinquency will appear on the credit report and the FICO score will be lowered. If the thief does make payments, the score will not be much lower, but a new line of credit will appear on the report signaling an identity theft. With identity theft becoming more prevalent, the ability to check one's credit report and score is an important tool.

Accuracy of FICO Scores in Determining Credit Risk

Do People Know What Determines Their FICO Score?

The first step in analyzing the usefulness of FICO scores is to gain insight as to whether or not people understand what a FICO score is, how it is calculated, or how their actions affect their FICO score. If people do not understand how or why their credit scores change, they may not act in the same manner as they would if they had more knowledge on the subject.

At first glance, maintaining good credit may seem simple, but merely paying all bills on time does not ensure a high FICO score. As addressed previously, there are more factors that contribute to the credit score than just payment history. Out of 118 people surveyed, only 58% knew what a FICO score was. Furthermore, only 48% of those surveyed claimed to have *any* understanding as to how a FICO score is calculated. 57% knew that payment history has a greater affect on a FICO score than the length of credit history, but only 42% knew that debt as a percentage of credit limits has a greater affect than length of credit history. The survey results suggest that there may be a significant deficiency of FICO score knowledge, especially among new users of credit, since college students represented the majority of the sample.

Inefficient lending may be taking place because there does not seem to be a connection between what people think they know about FICO scores and how they are actually calculated. Borrowers may be acting in a way that hurts their credit score without knowing it. If these borrowers had a better idea of how their score was affected by their activities, they would likely be more careful with their credit. Of people surveyed, roughly 19% carry balances on their credit cards even if they have the money to pay them off (for various reasons). These people's credit scores are likely lower than if they did not carry balances because their outstanding debt is higher as a percentage of available credit. If they knew that a high debt to available credit ratio negatively impacted their FICO score, they might be more likely to pay off their debt with available cash.

Statistical Accuracy: FICO Scores as a Predictor of Credit Risk

FICO scores are used by almost all of the lending industry as a measure of risk for individual borrowers. Lenders are able to maximize profits by minimizing the risk they take on relative to the return they receive from the loan. The return they are getting from the loan is the interest rate the borrower pays. The lower the credit score (higher risk), the higher the interest rate and expected return. This represents the risk reward payoff of the loan. Figure 2, below, illustrates the relationship between FICO scores and negative loan performance. This evidence suggests that FICO scores are good indicators of *average* expected credit performance which means when all the loans are taken they work out to show a good prediction rating, but when just one loan is looked at, it may not be the case.

Figure 2. Source – The Fair Isaac Corporation.

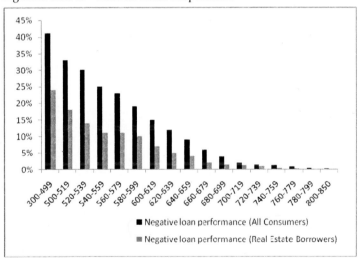

As can be seen in Figure 2, negative performance in each bin, or score range, of FICO scores is much lower for real estate borrowers than for all consumers. This suggests that people may not have the best understanding of how their activities affect their credit. The reason some borrowers have low FICO scores in the first place may be because they do not fully understand what goes into the score. An example of this could be if a person makes mortgage payments on time but has missed student loan payments because they see them as less important. Another consideration is that when a mortgage is made by a lender, much more information is gathered about the borrower. Intuition suggests that when more information is collected, a better assessment of risk can be made. This also illustrates the point that commercial lenders must consider many other factors when making loans.

Although there are some differences in default rates between loan types, these differences tend to converge over time. Past research has shown "… that ARM default rates increase by a factor of 1.5-2.5 times, whereas fixed default rates double or triple over the extended time horizon" (Kraft 8). This research implies that the predictability of defaults comes more from FICO scores than from loan type. More recent research, however, implies the opposite.

> New data from the Mortgage Bankers Association show that mortgage credit quality problems go well beyond the subprime sector. This can be seen from the fact that delinquencies on prime adjustable-rate mortgages are rising quickly – much more quickly, in fact, than those on subprime fixed-rate loans (Hatzuis 1).

Definitions of "prime" and "subprime" vary from source to source, but an acceptable cutoff is at a FICO score of 675. People with scores below 675 are classified as "subprime" borrowers and those with scores above 675 are classified as "prime" borrowers. This relationship can be seen in Figure 3 below through the increase in delinquency rates for prime and subprime, adjustable-rate and fixed-rate mortgages.

Figure 3. Source – Mortgage Bankers Association.

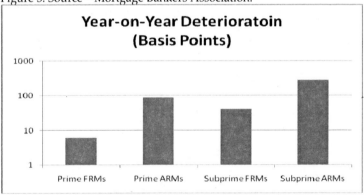

On average, FICO scores are a good measure of risk. This can be seen clearly in Figure 2; as FICO scores increase, negative loan performance decreases. However, Figure 3 suggests there are other important variables to consider when determining credit risk. In Figure 4 below, the default rate on adjustable-rate mortgage loans for the FICO bucket 800-850 is higher than that of the 700-719 bucket. Therefore, it is dangerous for lenders to rely too heavily on FICO scores as the sole measure of credit risk.

Figure 4. Default Rates

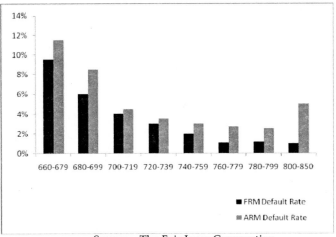

Source – The Fair Isaac Corporation

Issues Relating to Privacy and Technology

As the processes for developing credit risk indicators become more efficient, the speed with which lenders are able to make decisions increases dramatically. The increased use of FICO and other credit scores has helped the entire lending industry. "Especially for consumers with relatively good credit, approvals for loans can be given in a fraction of the time previously required, without any manual review of the information" ("Credit Score Accuracy" 4). It is unlikely that the recent boom in loan originations, particularly in the mortgage sector, would have been possible without the use of FICO scores ("Credit Score Accuracy"). Aside from the added speed credit scores can bring to lending, there are also the specialized products and services now available. Borrowers can shop around for the best prices on loans and lenders can create exotic loan choices to best cater to the needs of both parties. Overall, lending has become much more efficient since the advent of credit scoring, but the costs of this added benefit could be considered high.

Scores That Imitate the FICO Score

A VantageScore is a credit rating score distributed by the 3 credit reporting agencies: Equifax, Experian, and TransUnion. This score uses the same credit information but is calculated differently than a FICO score. Although this score basically measures the same types of risks, it is not directly comparable. A VantageScore is measured on a scale of 501 to 990 which is much higher then the FICO range of 300 to 850. One of the major problems with using this score is that not many lenders use it when evaluating the risk of a borrower. Problems tend to arise when someone gets what they believe to be a relatively high VantageScore, 678 for example, and thinks they will get a prime rate on a mortgage. In all actuality, the same person would likely have a much lower FICO score, possibly around 578, which would drop them into the category of a subprime borrower. "It's as if she turned on the radio, heard it was 32 degrees outside, put on a coat and stepped out, only to find that the temperature was 32 degrees Celsius -- about 90 degrees Fahrenheit" (Lewis).

The development of VantageScore was put in place so the credit bureaus would not have to share profits from releasing this score with Fair Isaac. The credit rating bureaus claim this imitation score is easier to understand and will help people be educated about their credit. "A lot of people are finding themselves in this situation -- they think they have this score and they find out the true FICO score is different," says Michael Moskowitz, President of Equity Now, a mortgage lender in New York City. Consumers get a score that is totally useless to them, and in many cases they are not even notified that this is not the score most creditors will use. While consumers are starting to become aware of the use of the VantageScore, the institutions that utilize credit scores are not planning on using it. "With billions and billions of pieces of data, it's becoming more and more refined with each transaction" (Lewis). The amount of data that are available using FICO scores makes the possibility of changing to the VantageScore almost impossible. Even though the credit bureaus are aware this scoring method is not going to be adopted by the mortgage industry, they are trying to market it to other industries. The marketing and use of this new credit score likely creates even more confusion for borrowers regarding their credit rating.

Personal Information and Privacy

Many find the idea of tracking credit histories somewhat intrusive. When surveyed, 18% called the information collected for the calculation of FICO scores an "unnecessary invasion of privacy." 32% claimed that this collection is "necessary for efficient lending" and 48% said that it is "necessary for efficient lending but still a slight invasion of privacy." While some may view the calculation of FICO scores as invasive, if they choose to use credit, they have no choice as to the method of tracking their credit habits.

Privacy issues go beyond just the collection of credit information for credit score calculations. In many cases, when borrowers apply for credit, the lender will request several pieces of information beyond their FICO score to accurately assess the risk. For example, a borrower applying for a mortgage would likely be asked for employment status and history, previous home ownership, assets, income, bank statements, debts, monthly obligations, etc. This information is important to lenders when making their decisions, but at the same time, borrowers may not want every company they apply for a mortgage through to have this much information about them. Of those surveyed, 87% said that they would divulge this personal information to a lender in order to receive a lower rate. While there are no laws requiring this information be given, it may be necessary if people wish to save money on loan payments.

Implications For Individual Borrowers, Primary Lenders, and the Financial Markets

Individuals should be aware of their score and how their actions affect it. A borrower in the lowest basket of FICO scores will likely pay the highest rate for a loan, if they are able to get a loan at all. There are times when it is impossible for an individual with a very low FICO score to get a loan because of laws that restrict the interest rate a lender may charge. If this is not high enough to compensate for the chance of default, the lender will refuse the credit application.

Lenders must also be aware of the mechanics of FICO scores. There are two ways a FICO score can misrepresent the underlying risk of the borrower. The first is by giving too low of a score to a particular person. Because the FICO score is understated, the lender will charge a higher interest rate to compensate for the higher perceived risk. This hurts borrowers because they will have to pay a premium for the loan. The alternative is when a FICO score is higher than it should be. This is beneficial to the borrower, but can have a negative effect on the institution that is lending the money. This higher FICO score would portray the borrower as a less risky loan candidate, charging them an interest rate that is too low for the level of actual risk involved.

Since the evidence for the statistical validity of FICO scores indicates that they are a good indication of *average* credit risk, institutional investors do not need to be as concerned with a specific individual's FICO score accuracy. The securities that are backed by individual loans are grouped together in large pools. When the loans are aggregated in such a way, it creates a situation where overstating and understating inefficiencies in FICO scoring cancel out, leaving a good average indicator of the credit risk. However, institutional investors do need to be mindful of other factors that can lead to delinquency such as the type of loan, refinancing rates and other market factors.

Future Research of FICO Scores

There is still more research to be done in this area. The findings of this chapter are not conclusive as there is no way to definitely determine the accuracy of FICO scores. The survey was from a sample comprised mainly of college students. Future research should include a much wider range of ages to better estimate the entire population. Also, correlations of information such as age and gender would be useful to combine with FICO scores. As credit markets are always changing, so should the research. Issues relevant today may be less important tomorrow and the scrutinizing of processes in place should be ongoing.

Conclusions for FICO Scores as a Measure of Risk

Our research has shown that while the FICO score is a good measure of risk for the population as a whole, it does not represent risk very well on an individual level. Some people are riskier than their scores would indicate, while others are less risky than their scores show. Therefore, when considered in aggregate, FICO scores are a good indicator of credit risk. Our findings also show it is almost impossible to manipulate a FICO score due to the protection of proprietary models. Even if this manipulation were possible, an efficient market would likely pick up on this and everyone would be doing it. This would in turn push scores higher and adjustments would have to be made in the model to calculate the score based on the new set of parameters. Statistical evidence and data collected through surveys suggest that many new borrowers do not have a very strong understanding of how their actions affect their credit. If the general population were more educated on credit rating systems, the lending industry would possibly become more efficient. However, this efficiency could come at the expense of personal privacy. This returns the essential theme relating to privacy and technology, the tradeoff between privacy and convenience, cost verses benefit.

Works Cited

Credit Score Accuracy and Implications for Consumers. Consumer Federation of America, 2002.

Fair Isaac Corporation, Consumer Federation of America. Your Credit Scores, 2005.

Hatzuis, Jan. Mortgage Credit Quality Problems Go Well Beyond Subprime. US Daily Financial Market Comment, 2007.

Kraft, Dennis F., and Jim Anderson. Structured Products Research: Consumer ABS. Wachovia Securities, 2004: 1-15.

Lewis, Holden. "Conflicting credit scores cause confusion." 07 DEC 2006.

Bankrate.com. 21 Mar 2007 <http://www.bankrate.com>.

myFICO. Understanding your FICO Score, 2005.

Schrock, Jason, and Ron Kirk. Credit and Insurance Scores. Colorado Legislative Council Branch 02-09, 2002.

4

Privacy Issues Pertaining to Gender Identity and Sexual Orientation

Madison Buske and Lauren Griffin

Introduction

Almost every college student faces challenges upon entering a new school; choosing the right classes, learning to live with a complete stranger, and finding a group of friends where one feels comfortable can be very taxing at times. For Annie*, a college freshman in 2003, the biggest challenge was her gradual physical transition from a male to a female under the prying eyes of her peers. As if fitting into a new environment is not grueling enough, she also had to battle the complete loss of privacy at a very crucial and intimate period in her life. Dorm rooms tend to be small enough as they are, let alone being forced to share the limited amount of personal space with another person or persons. Even in resident halls where the bathrooms are not co-ed, the community style bathrooms can be an intimidating environment for college students sharing the same facilities for showering and other daily rituals in various stages of dress. The dorms proved to be difficult for Annie, but progressing into the corporate world opened up a Pandora's Box of issues relating back to her gender identity, which will be addressed later in this chapter.

Dealing with the issue of expressing one's gender identity yet still maintaining privacy in a world that can be unaccepting, can cause a strain on everyday life. However, worrying about how to make a living to support this type of lifestyle is even more unsettling. Should the corporate world have knowledge of the gender identity and sexual orientation of an individual when hiring? Do they have the right to hire or fire an individual based on knowledge of their sexual orientation? Is it acceptable even if this information is voluntarily submitted? What type of rights do these individuals have to protect their privacy and do they stand up to the law?

This chapter will provide readers with a general overview of what exactly gender and transgender identity, sexual orientation, and gender expression are is and how they may affect an individual's private life. The topic will be explored further through real life cases where a person's privacy was compromised through the use of technology. This chapter will delve into the issues surrounding college-aged students and young adults who identify themselves in a category that is different from the norms of society. A series of questionnaires and interviews were conducted to determine their knowledge of the discrimination against their "unprotected class." A number of employers were also interviewed about their hiring policies that are not mandated by the Equal Employment Opportunity Commission (EEOC), and if the use of the Internet has any impact on their hiring decisions.

The Difference between Gender Identity, Sexual Orientation, Gender Expression, and Transgender

The Human Rights Campaign (HRC) is America's largest gay, lesbian, bisexual and transgender organization. They "effectively lobby congress; mobilize grassroots actions in diverse communities; invest strategically to elect a fair-minded Congress; and increase public understanding through innovative education and communication strategies" (Sheehy). This organization hopes to increase equality based on sexual orientation and gender expression to better improve the lives of gay, lesbian, bisexual and transgender individuals in their community and at work.

Below are terms Catherine Sheehy, a member of the HRC, defined, which have been included to help readers fully grasp the context of this chapter:

- *Gender expression* is all "external characteristics and behaviors that are socially defined as either masculine or feminine, such as dress, mannerisms, and physical characteristics."
- *Gender identity* is a person's "deeply felt psychological identification as male or female which may or may not correspond to the person's body or assigned sex at birth."
- *Sexual orientation* refers to an individual's "physical and/or emotional attraction to the same and/or opposite gender."
- *Transgender* individuals are those "whose gender identity falls outside stereotypical norms and do not wish to permanently change their physical characteristics (sometimes referred to as a cross dresser)."

- *Transsexual* people identify with the "roles and expressions associated with a sex that is different than the one they were assigned at birth." A transsexual changes his/her physical characteristics and mannerisms to satisfy the standards of membership of another gender (Sheehy).

What's in a Name: Story of Sebastian Colon

Sebastian Colon is like any other student attending their first day of college. Most people are filled with excitement and terror. The one thing that differentiates Sebastian from the other students is the reasons behind his fear. It is not the dread of having a horrible teacher or no friends in class, it is the fear of which name he will be called when the teacher takes attendance.

Sebastian is a first year graduate student in the School of Social Work at the University of Michigan. He considers himself to be a transgender male and prefers to go by his male name, Sebastian, instead of his legal female name. He is in constant fear that his classmates will discover and use his legal name, which makes him uncomfortable and concerned for his safety. Because of the rampant discrimination against transgender individuals, there is always the threat a person may purposely target him because he is different.

Students have learned his female name in the past through the University directory or by seeing the name that appears when he posts his discussion documents or papers on Ctools (a web-based system used for coursework and collaboration at the University used by the entire campus). This has led to an embarrassing situation in which Sebastian was forced to reveal his sexual identity to avoid confusion within the class between the two names.

Sebastian has made many pleas to CTools administrators, but each time he is told it is not possible to have the male name he prefers appear in public University directories and web based services in place of his legal female name. The University spokeswoman, Kelly Cunningham, says that a student can change their name on CTools by changing their legal name and notifying the Office of the Registrar of the change. Although the University would like to accommodate Sebastian as best they can, they are legally bound to use the name that was on official documents such as his application and financial aid files. However, Sebastian does not want to legally change his name due to familial ties and connections to his Puerto Rican heritage. He believes both names are important to his identity, but if he prefers to be recognized as his chosen name in a public setting, then the University should fulfill his requests (Frank).

In this case, Sebastian had to deal with changing his name on a legal document. There are other cases, however, where an individual desires to change their sex on a public record, such as a birth certificate, to express the identity they feel internally. The question is whether or not a person should be allowed to change a record that documents something that occurred in real time. Modifying or completely changing a legal document is a complex process that takes much commitment, and many states do not agree on whether they should be allowed at all.

Changing the Sex on a Birth Certificate

There is much debate as to whether an individual who changes their physical sex should be able to change the sex on their birth certificate and be reissued a new one. Each state varies on where they stand depending on state jurisdiction and some states do not allow any change at all. Although some will issue an amended birth certificate, noting the change of name and sex, other states will not issue a new birth certificate replacing the original. Even amending a birth certificate is not an easy task. In Alabama, an individual must submit an original letter from the Sex Reassignment Surgery (SRS) surgeon stating completion of the surgery. He or she also needs an "original or certified copy of the court order for [a] name change, as well as an original or certified copy of a court order for change of sex, not just the surgeon's letter"

(Allison). This enters another step into the procedure and is best handled through an attorney, although at extra cost. The individual must then file a "petition to amend a vital record," stating what he or she would like to amend, provide documentation of the reason for petition and name the Center for Health Statistics as a defendant (Allison).

The amending or issuing of a new birth certificate reexamines the issue of a legal marriage between a man and a woman. In the past, SRS surgeons recommended the change of sex on a birth certificate for legal reasons. This subject was challenged by the court in two separate cases involving male-to-female transsexuals who acquired updated birth certificates but were unable to have their subsequent marriages recognized by the courts. In both cases, the state supreme courts rejected the concept of a legal sex change. [Littleton v. Prange (Tex. Civ. App. 1999), (2000) and In the Matter of the Estate of Marshall G. Gardiner, 2002 Kan. LEXIS 117 (Sup. Ct. Kansas 2002)] (Human Rights Campaign).

In the debate between the Transgender Legal Defense and Family Research Council, Executive Director Michael Silverman, argued that transgender and transsexual individuals are one of the most discriminated classes when it comes to hiring. As a result, transgender New Yorkers experience "high rates of unemployment and poverty, and are often unable to access health care and social services" (Silverman). When a person applies for a job, they must present identification to prove eligibility to work. If this identification shows a gender different than what is physically presented, the fear of rejection arises. Silverman states that in "99 out of 100 cases," that individual does not get the job. This has led to an overwhelming amount of unemployment and poverty within this group of individuals.

Workplace Issues

With the rising popularity of networking sites, such as MySpace.com and Facebook.com, any person participating in one of these sites is inadvertently allowing any number of people to check these websites for incriminating information, even if it is voluntarily submitted. Future employers may investigate the character of a potential applicant and refuse to hire him or her upon discovering information that does not meet their standards. Websites have the potential to reveal private data that would have previously gone undisclosed, thus narrowing down the pool of applicants before an interview is ever scheduled. Some influencing factors that have affected hiring at different companies include underage drinking, illegal drug use as well as other types of behaviors companies may find inappropriate. With the abundant discrimination against individuals who violate sexual norms, an employer can refuse to hire an individual without giving a reason for the decision.

In the case of Annie*, which appeared earlier in this chapter, the company that had recently hired her decided to run a background check online after she accepted the job offer. Using a typical search engine, her full name alone brought up a website with the title "male-to-female transgender college student", directing the browser to a picture of her. Although she was not fired, the employers did question her about what they had found. The issue was addressed and they later recommended she remove her middle name from her resume to give her more ambiguity in the future. Annie feels fortunate to work for such an open-minded company and is happily still working for them today.

Not every person in a similar situation has experienced such affable results. It is surprising to think that people such as Annie are not protected under laws such as Title VII, which under the Civil Rights Act of 1964 forbid sex discrimination in the workplace; but federal courts ruled in the past that transgender individuals are not protected under Title VII (Sheehy). In 34 states, employers can legally fire someone based on their sexual orientation. In 44 states, it is legal to do so based on gender identity (Human Rights Campaign). For Annie, a person who identifies herself as a bisexual-transgendered woman, it would have been completely legal for her employers to fire her after viewing her MySpace.com page and seeing information relating to her sex reassignment surgery and her preference for both men and women. Although the above statistics seem harsh, companies are already attempting to further their recognition of gender identity or expression in their non-discrimination policies and these numbers are constantly increasing.

A majority of the Fortune 500 companies seem to be jumping on the bandwagon of improving their non-discrimination policies and catering them to gender identity and sexual orientation. According to HRC WorkNet data, "as of May 15, 2004, a total of 35 Fortune 500 companies included gender identity or expression in their nondiscrimination policies, 11 of which added such protections in 2003 alone. There was an annual increase of 120% over 2001 when only five companies had such protections" (The State of The Workplace). This information is from 2004 and shows a high increase to the number of companies adding gender identity and expression protection to discrimination. As of June 29, 2006, "430 (86 %) of Fortune 500 organizations include sexual orientation in their non-discrimination policies, and 81% include gender identity and/or expression, marking a ten-fold increase from 2001" (The State of the Workplace). Below is a graph indicating the 81% of the Fortune 500 Companies that have written non-discrimination policies. It also reveals the steady increase of companies that have changed their policies from 1999 to 2006 (The State of the Workplace).

Fortune 500 Companies with Written Non-Discrimination Policies That Include 'Gender Identity and/or Gender Expression,' by Year*

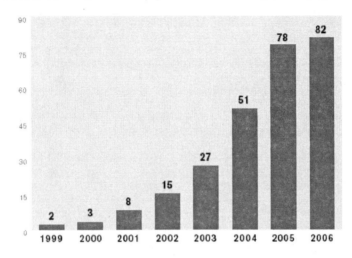

* Data for 2006 are derived using *Fortune* magazine's 2006 Fortune 500 list.
Data for all other years are based on the corresponding year's Fortune 500 list.

Discrimination outside of the workplace is so extensive that transsexual and transgendered individuals are harassed and assaulted in public places. There have even been cases where individuals were found on the Internet, tracked down and murdered (First National Survey of Transgender Violence). Granted this is an extreme case, it should not be ignored that peoples' sexual preferences are discovered through the use of technology everyday. When posting information on the Internet, it is a gamble as to who will have access to it. Since the World Wide Web is a public source of stored information, some data is never fully protected. Sometimes the user voluntarily provides this information and other times information is gathered by breach in security, such as accessing passwords or hacking into data systems.

Breach of Privacy in the Workplace through the Internet: Janet's Interview

Janet* is a 27 year old engineering genius who graduated at the top of her class in college. She held prestigious internships throughout college and was very involved on campus. Although she had only worked in her previous job for two years, she had a lot to offer any company that wished to hire her. She decided to look around for a new job that would better fit her liking and be appreciative of the knowledge and skills she had to offer.

When Janet intervieedw for the job of a project, she was told that she was only 1 of 5 applicants chosen for the interview out of the 23 who applied and went through the first round of phone interviews. She was feeling very anxious and a bit flattered that she was chosen against the odds as the interview began. After she had answered all the questions about the company and the job perfectly, the interviewer began to ask about the campus groups she had been involved in and where she went to college. This is where the problems started.

Janet was a male-to-female transgender individual that had gone through her full transition just a year ago. But throughout the years she attended college, she was a strong activist in the gay, lesbian, transgender community and even served as the president for one of the transgender groups on campus. Being a part of these groups and even holding a position was a major accomplishment to Janet, so she added them to her resume. However, she wrote nothing about her sexual preference and how she changed from a male-to-female because she believed that information should remain private and should not hinder the fact that she is capable for a job. Applicants are not asked to list their sex when filling out an application. During the questioning of her campus involvement, she held great poise and appreciation for all she had done and answered in a noble manner. The interviewer abruptly ended the series of questions and told her they would get back to her within a week or so. When Janet left the office, she felt as though the groups she was involved in had bothered the interviewer, and sure enough, they did.

This involvement probed the interviewer to search further into Janet's record to see if she was hiding anything. She had a MySpace.com page in college and had pictures of herself at meetings and other events, but she was not fully transitioned to a female yet, so her male characteristics were still identifiable stood out. She deleted her MySpace page all together once she entered the career world, but her pictures stayed archived deep within the Internet for others to find. She was also linked to a campus newspaper where she was featured on the front page as an activist for the transgender community, not quite looking like a woman due to not having had sex reassignment surgery yet.

About three weeks later, Janet got the call from the company she interviewed for telling her they found a better applicant for the job and thanked her for her consideration in their company. Feeling a little downhearted, she continued her job search and a month later found a new job that where she was hired instantly. Ironically, Janet received an anonymous e-mail from an insider within the Human Resources department for the company she had just been denied a job from. He told her the company questioned her sexuality, so they had two men working numerous hours probing into Janet's hidden secrets that might be found on the Internet. This anonymous e-mail told her what the company had found about her on the Internet and how they found it. He also informed her that he had quit the company because he was a gay man who had not yet come out, but respected the community she had worked so hard for as an activist in college. He was ashamed to work for a company that discriminated against a person simply because of their gender identity and/or sexual orientation.

Janet decided not to file a lawsuit against the company because she was working in a great job, where she has now been working for the past two years. Instead, she uses her story to educate others when applying for jobs. She is now an avid speaker in the transgender community in her current place of residence and no longer dwells on the past, but the good that the past has brought her. She does not believe any person should lie about their sexual orientation, gender identity, sexual preference or any other factor relating to their personal lives when applying for a job, but rather believes that companies need to change their policies to combat discrimination against this community within the job process.

Research

A sample size of 40 college-aged students and young adults, who consider themselves to be either gay, lesbian, bisexual, transgender, transsexual, or expressing their gender identity in any way deviating from the norm, were surveyed and interviewed. These surveys were distributed at the Gay Lesbian Bisexual and Transgender (GLBT) Resource Center at the University of Colorado – Boulder, and were also personally administered either via e-mail or telephone. The research was gathered from this population because the authors were interested in the opinions of those to whom these issued pertained. Seven employers who did not necessarily identify with any of the above groups were also interviewed to find out their hiring policies toward gay, lesbian, bisexual and transgender individuals and to learn about the use of information found via the Internet affected their hiring decisions.

The surveys dealt with topics concerning how much the respondents knew about the information that was being researched on them, and if they knew what effect this had during the job process. Out of the 40 respondents, almost all (95%) had an account on one type of social networking site, such as Facebook.com or MySpace.com and only 62% had private profiles. Slightly over half of the respondents knew that employers were using these public networking sites to investigate potential applicants, but only 33% believed it was ethical.

In the sample we surveyed and interviewed, an outstanding 72% felt they had been discriminated in the workplace for issues concerning their sexual orientation, gender identity, gender expression, or transgender nature. This discrimination was noticed within hiring, promoting adverse impact or disparate treatment in the workplace. Every respondent believes anything relating to his or her sexuality should not be taken into account when being considered for a job, especially if the information is retrieved from the Internet.

Of the seven employers we interviewed, none admitted to having a policy where they would not hire an individual based on sexual orientation or gender identity. Yet in the survey, 75% admitted that finding out information relating to one's sexuality may have some impact on whether they offered that individual the job. Many employers stated they keep an open mind and look at an applicant based on their qualifications, not on the basis of their sexuality.

Conclusion

In the past, it has appeared that individuals who deviate from society's sexual norm have largely been discriminated against in the workplace. Because of this type of discrimination, these classes of people have been associated with high rates of unemployment and poverty, and are often unable to access health care and social services. Much of this information is discovered via the Internet. Social networking sites, search engines, directories or data bases have the potential to divulge personal information about an individual that they do not necessarily wish to share with the world. Because of the freedom and accessibility of the Internet, many employers are able to research a candidate before even meeting them face to face, and disregard an applicant based on their sexuality. During the interview process, questions pertaining to gender, sexual orientation, etc., are not allowed because they are protected by the Equal Employment Opportunity Commission (EEOC). However, with access to this type of information before the interview, the EEOC cannot regulate how an employer makes their decisions based on this.

Based on interviews, case studies, and surveys, it is obvious that this type of discrimination exists. Many believe it is unfair to judge a person based on their private preferences, and not on their qualifications but potential applicants have very little privacy in a world dominated by technology. Until every company adopts a policy protecting against the discrimination of individuals based on their gender identity or sexual orientation, this problem will continue to survive, along with the Internet as its catalyst.

Works Cited

Allison, Becky. Changing Birth Certificate. 5 Mar. 2007 <http://www. drbecky.com/ birthcert.html>.

Anonymous, Annie. Personal Interview. 8 Feb. 2007.

Anonymous, Janet. Personal Interview. 15 Mar. 2007

Frank, Laura. "What's in a Name? A Lot Transgender Student says." Michigan Daily 6 Dec. 2005. 5 Mar. 2007

"First National Survey of Transgender Violence." General Public Advocacy Coalition. 13 Apr. 1997. 21 Feb. 2007

Human Rights Campaign: Workplace Discrimination. Human Rights Campaign. 21 Feb. 2007 <http://www.hrc.org/Template.cfm? Section=Workplace_Discrimination>.

Sheehy, Catherine. Transgender Issues In The Workplace: A Tool for Managers. 2004. 21 Feb. 2007 <http://nmmstream.net/hrc/ downloads/publications/tgtool.pdf>.

Silverman, Michael. Interview. <u>The New York Daily News.</u> 5 Mar. 2007
      <http://www.nydailynews.com/news/ideas_opinions/story/47046
      6p-395981c.html>.

"The State of the Workplace 2005-2006." 2006. Human Rights Campaign
      Foundation. 21 Mar. 2007 <http://www.hrc.org/Template.cfm?
      Section=Get_Informed2&CONTENTID=32936&TEMPLATE=/Co
      ntentManagement/ContentDisplay.cfm>.

5

Politicians and Privacy
Alexa Cowen and Lindsey Gross

Introduction

Imagine running for a position in a political office when your confidential medical records are released to the public. Let us assume that you have a previous history of a life-threatening illness which could be detrimental to your future career. Could certain private information that is leaked out to the public affect the results of the election?

Many ethical dilemmas arise when it comes to private information escaping into the media. Furthermore, this information could have a major impact on voters' decisions. For example, during the 1972 presidential campaign, Thomas Eagleton ran for Vice President until the public became aware of his previous struggle with depression. Presidential Candidate George McGovern selected Eagleton as his running mate initially, vowing to "back Eagleton 1,000 percent" prior to the public announcement of Eagleton's previous mental illness. Once information about his electric shock therapy treatment was revealed to the public, McGovern eventually chose Sargent Shriver, an in-law of the Kennedys, to replace Eagleton as his running mate ("Former Senator"). Although Thomas Eagleton was dropped from the election process, he remained in the senate until 1987.

Would it be fair for the public to base their votes on the details of Eagleton's private life? Are the specifics of a politician's private life helpful to voters? Could an issue such as depression seriously affect the success of a leader? How much information about politicians should be disclosed prior to elections and does that information affect a reelection? Scandalous issues such as racism, sexual encounters, illicit drug use, and alcoholism will also be discussed while addressing how these issues have affected the election or re-election of politicians. Is being deviant avoidable, and how much should a politician try to hide from the public?

Legal Rights to Privacy

The only legally protected privacy rights politicians have are all related to their medical history. Information about the medical status of a politician is closely guarded, not only to protect his privacy but also to ensure the national security of the country.   Legally, everyone has a right to confidential medical records but according to CNN.com, if the president was to become incapacitated, the "facts would be made public and the orderly transfer of power would take place." On one hand, people may believe that there should be no reason to violate the medical privacy of an existing or potential leader, but others believe they need to know if the candidate they are voting for is physically and psychologically fit for the position.

The United States' medical system is becoming more urbane and computerized which makes it easier to access health records making them more vulnerable to unauthorized disclosure.   This increases the risk that medical information will leak to the press and become public.

The Health Insurance Portability and Accountability Act (HIPAA) prohibits doctors and hospitals from releasing medical records, in most instances, without patient consent. Candidates' medical records can only become public if they release their own information or authorize their doctors to discuss their health with the media (Goldman). The White House has a different approach: "they feel it is ethical to allow reporters to read, but not copy, the medical documents of a politician" (Goldman).

The American Medical Association's Council on Ethical and Judicial Affairs instructs physicians to "cooperate with the press to insure that medical news is available more promptly and more accurately than would be possible without their assistance if their patient authorizes them to disclose medical information." The Council strongly advises physicians not to release any information without patient consent to avoid any potential lawsuits (Goldman). On the other hand, the media can legally photograph or document any person, place, or thing they have seen in public.

Types of Scandals and Incidents

A large concern for politicians is the release of confidential medical information to the media. In addition, there is much paranoia for politicians about their private lives with friends and family being exposed to the public eye. For example, politicians have cheated on their significant others, had sexual relations with drastically younger persons, participated in prostitution, were involved with child pornography and in other scandals. In addition, many public officials have dealt with or are still dealing with alcoholism or drug abuse. Less common scandals can even involve violence or murder. Various types of scandals or incidents that occur can have an effect on a politician's present or future career. Despite an incident occurring many years ago, information can always get exposed to the public leading to problems with the politician's constituency, and have an adverse impact on their ability to properly carry out the mandate of their office.

The Lose-Lose Situation

From a politician's perspective, being honest can potentially be a lose-lose situation. Honesty is one value that many Americans hold in high esteem. This value has often been forgotten with politicians of the past, hurting their reputations as leaders. On one hand, the media has the resources and technology to uncover any mistakes one may have made in the past. The media can proceed to present those mistakes to the public which in turn, may help competitors win an election, or cause voters to lose respect for the politician in question. On the other hand, if a politician keeps secrets and blatantly lies about past mistakes and the media discovers the deception, voters may no longer respect that politician due to his or her dishonesty. A report from CNN.com states, "In today's political environment, saying no is tantamount to admitting there is something to hide and so many candidates have taken to releasing sometimes voluminous medical records in an effort to answer questions and thwart further digging." This situation has put politicians under a magnifying glass with an expectation of perfection, which could arguably be unattainable and can certainly add a twist to politics and voting behavior.

Interview with Colorado Senator

Politicians are aware of how technology is providing easy access to their private lives and the potential negative consequences to their career. Colorado Senator Brandon Shaffer outlined three areas where he saw a paradigm shift in reference to privacy. These areas of technology include email, media publishing material, and negative campaigns.

The media, as well as campaign candidates, are on the prowl for any controversial topics that would make a good headline. With the innovation of email, camera phones and fast-paced blogs, private information can circulate more quickly and with greater ease than before. Private information can be published rapidly, which leaves little time for the public to question the accuracy and credibility of the source, not to mention whether a politician was truly guilty of the claim. In addition, this can lead to the slandering of campaigns of opponents.

During election time, the public is exposed to a large amount of negative campaigns that aim to back stab and nit pick the private lives of opponents. Increasing technology today assists the media and the public to record, publish, or capture private and inaccessible information that could not be acquired without these innovative tools.

Medical Privacy

How deep should the media dig in order to obtain medical information about politicians? Should voters use this information to decide if a politician will make a worthy candidate or is it irrelevant to the voting process? People are essentially going to want to know if their future president is mentally and physically fit for the job, but should past medical records affect the way people vote? Would the average person vote for the candidate who suffers from an illness that may impair his ability to function, or even put a stop to the completion of a four-year term? Even though medical records are supposedly confidential, these records can be found by the click of a button at a doctor's office or hospital. The media has obtained private medical files, which could also be used for negative publicity or campaigning.

Although it may not be the first thing that crosses a person's mind, voters may have legitimate concerns about whether a candidate will be able to finish out his or her term. For example President Warren Harding, who hid his heart disease for many years, died of heart failure in his first term in office. Another incident occurred when President Franklin Roosevelt concealed his polio and hid the hypertension and heart failure which he developed during his third term in office (Goldman). During his fourth term, Roosevelt died leaving his country and citizens without a president. President John F. Kennedy suffered from various conditions such as Addison's disease but denied to the public he had any such illness. Kennedy did not want the fact that he may have been physically unstable to jeopardize his career as President. When candidates cannot physically and mentally finish out their terms, it puts a burden on the government, and most importantly the citizens of the country.

Recently, Americans have been with faced with the question of whether current Vice President Dick Cheney is medically fit to serve in his post? Cheney has a history of medical instability, including cardiovascular disease, which led him to his first of four heart attacks beginning at age 37. He underwent a coronary artery bypass, coronary artery stenting, and coronary balloon angioplasty. In addition, he currently lives with an implanted cardioverter-defibrillator used to shock the heart if the monitor notices any unsteady cardiac rhythm (American Heart Association). Additionally, Cheney suffers from atherosclerotic disease and had an endo-vascular procedure in 2005 for his knee. He also suffers pain in his foot which usually requires him to walk around with a cane. On top of these medical problems, Cheney is a former chain smoker. Do these illnesses impair his ability to function as an elected official?

Due to Cheney's experience, skill, education, and job tasks as vice president that did not require extreme health and fitness, his medical history should not affect the overall performance of duties as a political officer. However, the public should be aware of the time commitment that each medical procedure and follow-up treatment requirements. Since a vice president's position does involve long work hours in order to perform his duties as a leader and serve the country effectively, physical and mental health is an advantage ("Cheney, Dick").

In another example, New York City's former Mayor Rudy Giuliani battled an extremely private cancer in front of a very public audience. Although Giuliani knew he would be suffering from embarrassing symptoms such as frequent bathroom trips, pelvic discomfort, weight loss, and persistent lower back pain, Giuliani fought through prostate cancer in a way that proved his leadership ability and his heroism to New Yorkers and the country. Giuliani served two terms from 1994-2001 and was named Time magazine's "Person of the Year" in 2001. Giuliani's next feat will be his candidacy in the 2008 presidential election (Time).

Marital Infidelity and Sexual Relations

Private controversies have occurred since the U.S. government was founded ("Cheney, Dick"). The First Secretary of Treasury, Alexander Hamilton, became intimately involved with a married woman named Maria Reynolds. Hamilton was blackmailed by Reynolds' husband, which leading Hamilton to admit to the affair and resign as Secretary of the Treasury in 1795.

Of all the types of political scandals, marital infidelity and sexual relations appear to be the most publicized. People who lived through Bill Clinton's presidency are keenly aware of his affair with White House intern, Monica Lewinsky. Initially, Clinton denied the accusations of the affair, but as physical evidence surfaced the President finally admitted to having "sexual relations" with Lewinsky. After Clinton acknowledged the affair on national television, his career and reputation were in jeopardy. Not only was his family devastated by his actions, but some Americans felt betrayed and lied to, as well.

Although the affair was considered inappropriate behavior, was it fair for the public to critique Clinton's whole job performance based on his personal sexual relationships? Or was Clinton judged not because of his sexual relationship, but because he told a lie? Unfortunately there is no easy way to know what Americans truly thought of the Monica Lewinsky scandal. Clinton's publicized scandal shocked the media, but nonetheless settled with Americans, proven by the example of his wife Hillary Clinton becoming Senator for the state of New York.

Additionally, 53% of Americans felt that marital infidelity had little to do with a president's ability to govern, according to a Gallup Poll taken after the affair. As a result of perjury, President Clinton was put on trial for impeachment from office but after being acquitted, continued to serve for the remainder of his term. Many Americans may not have necessarily disputed with Clinton's affair. However, they may have felt uneasy about his public announcement, which many felt consisted of lies. Following his two presidential terms, Clinton became involved in public speaking and humanitarian work, but has yet to dive back into the political arena.

An additional example was the affair between Colorado Senator Gary Hart and his mistress, Donna Rice. Rumors began to circulate about an affair prior to the presidential election in 1988. After hearing these claims, Hart stated, "Follow me around. I don't care. If anybody wants to put a tail on me, go ahead. They'd be very bored" (Time). Taking him up on his word, reporters waited outside his home to watch for suspicious activity. Sure enough, an unfamiliar woman, who was not Hart's wife, but rather Donna Rice, was seen leaving Hart's home numerous times. Following up on Hart's suspicious activity with the unknown woman, the media followed both of them down to Gary Hart's yacht. Days later it was revealed that Hart was having an affair with 29-year-old model Rice. As a result, Hart immediately dropped out of the presidential election. Though his chances in the presidential election were lost, Hart resumed his law practice, served on the Hart-Rudman Commission to change security policies, and furthered his degree in politics to remain active in the political scene.

In 2004, Neil Goldschmidt, the Governor of Oregon for four years, finally admitted to having a lengthy sexual relationship with a 14 year old girl in the mid-1970s (Jaquiss). Goldschmidt proceeded to resign from his positions with the Texas Pacific Group and the Oregon State Board of Higher Education. Much of the public believed that the relationship with the minor was the true reason why he had not run for re-election as governor or for a seat in the United States Senate. After he admitted to the affair, his political reputation with citizens declined, which forced an end to his career in politics.

Alcoholism

In 1952, Thomas J. Dodd was elected into the House of Representatives, serving two terms. He later served as Connecticut's senator in 1958 and was reelected in 1964. In 1965, Dodd was reported drunk on Capitol Hill. Subsequently, rumors circulated about potential alcoholism. Dodd then suffered a heart attack in 1970 and did not run for reelection. Dodd continued to serve as senator until several months before his death.

Alcohol abuse affected another reported public official, Herman Talmadge. Serving as governor of Georgia from 1947 to 1955 and then senator from 1957 to 1981, Talmadge was a committed political leader. However, he was defeated for reelection in 1980 due to a combination of factors. Primarily his self-admitted alcoholism spun out of control after his son drowned in 1975, leaving Talmadge depressed and incompetent (Talmadge, Herman). His depression led him to retire after realizing he wasn't capable of being a strong, influential political leader any longer.

Suspicious Occurrence

The Chappaquiddick incident which involved Edward Ted Kennedy quickly became a national scandal and was very influential on his later career as a politician. After a night of heavy drinking at a political event in 1969, Ted Kennedy agreed to drive his campaign worker Mary Jo Kopechne home. Unfortunately, he swerved off the bridge he was driving on and drove into a channel of water below. Kennedy claims he tried to save Kopechne but was unsuccessful. After the crash, he returned back to the party and was later charged with drunk driving and fleeing the scene. After this incident, his campaigns received substantial negative press, which may be the reason Kennedy decided against running for president in 1972. Despite the shocking Chappaquiddick incident, Ted Kennedy has remained politically active and began a new term in 2007 ("Sentaor for Massachusetts").

A Mix of Segregation and Statutory Rape

Holding the record for the longest serving senator of his time, Strom Thurmond, Governor of South Carolina and U.S. Senator, did not hold a record on purity. Thurmond conducted the longest filibuster ever conducted by a United States Senator in opposition to the Civil Rights Act of 1957. Thurmond later moderated his views on race, but continued to defend his early segregationist campaigns on the basis of states' rights. Thurmond was elected as Governor of South Carolina in 1946 and ran for the 1948 presidential election. He served as Senator of South Carolina from 1954 until 2003. Following his death in 2003, Essie Mae Washington-Williams announced that she was Thurmond's illegitimate daughter, and that her mother was an African American maid who worked for the Thurmond family. She gave birth to Essie when she was only sixteen. Strom Thurmond did not consider himself to be a racist, but he did support segregation. His beliefs contradicted his actions when America found out that he was guilty of statutory rape of an African American woman while she worked as a maid in the Thurmond household. Essie Mae, her mother and Thurmond agreed to keep their connections a secret. This controversy did not have an impact on Thurmond's career, due to the fact that Washington-Williams waited until after his death to reveal this information.

Politicians and the Future

Ed Schrock, a member of the United States House of Representatives from 2001 until 2005, and a member for the Second Congressional District of Virginia, firmly opposed gay rights and same sex marriage unions. Schrock abruptly declined election for a third term once rumors of his sexual preference were publicized. Audio recordings on a blog were found of Schrock soliciting homosexual phone-sex. Politicians have viewed this example and learned how the media exposed Schrock's private life. The following quote comes from Jim McGreevey, a former New Jersey Governor who left office three months after announcing his affair with a male co-worker:

> As glorious and meaningful as it would have been to have a loving and sound sexual experience with another man, I knew I'd have to undo my happiness step by step as I began chasing my dream of a public career and the kind of 'acceptable' life that went with it. So, instead, I settled for the detached anonymity of bookstores and rest stops — a compromise, but one that was wholly unfulfilling and morally unsatisfactory.

McGreevey's situation only further proves the "lose-lose" situation confronted with complete honesty, while serving a public office position. This has not yet affected Schrock's career, as he is still politically active.

Newt Gingrich, a potential 2008 presidential candidate, has been had several past extra-marital affairs, which may affect the way people view him as a person. Gingrich married his high school teacher, Jackie Battley, but filed for divorce while Battley was recovering from cancer surgery. He told the media that, "she's not young enough or pretty enough to be the wife of a president, and besides she has cancer" (Jeffery). Several months after this harsh statement and a divorce settlement with Battley, he married Marianne Ginther. Eighteen years later Ginther and Gingrich divorced, and Gingrich admitted to an extramarital affair with 33-year old Congressional staffer Callista Bisek (Time). He married Bisek only one year after the divorce with Ginther. Newt Gingrich has gained some negative publicity from his messy marriages and divorces, yet he remains as a potential candidate for the 2008 election.

Recently, Barack Obama, Senator of Illinois and 2008 presidential candidate, publicly addressed his history of drug use in his book *Dreams From My Father*. Before Obama entered the political scene, he experimented with marijuana, cocaine and until recently, chain-smoked. By making a choice to be completely open and honest with America about his past struggles, Obama is taking a huge risk, which may be judged negatively against him in the 2008 election. His honesty comes as a shock, which begs the question as to whether his confessions were revealed only because most privacy no longer exists, and what little does exist may be in jeopardy of being exposed. Perhaps, Obama's new approach to honesty will translate to a successful trend throughout candidacy.

Recently it was announced that North Carolina senator John Edward's wife has been diagnosed with a recurrence of breast cancer. Edwards says he still plans to run in the 2008 presidential race, although a USA Today/Gallup Poll found that a third of those surveyed believe Edwards will eventually be forced to withdraw from the campaign due to her illness (Page).

Hillary Clinton, a 2008 presidential candidate, will soon find out the influence of her husband's past scandal when voting time comes. In an article from *USA Today*, the author questions, "Will memories of the Monica Lewinsky scandal haunt Hillary Clinton's campaign and drive away voters" (Lawrence). According to a USA Today/Gallup Poll, an surprising 70% of Americans say Bill Clinton will do more good than harm for his wife's campaign (Lawrence).

Currently, it is unclear how personal information and private scandals will affect the voting process for these future candidates. As illustrated above, some candidates have been greatly affected by their personal incidents, while others have not had any affect on their electability as a political officer.

Conclusion

No one is perfect, but how can Americans decide who is most honorable to lead a country? Honesty, guidance, and leadership can be viewed as imperative characteristics of politicians. These previous examples have illustrated that a public scandal can not only disappoint Americans, but also end a political career and reputation. For instance, a breach of medical privacy can show weakness and lack of thoroughness on the job for a candidate. Controversial scandals have resulted in resignation, wasted time, investments, and at times, caused an exit from the political scene. Conversely, some of the previous examples show that politicians have continued on with their political careers long after private incidents surfaced to the public. In the end, technology and the media have enabled a new age, which has opened the closets of any politician and exposed every one of their secrets, regardless of size.

Voting citizens must choose whether or not to see beyond the surface of a politician and decide what values a politician can offer as a leader for the country. If Americans were to vote solely based on scandals and historical details of a candidate's private life, they may be failing to vote for the integrity of the country. The challenge for Americans lies in critically examining the facts presented by the media. By understanding one's personal values and placing initial judgments aside, a wiser and more informed democracy could be established.

"Oh that lovely title, ex-president"

-Dwight D. Eisenhower

Works Cited

"Cheney, Dick." Encyclopaedia Britannica. 2007. 21 Mar. 2007
    <http://search.eb.com/eb/article-9345386>.
Former Senator, Vice Presidential Nominee Thomas Eagleton Dead At
    77. FOX News Online. (2007). 19 Mar. 2007
    <http://www.foxnews.com/story/0,2933,256518,00.html>.
Goldman, Janlori, and Elizabeth I. Tossell. "Presidential Health: Do We
    Have a Right to Know?"
IHealth. 1 Apr. 2004. California Healthcare Foundation. 20 Mar. 2007
<http://www.ihealthbeat.org/index.cfm?action=dspItem&itemID=12892
    5&changedID=101580>.
Jaquiss, Nigel. "The 30-Year Secret." Willamette Week Online 30 (12
    May 2004): 20 Mar. 2007. <http://www.wweek.com>.
Jeffery, Kahn P. Public Office and Private Lives: Do Politicians Deserve
    Medical Privacy? 20 Mar. 2007. <http://archives.cnn.com/2000/
    HEALTH/08/08/ethics.matter/>.

Lawrence, Jill. "Big Question for Hillary: What Will Bill's Impact Be?" <u>USA Today</u> 29 Mar. 2007, sec. A: 1-2.

Page, Susan. "Edwards Gains Support as He Remains in the Race." <u>USA Today</u> 27 Mar. 2007.

Shaffer, Brandon. Personal interview. 6 Mar. 2007.

Senator for Massachusetts, Edward M. Kennedy. 2007. 21 Mar. 2007. <http://www.kennedy.senate.gov>.

"Talmadge, Herman". <u>The New Georgia Encyclopedia.</u> 2007. 21 Mar. 2007 <http://www.georgiaencyclopedia.org>.

<u>Time.</u> Mar. 2007. <http://www.time.com>

II

CONSUMER PRIVACY

6

International Privacy and Travel
Brittany Burgess and Krista Fox

Introduction

Since the start of humanity, people have embraced the idea of travel. Whether to fulfill physiological needs, such as food or shelter from enemies, to engage in trade, or to arrange technical business deals in the 21st century, travel has remained a commonly accepted and often unavoidable activity. Since medieval times, people have been required to carry travel documents with them containing personal identification information. This identification, known today as a passport, began as a list of cities through which the user could pass and has now become a much more personalized document (Marrus).

With the growth of globalization, international travel has become almost as frequent as travel within one's own country. Each day hundreds of thousands of travelers pass through international airports, cross through national border checks, or enter a foreign country in another way. In the U.S. alone, Customs and Border Protection processed the information of an estimated 430 million travelers (Our Travelers). Each person must provide a government-issued document such as a passport in order to identify themselves, their nationality, and the purpose of their visit.

Travelers will give a foreign government access to this personal information without question because it is considered a routine and necessary process. But can these governments be trusted with this information or does international travel put travelers' privacy at risk? How much information is really available when the passport is scanned? Who receives this information and how accessible is it to those who are interested in collecting this information? Which countries are the riskiest for the travelers' most private information to be released? Analyzing these issues and attempting to give new insight into the privacy risks involved with international travel will provide answers to some of these questions.

International Travel, Security, and Privacy Overview

The rules of international travel differ greatly between countries. Today, a passport is generally required to get into most countries. There may also be health requirements, such as vaccines, and avoiding being on lists of people who pose a high risk to the country and are not allowed across the border. A common practice now is that a visitor must show proof of an outbound ticket or roundtrip itinerary proving they have plans to exit the country. Some countries, like North Korea, do not allow citizens to leave the country and prohibit many visitors from coming in. Although a visa is required to enter North Korea, since 2004, the government has refused to issue visas to U.S. citizens. Surprisingly, some smaller countries have the toughest travel requirements because of political rules, such as restrictions between the U.S. and Cuba, and environmental concerns. Some countries, especially Middle Eastern ones, even change travel policies depending on the citizenship of the traveler and the location he or she is entering the country from.

For travelers who wish to visit a foreign country for a longer period of time, usually over 90 days, visas are usually required. Different types of visas are available, such as a travel visa, student visa, and work or business visa. The following list is a collection of the information commonly requested on visa applications:

- Current Name
- Name at Birth
- Name(s) of Parent(s)
- Marital Status
- Name of Spouse
- Date and Place of Birth
- Citizenship/Nationality at Birth
- Passport Number
- Date and Place of Issue of Passport
- Home Address
- Occupation
- Name/Address of Employer
- Religion
- Previously Visited Countries
- Dates of Visit
- Was a Visa Application Previously Rejected?
- Names of Relatives/Friends to Visit
- Purpose of Visit

- Desired Duration of Visit
- Desired Number of Entries
- Intended Date of Arrival
- Intended Place of Entry/ Exit
- Places to Visit
- Local Sponsor (Hasbrouck)

This extensive list is then filled out and sent to the foreign consulate in the U.S., where it is processed and eventually sent to foreign authorities. If deemed acceptable, the applicant will have the visa attached to their passport and mailed back to them.

The U.S. Department of State publishes a list of countries, travel to which is not recommended. It has been suggested that when a person engages in foreign travel, she should register with the State Department, so the government is aware of their location and plans, but how far does this information go? Is it possible for the government to track travelers using this information without their knowledge (Clear)?

International Identification – Passports

A passport is a nationally-issued travel document requesting that the identified person be allowed to enter a foreign country for a period of three months or less (Lansky 2006). Based on world-wide standards created by the League of Nations and later the International Civil Aviation Organization, the passport now has a standard format that includes a cover and title page identifying the issuing country and personal information about the holder. This information includes the holder's name, date of birth, signature, and photograph, as well as blank pages for official stamps and a serial number assigned by the issuing government (Hasbrouck).

In order to obtain a passport, citizens must go to a passport acceptance facility, fill out an application, and provide specific documentation. There are over 8,000 such facilities in the U.S., including post offices, courthouses, municipal offices, and even public libraries. Along with giving personal information on the application itself, all applicants are required to submit proof of U.S. citizenship, current proof of identity, a social security number, two photos, and an application fee. This information is reviewed by the person accepting the application and then sent to the State Department for further review. Once information has been reviewed, verified, and accepted, the passport is printed and mailed back to the applicant's unsecured mailbox (Foreign).

The following graph shows the increase in passport applications and issuances over the past 30 years.

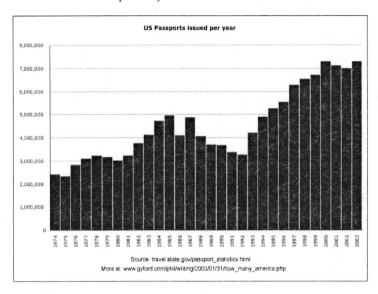

US Passports issued per year

Source: travel.state.gov/passport_statistics.html
More at: www.gyford.com/phil/writing/2003/01/31/how_many_america.php

While the U.S. government processes over seven million applications every year, less than 20% of Americans currently hold a passport. International travel is not very popular in the U.S., probably because other countries are not as easily physically accessible as they are in Europe. However, the numbers are increasing about 10% per year (Foreign). The application process is not difficult, but the information required for the application passes through many hands before the passport is received. Not only that, but it remains in many databases indefinitely. With the growing numbers of passports being issued, the risk of losing privacy grows as well.

The most commonly used passport today is the machine-readable passport. Contained in this document is textual data as well as strings of alphanumeric information that is read via an optical character recognition (OCR) machine (Machine). What this means is that each passport has a unique combination of numbers and letters that, when passed in front of the proper technology, will retrieve and display all the correlating information stored in government databases. All countries requiring passports upon entry are capable of processing information in this format, either manually or electronically.

The area of largest concern when it comes to machine-readable passports is their ability to be copied and recreated. Governments around the world are constantly trying to suppress the use of fraudulent passports and other identification materials. The U.S. is one of the most dangerous places for criminals using fraudulent identification, because agents have extensive training and access to cutting-edge technology in detecting fraudulent materials (CBP).

Many governments are beginning to look at the possibility of using biometric technology to add information to passports. New passports will contain Radio Frequency Identification (RFID) chips, on which data can be digitally stored and remotely retrieved. The chip will contain an identification number and digital signature, and once printed, the chip cannot be altered. Current identification methods linked with biometrics are facial recognition, fingerprint analysis, and retina scanning (Our Travelers). The personal information provided will be stored in central government databases and accessed through the two numbers assigned to the chip. Many governments are moving toward this form of passport because identification methods such as those listed above are nearly impossible to duplicate and levels of fraud will be drastically decreased. This new technology will also allow for even faster confirmation of identification and more timely security clearance at travel ports.

A primary concern with adding RFID chips to passports is that the chips can be read from a distance. While government officials have said that the chips are readable only within "close proximity," experts in RFID field say they can be accessed from 30 to 65 feet away. Although state officials are going to take precautionary measures to help protect travelers, the risk of having the transmitted personal information intercepted obviously leads to the fear of identity theft (Passport).

As international travelers embark on their journeys, they are required to pass through customs. Using the U.S. as an example, when a traveler prepares to board a flight entering the U.S., the information found on their passport is sent via the Advanced Passenger Information System to the National Targeting Center, a data analysis center operated by Customs and Border Protection (CBP) units. This system is used to screen passengers prior to their arrival to the U.S. and gives CBP more time to process and review traveler information. Once at the airport, the traveler has to pass through American customs. Their passport is scanned for a second time; this time border control and the Transportation Security Administration access the information that had been previously received by the CBP. The person is either identified as a "low-risk traveler" and allowed entry, or they are suspected of criminal activity and pulled aside for further investigation (Keeping it Real).

Integrated Automated Fingerprint Identification System, which is directly linked to an individual's biometrics, is the future of passport technology, which law enforcement officials use to access criminal and immigration databases. "This system, housed by the FBI, is the largest biometric library in the world and contains the fingerprints and corresponding criminal history information for more than 47 million subjects" (Our Travelers). Once a traveler is flagged for suspicious activity, the information found on their passport is matched with the data from this system to verify the individual's identity. It takes customs officials less than 30 minutes to find and receive original passport applications, photos, and signatures via photo-phones (Keeping it Real). In this way, the U.S. government is using personal information contained on passports to seize criminals and try to prevent terrorism. However, if there is an error in this methodology, it could very well affect unsuspecting and innocent travelers as well.

National Identification – Citizen Cards

Government agencies can also track individuals internally through national identification cards. National ID cards are rapidly becoming a hot topic within the U.S. because of the implementation of Biometric Passports. The cards are already in place in many regions of the world, including the United Kingdom. With ID cards' popularity growing, the following questions must be asked: do they allow more personal access to citizens, do they impede on civil liberties, and are they yet another tracking device? Some fear that the government or corrupt individuals are slowly moving in on personal privacy and each program must be assessed in order to decide what is acceptable for the good of the population.

The countries that have adopted the national ID card systems have generally made the cards obligatory. Most developed countries currently have some sort of personal identification card, such as the social security card issued in the U.S., but most do not require the card be carried at all times. Soon, it may be required to always have the identification card, in case an authority figure requests to see it. The information provided on national identification cards varies, but most cards state the name, gender, and date of birth of the individual. Some have signatures, pictures and expiration dates.

Although there are many advantages to the National ID card system, there are also many disadvantages. Some advantages include improved safety, the ability to move quickly through places such as public transportation, and reduction of fake ID use. Disadvantages include invasion of privacy, increased opportunity for identity theft, and unknown users having the ability to track people without their knowledge. The privacy issues are endless with these sorts of cards; for this reason, many countries have already rejected the idea (Foreign). On the other hand, an increasing number of countries have adopted and mandated them. The countries include the UK, Poland, and Russia. The U.S. has not yet implemented them, but there is a strong possibility that the cards could be required for citizens as early as 2008.

Registered Traveler (RT) Program

Increased travel risks after September 11, 2001 have changed air travel dramatically. Airport security is heightened, but along with increased safety comes longer wait time and frustration. To combat some of these new issues, the U.S. government agency, the Transportation Security Administration (TSA), and a private company, have created a new program.

The Registered Traveler (RT) program allows for an expedited security screening in airports by providing people who volunteer their biometric and biographic information prior to travel with a card that allows them to pass through a different and shorter security line. Once their information is analyzed, their security threat is assessed, and they are deemed non-threatening, they pay the fee and receive a card. The fee is $99.95 for the first year, which includes the $28 TSA portion. Once the new security lanes are established throughout the country, the airport security process for registered travelers will be much more efficient (Our Travelers).

The program sounds straight forward although it does require individuals to provide extensive personal information that individuals must provide in order to receive the card is rigorously studied and therefore, the card is not easily attainable. The requirements include, but are not limited to:

- Other Names Used
- Social Security Number
- Citizenship Status
- Alien Registration Number
- Current Home Address
- Primary and Secondary Telephone Numbers
- Current E-mail Address
- Date of Birth
- Place of Birth
- Gender
- Height
- Previous Home Addresses
- Employer Name
- Employer Address
- Driver's License Number

This information is kept on the system's computers and is used to correctly identify individuals and eliminate possible misuses. It can also be used to communicate with people when suspicious behavior is recognized. The system is now being called "Clear" and is available in five major cities including: Cincinnati, Indianapolis, New York, Orlando, and San Jose. Once in one of the equipped airports and in the "clear lane," a government issued ID must be presented, like a driver's license, the biometric card is read, and then the individual's fingerprint or iris is read. After all of these have made a positive match, the boarding pass is marked and the person is allowed to proceed through X-ray and metal detector machines. The advantage of the "Clear" line is that it is much less crowded and moves quickly.

To keep the system accurate and as secure as possible, every registered member's information gets screened on a regular basis. If they are no longer deemed suitable to use the "Clear" card, they receive an e-mail notification and are reimbursed for the unused portion of the fee. Although there are always risks to these types of systems, third party audits have been conducted and have shown the system to be safe. Members are guaranteed that their information remains private. The private issuing company even provides users with an Identity Theft Warranty. While this program is being implemented as a safety measure, it is possible that it allows possible terrorists the luxury of finding out if the government recognizes them as a threat. If they are not recognized as a security threat, they are able to travel more easily and are subject to less security. If identified, they can pass the job on to a colleague.

Travel Warnings

The U.S. State Department issues Travel Warnings about countries to which it is recommended that Americans not travel, accompanied by the actual posted warning is a Consular Information Sheet. This document is available for every country, but for countries that have been added to the Travel Warning list, the information sheet gives detailed explanation as to why. This serves as a general public announcement to inform citizens of travel dangers, such as terrorist threats or sudden disease outbreaks.

Being added to the Travel Warning list occurs most often in lesser-developed countries with unstable governments. Often, warnings are posted about anniversary dates of previous terrorist attacks or sudden coups. The Consular Information Sheet provides information about embassy locations, unusual regulations, crime, drug penalties, or any condition that is considered potentially harmful. However, not all unstable countries are on the warning list, just ones that at the time pose a specific danger or threat.

The following is an example of a country that has been added to the list of Travel Warnings, with an example of its Consular Information sheet:

- Côte d'Ivoire (11/28/2006)
  - 12/18/2006 Travel Warning
  - Avian Flu Fact Sheet
  - International Financial Scams
  - Intercountry Adoption Cote d'Ivoire

Within each of the sheets, a traveler can view details into the occurances for each country, in this case, Cote d'Ivoire (Foreign).

International Travel Entry Requirements Data

In order to determine which countries are the least accessible to international travelers and riskiest to give their personal information to, primary data was collected comparing approximately 200 countries of the world.

First, a list of entry requirements was collected from the U.S. Department of State website (http://www.travel.state.gov). This list includes the following 18 requirements: passport, visa, proof of travel itinerary, sufficient funds, birth certificate, vaccination records, daily tariff, departure tax, entrance fee, health insurance, HIV test, letter of consent for minors, letter of invitation, letter of purpose, limited entry points, personal interview, police registration, and travel insurance. Then, for requirements that applied to each country, the country received a score of one and for requirements that did not apply, the country received a zero. Finally, the totals were calculated out of 18 and the countries were sorted in order from the countries requiring the most items off of the list to the countries requiring the least. Based on the data collected, the most difficult countries to enter are Angola, Eritrea, Saudi Arabia, and Sudan. Countries that are easier for international travelers to visit include places like the United Kingdom, Gibraltar, Switzerland, and Morocco.

Another calculation was done based on each entry requirement to determine the percentage of countries addressing that specific requirement. Results show that 98% of all countries require international visitors to have a passport. 53% of these countries also ask for proof of an outbound flight or roundtrip tickets to ensure that the visitors will not be residing permanently. The next most prevalent requirements from countries are visas and entrance fees. As stated earlier, there are multiple types of visas and entrance fees are included in the visa application fee and paid to the foreign governments. Bhutan, one of the more difficult countries to visit, is the only country to require a daily tariff from visitors, so the percentage is less than one percent. Also at a frequency of less than 1%, upon entering China, a traveler may be stopped for a personal interview.

Conclusion

As international travel becomes ever more accessible, more privacy risks present themselves. In the process leading up to, and in experiencing the journey of a lifetime, the traveler must give up certain personal information to a multitude of governmental and non-governmental agencies. Postal workers, government employees, foreign government members, customs agents both foreign and domestic, and essentially anyone else who has the tools to hack into the databases that this information is stored in are able to review it. There is an obvious difference in risk level between a country like the U.S., where security of personal information is a top priority, and a Middle Eastern country where even legally crossing borders can be risky. The truth is it is ultimately up to the traveler to decide who can be trusted.

Works Cited

"CBP Travel Spotlight." US Government and Border Protection. http://cbp.gov. 22 Mar 2007

"Clear's Commitment to Privacy." Fly Clear Company. http://www.flyclear.com/privacy.html 22 Mar 2007

"Foreign Entry Requirements." US Department of State. http://travel.state.gov. 22 Mar 2007

Hasbrouck, Edward. The Practical Nomad: How to Travel Around the World. California: Avalon Travel Publishing, 2004.

"Keeping it Real." US CustomsToday. March 2002 Vol. 38 No. 3

Lansky, Doug. First Time Around the World. New York: Rough Guides, 2006.

"Machine Readable Travel Documents (MRTD)." ICAO. Retrieved on 22 Mar 2007

Marrus, Michael. The Unwanted: European Refugees in the Twentieth Century. New York: Oxford University Press, 1985. p. 92.

"Our Travelers." Transportation Security Administration. <http://www.tsa.gov/what_we_do/layers/rt/index.shtm.> 22 Mar 2007

"Passport." Wikipedia: The Free Encyclopedia. <http://wikipedia.org>. 22 Mar 2007

Pelton, Robert Young. The World's Most Dangerous Places. New York: HarperCollins Publishers Inc., 2003.

7

Biometrics: Does Convenience Outweigh Privacy?

Jarret Roberts and Sejal Patel

Introduction

Eight years ago, the tiny ridges that make up a fingerprint meant little more than a way for crime scene investigators to identify suspects. Now, in the world of 2007, they are linked to everything from bank accounts to national identification systems. Consumers can pay at grocery stores literally with the touch of a finger, and employees do not need to carry around security cards because they can use their fingerprints to gain access to restricted areas. "Biometrics is the science of measuring biological characteristics and behaviors for the purpose of determining or verifying identity" (Langenderfer and Linnhoff 314). Even though fingerprint scanning is the most widely used and known form, the entire biometrics field is quickly becoming integrated as a standard in both the consumer and business world. The rapid expansion of an industry so closely tied to extremely personal information raises the question: are the conveniences created by biometrics worth the sacrificed privacy?

Much of the attention surrounding biometrics has focused on accuracy and reliability (Carpoor 48). While this chapter will touch on the topics of accuracy and reliability, the main focus will be to explore the ethics, convenience, and security issues integrated within biometrics. The first section of this chapter will present a brief introduction to the topic of biometrics. From there, the role of this chapter will be to present research findings on the perceptions surrounding biometrics, regarding the trade off individuals face between ethics, convenience, and security.

An Overview of Biometrics

Biometrics originally stemmed from the need to identify victims though forensics (Carpoor 48). While early forms of the technology required an expert to analyze and make conclusions based on human experience, the integration of technology allowed biometrics to be implemented on the mass scale seen today. In early 1998, Visa began the first commercial integration of biometrics by linking credit accounts to the fingerprints of participants in a pilot study (Cuneo 24). From there, the industry grew to reach revenues of over $800 million in 2003 and is now projected to more than triple by 2008 (Allan 77). In addition to the aforementioned fingerprint scanning, biometrics includes face recognition, hand geometry, iris scanning, voice recognition, signature recognition, retina scanning, ear/lip motion recognition, body odor analysis, skin reflection analysis, nail bed analysis, body shape analysis, dental analysis, and DNA recognition. (Langenderfe and Linnhoff). All of these functions require a two-step process, "enrollment" and "authentication," to verify identity (Langenderfe and Linnhoff 315).

How It Works

Biometrics works by first enrolling information and then later using that information to authenticate an individual's identity. In the first step, enrollment, data collected and the individual's data points are linked to her identity. The purpose of this first step is to create a data set that can later be compared to data points during authorization. In the case of biometrics, enrollment is unique because of the biological and behavioral information collected. Unlike many current forms of collected identifiers, such as Personal Identification Numbers (PINs), the data collected for a biometric data set is physically linked to its owner. For example, an individual's fingerprint could be scanned into a database, and then linked to the identity of the individual it came from. As will be seen, this link to the physical form is the source of much convenience, but also a great deal of ethical debate. After enrollment, new data can be compared to the existing data set through the second step, authentication. The data being collected is in the form of biological or behavior attributes. Again using fingerprints as an example, an individual scans a fingerprint into a system that searches a data set of fingerprints to determine if there is a match.

Matching is not a simple process. To authenticate these individual data points against the data set, they must first be translated into a form that is easily comparable and readable. In order to accomplish this conversion, physical information, such as fingerprints, is translated into vectors or equations (Langenderfe and Linnhoff). The equations generated are easily read and compared to each other by computers when run through algorithms. Authentication is granted if the equation fulfills the requirements of the algorithm. In the case of fingerprints, the scanner would take a digital image of the fingerprint. From this image an equation would be written describing features, such as a ridge splitting or the center point, along with the location of these features.

This equation is then run through an algorithm and if the features and their locations match, authentication is granted.

If authentication is granted it can come in two distinct forms: identification and verification (Hong, Yun, and Cho 502). Identification, the first type of authentication, occurs when a newly acquired data point is compared to a pre-existing set to see if the point can be identified via the set. In this case, a name or some other identifier would identify an individual by scanning their fingerprint individually. In the other type of authentication, verification, a data point is compared to a set in which it may or may not exist. If, for instance, a security guard scanned his finger, and that data point existed in the authenticating data set, he would be verified and granted access without actually being identified as an individual.

No two scans will ever be exactly alike even if they are of the same image. For example, fingers placed at slightly different angles create a much different image than the one created during enrollment. Further, an individual may have a paper cut, or some other new abnormality, running across the middle of a finger which was not there when the original enrollment image was scanned. Thus, even with the most advanced technology the vector renditions are never exact and limits must be set as to which data points pass and which do not. Setting very stringent criteria for matching ensures a much lower likelihood of false positives. However, setting such stringent limits also drastically increases the number of false negatives. The opposite is true for setting an intensely lenient limit. There will be fewer negatives that should have been authenticated, but false positives will register more often. While finding a balance between stringent and lenient limits is a constant source of debate, the effects on society from a false positive often outweigh those of a false negative. From a company perspective, it is better to wrongly lock out someone who belongs in a restricted area than to wrongly grant access to someone who does not belong there.

Users of Biometrics

Biometrics reaches into three main user segments: government, consumer, and business. With the recent increase in global terrorist activities, governments are pushing even harder for identification technologies that are reliable and secure. For example, "the U.S. government is pressuring twenty-six visa-waiver nations to embed biometric data into their passports" (Allan 77). Additionally, "next generation smart cards in Europe, Asia, and Japan promise to include biometrics for identification, passport visa, and driver's license purposes" (Allan 77).

The implications of such large-scale implementation are enormous. If the UK government were to utilize biometric technology in their national identification cards, it would create a biometric database with over 50 million entries (Dettmer 26; Hornung 502). Aside from national implementation, the consumer segment will be the largest group affected by biometrics. Companies such as Piggly-Wiggly grocery store and Blockbuster Video are already beginning to allow consumers to link accounts and even payment to biometric identifiers (Langenderfe and Linnhoff 327). Finally, businesses are beginning to employ biometric technology into all aspects of employees' workdays, from authorization to print, to accessing restricted areas. For companies, the advantage of biometrics security is the inability to transfer access. While employees can let someone borrow an access card and clock each other in, a fingerprint scanning time clock would prevent such exploitation.

Ethics of Biometric Data Collection

While lost credit cards can be canceled, and PINs reassigned, the permanence of biometric data magnifies the ethical debate about its collection. Perhaps one of the greatest concerns revolves around the possibility of a breach in a biometric database. All too often, it is reported that personal information on a company's system or Website has been compromised. In the case of biometric data, a compromise of biometric databases would have much more permanence. Once a fingerprint is compromised, it is impossible to exchange it because of its physical link to the owner. Individuals cannot simply cancel their current fingerprint and get a new one. This physical link and permanence are, however, what make biometrics such a convenience.

The permanence and extreme individuality of biometric identification factors make data exchange and tracking easier than ever (Langenderfe and Linnhoff 330-334). The consolidation of identification biometrics provides, and often leads to one form of identification. In turn, this allows for easier tracking of individuals. At the same time, the biometric identification factors are both unique and universal, again creating an ease of sharing consumer information. While some argue linking databases could allow the capture of criminals that otherwise would have dodged apprehension, there is a greater cost to society to consider. Such ease in tracking could easily be taken to an extreme. It is possible that tracking could lead to a society where every violation, no matter how small, is tracked though the use of biometrics. If this were to escalate, the world could transform into a "Big Brother" society. It is also realistic for corporations to be able to track and link consumers' every interaction with a biometric scanner, permitting the formation of in depth consumer profiles. Individuals have always had to balance the convenience of technology with its intrusiveness. Now, however, technologies such as biometrics utilize one of the last unexploited pieces of information individuals have, their biological characteristics.

Convenience of Biometrics

While the ethics of biometrics are still a major debate, the potential convenience is often viewed as the beneficial contribution society will receive from the technology. Biometrics removes the inconvenience of being without identification. In a survey by New York based Biometrics Group, 240 random consumers were questioned as to their preferred form of security. According to a recent poll by US Banker, fingerprint scanning ranked nearly three times higher than traditional passwords. The reason given for such a high ranking was closely linked to the convenience. Imagine a society where a wallet or purse is a thing of the past. Additionally, biometric identifiers add convenience because, for the most part, they do not change over a person's lifetime, eliminating the need to physically renew cards. DNA and even finger print samples taken from a newborn will be nearly identical to those taken from the same individual decades later. Waiting in line for a license at the Department of Motor vehicles would no longer be necessary.

Next, since biometric data is a physically stored type of data it cannot be lost, forgotten, or easily stolen. Thus, remembering many different passwords or leaving behind credit cards after purchases would be a thing of the past. Having an identification or credit identifier that cannot be lost or physically stolen would greatly reduce the fraud currently seen with credit cards. Finally, biometrics has the potential to make life more convenient by reducing theft. If computers and cell phones were integrated with biometric sensors, they would be useless to anyone but the owners. For thieves, the desire to steal them would be greatly reduced because the stolen goods would have little value to anyone except the owner, whose fingerprint is needed to unlock the goods. The convenience linked to biometric sensors continues to fuel the debate over its ethics.

Security Implications of Biometrics

Biometric technologies have tremendous potential to strengthen national securities by uniquely identifying individuals. As previously mentioned, many governments are currently putting a great deal of effort into the development of nationally linked biometric identification systems. One major problem with such implications is enrollment. In order for an individual to be authenticated as a criminal or suspect they must first be enrolled and classified as one. It is unlikely that many criminals or terrorists will willingly enroll in biometric databases, and it is likely, these will not be the only groups opposed to enrollment. Some religious groups, such as Mormons, discourage or even prohibit the use of technology. If biometric systems were put in place, would these people then be excluded from societal interaction or would a by-pass have to be allowed? Any form of by-pass would compromise the security of the system. However, it will almost certainly be necessary for such bypasses to exist. It is inevitable that no matter how accurate the technology behind biometrics becomes, there will still need to be some way to by-pass the system. Due to the false positives that will occur, even at the smallest of percentages, and the potential for technology failure such as a power outage, the overall security of biometrics will only be as strong as its weakest part.

There are also security concerns about biometric tracking, which is "real-time or near-real-time surveillance of an individual," and mapping a person's past habits to make or reconstruct someone's path (Arthur 6). Such tracking could provide enormous security and is becoming closer to a reality. Iris scans now can take place from up to twenty-four inches away (Langenderfe and Linnhoff 319). The implications of such technology lead to the concern that individuals will soon be tracked with little knowledge of such happenings. In much the same way, hidden cameras now cover much of the public and consumer world; soon, biometric scanners could track individuals. Again, it is a trade off of convenience and privacy. It would be convenient as a society, if criminals could be located and apprehended in a matter of moments due to the tracking capabilities. At the same time, our society must weigh the ethical implications of giving up so much privacy.

Future Obstacles for Biometrics

The advancement and acceptance of biometric technology globally shows that consumer acceptance and trust is growing exponentially. Companies are also adopting biometrics at an amazing rate. The Aite Group, a research firm in Boston, predicts that in January 2009, 35% of financial institutions will have deployed biometric technologies (Allen 77). The International Biometric Group of New York also projected in January, that global biometric revenue would rise from $2.1 billion in 2006 to $5.7 billion in 2010 (Allen 77). However, biometrics must surmount some very real concerns before becoming common in everyday life, especially in the areas of cost and accuracy.

Cost is one major concern. Currently, the cost to produce and implement biometric technology is beyond what many companies can afford to pass on to their consumers. United Airlines mandated 400 of its employees to use biometrics technology to gain access to their network and log their work hours. The total cost for this one biometric project cost millions of dollars for the United States (Costanzo 6-11). For smaller companies, the cost of implementing biometric technology may not be realistic. "Eventually the industry will provide biometric solutions that will be more acceptable to a wider audience, making it more affordable to everyone," stated Ken Silveira, the chief information officer at Bridge Bank in San Jose (Costanzo 6-11). Until economies of scale combine with cheaper technology, cost will be a major hindrance on the growth of biometrics.

Another major obstacle facing biometric technology is the possibility of error. Even though the International Biometric Group states that in the last decade biometric technology has become "a lot more accurate, with less than a one percent False Rejection Rate (FRR)," error is still a major concern (Bruno 41). If in the aforementioned case of the UK implementing a national biometric system with 50 million data points, a one-tenth percent FRR occurred, it would mean that 50,000 data points would be falsely rejected. False identification could have implications just as harmful; "Oregon attorney Brandon Mayfield was wrongly jailed for two weeks because his fingerprint purportedly matched one found at the scene of the Madrid bombings in March 2004 (Langenderfe and Linnhoff 228). It is highly likely that accuracy will never reach 100%. With this in mind, society must consider the cost of error that will occur, compared to the convenience provided.

Research

Design, Methodology, and Approach

As mentioned, the research done for this chapter examined individuals' views regarding the sacrifice of privacy for the convenience that biometric technology provides. To allow the full exploration of this topic, in-depth personal interviews were conducted with twenty-four respondents. Respondents were selected to yield a balance of age, gender, profession, and interests. This allowed a greater variety of perspective on the subject. A set of ten predetermined questions was the concentration of the interview. However, respondents were encouraged to expand upon topics. The questions were designed to assess the sample perceptions surrounding biometric technology, the ethical obligation of collecting personal information, how security weighs in on technology today, and how important convenience is in individual lives. The interviews were conducted in person and lasted between fifteen and twenty minutes. Questions were designed with as little bias as possible to allow respondents to reply positively or negatively. The focus was to extract trends that either bridged the entirety of respondents or were isolated within homogeneous segments of respondents. Thus, major themes regarding ethics, convenience, and security of biometric technology in individuals' lives could be compared to trends regarding the sacrifice of privacy.

Responses on Ethics

"I do not think it is ethical. It's the last piece of privacy a human being has," one respondent begins. Nearly all interviewees expressed concern about the ethics of collecting biometric data. Additionally, respondents were concerned about the collection of personal information such as address and social security number. Nevertheless, a majority of respondents said they willingly gave up personal information without knowing its end use. As one respondent stated, "I give it to them, but I don't think they need it. I don't know what they do or might do with it." Individuals realized there were ethical dilemmas in giving up personal or biological information, but were still willing to do so. "We are getting to the point where we do so much of it [giving out information] that we are getting jaded as people," one interviewee stated. Another respondent affirmed this claim when she stated "it's kind of one of those things you don't have a choice on. It's like if they decided to get rid of the penny, do you really have any choice in it?"

The interviews revealed that while respondents immediately expressed concern about the implications of biometric data collection, they were not opposed and seemed optimistic regarding the possibilities it could provide. New technologies such as biometrics were seen as the solution to current problems, and the ethical implications were put aside in the minds of respondents. Consequently, while biometric information was viewed as the last piece of personal information left to be exploited, it was also something individuals were willing to consider sacrificing for a more secure and convenient future. As one respondent concluded, "it depends on how the information will be used, and what they tell me it will be used for."

Whether consumers consciously guide and limit the integration of biometrics, or simply accept it as the next progression, has yet to be seen. Holding biometric data collection to a high standard and limiting data exchange will reduce some of the ethical issues surrounding biometric systems. However, there will always exist some ethical debates on the collection of "the last piece of privacy a human being has."

Responses on Convenience

"Biometric technology would, in the end be more convenient," one respondent replied when asked to comment on how biometrics would affect his life. The majority of respondents believed that biometrics would, to some degree, add convenience to their lives. However, older respondents, over the age of forty, were more concerned with the tradeoff of privacy for convenience than respondents under the age of twenty. As an older respondent reported, concern is carried over from current technologies and projected on biometrics. "Well, you know when you pay bills online, you have to give them all your information, your credit cards. No, I don't think it's secure. But you do it, 'cause it makes your life more convenient."

The reported willingness to sacrifice privacy for technology lead to a few conclusions. First, individuals may not be informed about the privacy implications associated with technologies, such as biometrics. Second, individuals may understand, but may not be concerned with the implications. Finally, individuals may be subject to a lack of both understanding and concern. The qualitative data provided by interviews showed a variation of all three responses throughout the entire set of those willing to forgo parts of their privacy. One respondent expressed understanding but a lack of concern with privacy issues, when she described the security of technology in society as being an "illusion of security." Later, when questioned about privacy and convenience, this same respondent stated, "biometric technology would, in the end, be more convenient." A second respondent's comment exemplified the idea that individuals knowingly trade privacy for convenience. "[New technology is] part of the reason they're getting all the information. They can keep track of what you do easier (*sic*) because of all that stuff." At the same time, this respondent stated that, "you can really see the benefits of technology," showing a knowledge of sacrificing privacy, but also a willingness to do so. The overall trend found in respondents was an acceptance of new technologies that provide greater convenience, even at the cost of privacy.

Responses On Security

From the subjects interviewed, there was a general theme that respondents believed biometric technology would provide more security than current technologies. "I think they would be more secure. For instance, if they took fingerprints or retina scans, those are my distinct features and they are not easily copied or cannot be easily hacked using some computer" one respondent replied. The idea that biometric data would be carried by the owner and not left on a computer appeared in many interviews. However, the conclusion was also drawn that the perceived security of biometrics will be greater during the introductory phase of the technology and, then lessen over time. This is due to the belief by respondents that any technology can and will be broken into.

While respondents believed that a greater security would be provided by biometrics, they also thought it would only be a matter of time before it is exploited. As one respondent explained, "technologies are insecure because if someone can write it and make it secure, someone can hack it." Individuals' belief and trust in new technology may stem from this idea that new technology is secure for a short while, but later becomes compromised. One interviewee described, "I'm sure someone's going to figure out how to break it [biometrics] and there's always going to be someone who will figure it out." From this respondent's answers, it was inferred that the idea of security with emerging technologies has very little permanence, even with biometric technology. While there was a strong acceptance, and trust, in the promise of improved security from biometrics, there was also reason to believe that individuals would be quick to change their minds if biometrics does not fulfill its promise.

Research Concerns

The information collected for this paper provided many insights. Still, as with any research, there are limitations. This study was done over a period of two months. One of the major benefits of conducting research over a short period of time is the snapshot it creates. This is especially relevant for such a rapidly evolving topic. On the other hand, the short time frame limits both the quantity of data it is possible to collect, and the ability to track trends over time. In addition to these issues, the global aspect of biometrics raised some other concerns around the methodology and research findings. Using one location, Boulder, Colorado undoubtedly added bias to such a global topic. Given more time and the opportunity to expand the survey area, it would be interesting to see how geography affects the opinions on biometric technology's role in privacy and convenience. Not only would a larger geographic area reduce location bias, but it would also allow for a larger sample size creating greater statistical significance. Finally, a larger, more geographically balanced sample would provide a more even distribution within gender, age, and profession.

Conclusions

The research concluded that there were major trends in ethics: the convenience and security of biometrics, and the sacrifice of privacy. According to the sample of respondents, biological information is ultimately the last unexploited piece of individual's identity. However, many of the individuals were quick to consider its sacrifice in order to live a more secure and convenient future. While respondents had consideration, it was not black and white. There was concern about how the information would be used and if there would be policies in place to protect biometric information. It was clear that regardless of the policies, it would only help control the debate over biometric technology's ethics. Additionally, respondents' answers helped conclude that the idea of security is nonexistent in today's technology, and that the integration of biometric technology would only give the "illusion of security" for the short term. Finally, it was also concluded that many of the respondents see technology as ever changing and only a step ahead of being cracked.

Ultimately, this research paper sought to answer the question: is the convenience created by biometrics worth the sacrificed privacy?

Many of the respondents felt there would be an inherent beneficial implication of convenience in their lives from biometric technology. However, it was the respondents over the age of forty who feared and questioned the tradeoff of privacy and convenience. Conversely, the respondents from the ages of eighteen to twenty-five, who will be the leaders and consumers of tomorrow, were not as concerned with their privacy being exploited.

Today's world is a place where convenience is on the forefront of every consumer's mind. In this fast paced, evolving world, new technologies are proving to be a balance of intrusion and convenience. Biometrics is quickly becoming integrated into the consumer and business world. Clearly, biometrics will bring convenience to consumers; however, it will also cause a loss of privacy. In the end, the degree of the privacy lost will depend on how involved consumers are in the integration of biometrics.

Works Cited

Allan, Roger. "Biometrics Wields a Double-Edged Sword." *Electronic Design*; 6/30/2005, Vol. 53 Issue 14, p77-81, 3p, 4 diagrams, 1 graph, 2c.

Bruno, Mark. "That's My Finger."*Bank Technology News*; Mar2001, Vol. 14 Issue 3, p41-42, 2p.

Capoor, Sapna. "Biometrics as a Convenience." *Security: For Buyers of Products, Systems & Services*, Dec2006, Vol. 43 Issue 12, p48-50, 2p.

Charndra, Akhilesh; Calderor, Thomas. "CHALLENGES AND CONSTRAINTS TO THE Diffusion of Biometrics IN INFORMATION SYSTEMS." *Communications of the ACM*, Dec2005, Vol. 48 Issue 12, p101-106, 6p.

CHO, SUNG-BAE; HONG, JIN-HYUK; YUN, EUN-KYUNG. "A REVIEW OF PERFORMANCE EVALUATION FOR BIOMETRICS SYSTEMS." *International Journal of Image & Graphics*, Jul2005, Vol. 5 Issue 3, p501-536, 36p.

Castanzo, Chris "Suddenly Biometric ID Doesn't Seem Like Science Fiction." *American Banker*, June2006, Vol. 171 Issue 107, special section p6-11, 5p.

Cuneo, Alice Z.. "Let your fingers do the paying." *Advertising Age*, 10/4/2004, Vol. 75 Issue 40, p24-24, 2/3p, 1c.

Dettmer, Roger. "SAFETY IN NUMBERS." *IEE Review*, Nov2004, Vol. 50 Issue 11, p26-29, 4p.

Hornung, Gerrit. "Biometric Passports and Identity Cards: Technical, Legal, and Policy Issues." *European Public Law*, Dec2005, Vol. 11 Issue 4, p501-514, 14p.

Langenderfer, Jeff; Linnhoff, Stefan. "The Emergence of Biometrics and Its Effect on Consumers." *Journal of Consumer Affairs*, Winter2005, Vol. 39 Issue 2, p314-338, 25p.

Ploeg, Irma. "Biometrics and Privacy A note on the politics of theorizing technology." *Information, Communication & Society*, Mar2003, Vol. 6 Issue 1, p85-104, 20p.

"That's My Finger." *U.S. Banker*. Feb2001, p20 1p.

8

Advertising and Technology:
How Advertisers Are Trying To Get Into Your Head

Drew Woodcock & Caroline Sweeney

Introduction to Advertising and Technology

The following is a scene from Steven Spielberg's *Minority Report*:

> *Anderton walks in the door, gets his new eyes scanned, and we hear a*
> *voice say:*
> *Hello, Mr. Yakamoto! Welcome back to the Gap.*
> *Anderton stops cold as a holographic image of a huge Asian man now*
> *appears standing in front of him.*
> *How'd those assorted tank tops work out for you? (Frank)*

Many would think this scene seems like a stretch for the near future
of advertising, but consider this quote regarding technology
advancements in the last 50 years:

Fifty years ago, we were only beginning to have color television,
The Wizard of Oz had just premiered on TV, a remote control had just
been invented, and VCRs were still a long way ahead. Twenty-five
years ago, Pac-Man was a popular novelty, CNN was one year old, and
cell phones were yet to be introduced. Ten years ago, watching a movie

online was still a dream. Five years ago, the world didn't know anything about iPods and podcasts, Google had just begun to sell its ads, and blogging was still a fringe nerdy thing to do (AdvertisingLab).

Where is the technology going to be in the year 2030? What is in store for the future of advertising and the next twenty-five years of technological development? The holographic display technology mentioned in the scene above is already being implemented in the market today. Advertisers have started to embed advertising directly into every facet of life and the actual consumer is now an advertiser's most important medium. This chapter will discuss the future of advertising, as well as the possible threats this technology poses to consumer privacy.

Advertising Today

Many Americans, by the time they arrive to work in the morning, have already been exposed to over 200 advertisements such as billboards, monitors, bus stops, etc. Advertising and marketing agencies are constantly inventing new ways to expose consumers to a barrage of ads that will potentially convince the shopper to invest in a particular product or brand. The original idea behind advertising was to inform potential customers of the benefits provided by a certain product or service to create differentiation between competing brands, as well as contending in the race with market competitors. The issue today is that consumers have begun to reject the excess amount of advertisements, or simply "tune" them out, due to the extreme overexposure on a day-to-day basis. Agencies are trying to determine new ways to break through all of the clutter and appeal to consumers in a more personal and targeted manner. What new technologies will advertisers take advantage of in the pursuit of targeting specific consumer segments? Will these technologies breach the privacy of the individual consumer?

Research on Privacy and Technology

The topic of this chapter revolves around the future aspirations of advertisers and the lengths at which they are willing to go to reach the consumer. In order to reveal the future implications of these techniques and technologies, an extensive amount of secondary research was done. A plethora of information was used to investigate the future of advertising practices in conjunction with technological advancements. This extensive research included scholarly journals, online databases, electronic articles, related organizations, libraries, and accredited web pages. The following is a portrayal of the current and future on-goings in the world of advertising, technology, and the effects on consumer privacy.

Advertising and Technology

Digital Signage

A new gadget advertisers have been utilizing is digital signage. This fairly new technology allows retailers to use either projection devices or high definition monitors to effectively display advertisements which they hope will intrigue and inform the consumer. This advertising technology is being incorporated into malls and shopping centers across America and is very effective at catching the attention of potential customers within a close proximity. The idea is to grasp the attention of the customer long enough for sensors to pick up on certain physical attributes or characteristics. The sensors that are installed in the plasma screens and projectors have the capability to read the shopper's face and determine whether the person is male or female, along with their age and race. The readings are connected to software that also has the capability to determine what, if any, products the customer is currently holding or looking at. With this information brands can quickly and easily identify key competitors in their market along with ways to create stronger product differentiation for their target segment.

The main struggle of this technology for retailers and advertisers is getting a customer's attention long enough to obtain a reading or become influenced by the digital signage. Once the sensors have established who the customer is, the software displays an advertisement that could potentially appeal to the person based on the identified characteristics. But where do the advertisements come from? Advertisements are stored in a local computer that can be accessed by the retailer or any other authorized personnel, such as a firm that is always online with the signage source. Each ad has preset information assigned to it that tells the software which advertisement should be displayed based on the consumers' characteristics. Signage options are also based on other external factors such as location, time of the year, and weather (Terdiman). According to David Polinchock, the founder and chairman of Brand Experience Lab, such marketing can increase sales by up to 300%. Polinchock further explains that "the more that you can target an ad specifically to what a person is looking for, what they might need and who they are, the better you have a chance to connect with those people."

The problem with digital signage is that it is hard to obtain the attention of people in a distracting environment like a retail shopping center. This method of advertising is also very expensive to use. However, advertisers are inventing new ways to reach a cost effective method of using this high-tech platform. IBM has recently patented a system that could give advertisers the possibility of projecting images on walls at an angle. By putting this new technology in the corner of a room, the image could be projected on all four walls of a room, maximizing the effect. Another advantage of using a technology like IBM's is that the projectors are much cheaper than the plasma displays currently being used. Regardless of future advancements, this technology is a valuable resource for advertisers and a possible threat to consumers.

Privacy Issues with Digital Signage

A shopper walks into a Target store and notices that there are several monitors in the entrance. The sensors in the monitors take a reading and load the purchase history of this particular customer. After scanning past purchases, the software recognizes that it has been several months since the customer has purchased new socks. The software installed in the monitor can then inquire of the customer whether they would like the usual brand and size of socks sent to the checkout stand along with the number of units needed. Voice recognition software can then read a response of "yes" or "no" from the costumer. If the shopper responds "yes," the system will inform store employees to send the merchandise to the front and put it on hold for the consumer until they are finished shopping. If the customer responds "no," the software will recommend other items that the customer may potentially be interested in. This technology seems to be the ultimate in convenience. But what if the software becomes too personal? For example, an obese shopper enters the store and is picked up by the digital signage monitors. The software would recognize that this person's waist line has been increasing and decides to recommend some new exercise equipment. This may seem like an exaggerated circumstance, but what exactly will be considered crossing the line in regards to a shopper's privacy?

Shopping Buddy

One national supermarket chain, Stop & Shop, was searching for a way to address key issues customers were facing while shopping. Stop & Shop realized that finding competent employees who wanted to work for the long-term was challenging; so they looked into communications technology.

The grocery giant has recently implemented a new technology into many of its stores called the Shopping Buddy. Shopping Buddy is a "wireless touch screen browser device that attaches to a shopping cart and delivers personalized services and incentives to customers while they *shop*" (Tarnowski). When customers arrive at their local Stop & Shop, they grab a cart that holds a small monitor in the middle of the cart's push handle. Shoppers simply swipe their member card, and a list is presented on the screen with an index of previously purchased items as well as many other recommendations based on the customer's previous purchases.

Shopping Buddy contains a function that pinpoints where the shopper is in the store, ensuring that recommendations are relevant to the products the customer is currently looking at. The device also includes a wireless barcode scanner to give shoppers the convenience of scanning their items at the cart, saving potential check-out time. This tool is incredibly convenient for the customer and creates opportunities for companies who want to learn more about buyers' habits and possible future purchasing decisions. The question that always arises is, how is this massive amount of consumer information is going to be used? Will these new technologies prove to be detrimental to consumer privacy, or will they continue to add convenience to everyday life?

Privacy Issues with Shopping Buddy

Today's shoppers may be unaware of what exactly retailers are doing with personal information they have collected. Most shoppers are under the impression that the privacy policy they signed will protect the information they have so willingly given to retailers, and that it is the retailers' responsibility to comply with this policy. What they do not understand is that the policy is written to benefit the supermarket, and could be misused. Why people who would not normally give up such personal information decide that it is okay to give it to their local grocer is concerning. Consumers most likely still feel safe because the technology is still young, and there is little awareness about potentially serious privacy breaches.

An ethical dilemma could arise if the grocery giant Stop & Shop decided to increase revenues by selling all of a consumer's purchasing habits to a marketing research company, who could then release the information to that consumer's health care provider. If the provider had possession of the consumer's eating habits and noticed a pattern of unhealthy purchases, they could decide to increase insurance rates. On the other hand, shoppers who could prove excellent eating habits could have the possibility of their rates being lowered. So far, shoppers have only had praise for the new Shopping Buddy and have had no complaints about privacy issues, but it is possible that the use of these consumer information databases will soon have many customer issues and complaints regarding security and protection.

Mind Reading Computer

Professor Peter Robinson of the University of Cambridge, and a group of professors from the Massachusetts Institute of Technology have developed a camera-assisted computer that can understand what a person is thinking and feeling from their facial expressions, gestures and tone of voice. This technology was debuted at the Royal Society in the summer of 2006, which is the National Academy of Sciences for the United Kingdom and is on the cutting edge of newest technologies.

The program has had high accuracy in test results and a working prototype is being completed at the Massachusetts Institute of Technology. The computer program was as equally accurate as the top 6% of humans in picking out people's moods and feelings. Similar to a mind reader, the computer is being programmed with over 400 different expressions and minute facial movements, such as a raised eyebrow or a squinted nose. The computer's knowledge of emotions is being programmed by digitally recording actors, who make different movements and expressions to signify distinct feelings.

This technology could be used in many different aspects of human life in order to advertise to consumers in many diverse forms. It can be used to assist as well as advertise to people with Autism or Asperger's syndrome. It can be used to alert people with music advertisements while in their car, or it can be used to send advertisements based on a person's mood anywhere there is a camera with this technology.

People with Autism or Asperger's syndrome are generally seen as 'mind blind' because they have difficulty interpreting people's moods and feelings from facial expressions and other non-verbal clues. This technology will help them to better communicate and understand how other people feel, because it can relay to them, in words, what a person's facial expression might mean. In the same way the technology can help people with these disabilities, it can also help advertisers to target this special group of consumers, who have been harder to reach in the past. By relaying the mood of an advertisement back to these consumers they can better connect with the ads.

Professor Robinson is said to be working with a Japanese car company and has expectations that this video technology will be installed in cars within the next five years. Installation will probably begin as a luxury feature and then become a common addition to cars in the near future. The video camera in a person's car will be able to read their facial expressions and deliver alerts to the driver. If the driver appears tired and falling asleep, the monitor in the car may advertise a nearby hotel or gas station where the driver could get some coffee. It can also play music in an effort to change a person's mood. For example, if the program picks up facial expressions that symbolize sadness, the software might send a humorous advertisement or play cheerful songs.

Most importantly, this new technology is meant to tap into someone's mind in order to send them the perfect advertisement for their mood and for their needs. Advertisers are always looking for new ways to determine how people really react to certain advertisements they place or products they develop. To tap into someone's thoughts when they are making purchasing decisions or simply walking by is the next step in 'becoming one' with the consumer and is exactly what this new technology allows for (Scott).

Privacy Issues for Mind Reading Computers

As futuristic as the technology may seem, working prototypes and test results about the accuracy of this new 'mind reading' technology already exist. Now is the time to start thinking about how this might affect privacy and what the consequences might be. The biggest question will always be: who can get hold of the information collected and what can they do with it?

In the case of the video computer in a car, what if an insurance company or a potential employer received private driver information? If a driver is constantly about to fall asleep at the wheel or in an angry mood, this might suggest to an insurance company or employer that the person is not a responsible and may be a risky driver. An insurance company might in turn not want to insure the driver or give the driver good rates. Depending on the position, this information could potentially sway an employer not to hire a possible job candidate. Is this fair, or an invasion of personal privacy?

Offense could be taken, or someone's well being may be affected by this new technology that has advertisements popping up all the time based on their perceived mood. Someone could be embarrassed if their facial expressions consistently give the program the impression that they are depressed or sad, and the software continues to recommend psychiatrists or antidepressants. This could have an effect on a person's well being by perpetuating a bad mood or changing their mood for the worse by giving them the wrong readout. For instance, what is a person's typical reaction to someone asking if they are in a bad mood when in reality, they are not? They would probably get angry or frustrated that others have the wrong impression of them and consequently, they might be put into a bad mood. False readings are a drawback of this software technology and could affect its future implementation.

Blogging

Blogging can be a form of business-related communications via a website where anyone can make journal style entries and leave comments in an interactive format. Recently, companies have become much more aware of blogging and the effect it can have on their brand images. Companies are designating much more time and energy to monitoring blogs and Internet sites with comments and posts about their products. This gives them the ability to insert positive advertising into the communication stream to try and counteract any negative feedback people might be posting. (Steinberg)

In general, blogs are an anonymous way to share information and thoughts on any subject. This anonymity gives advertisers a way to insert subtle advertising and information onto a website without appearing biased, because no one knows who it is coming from. Before a lot of companies started harnessing the phenomenon of blogging, a consumer could be almost certain that the comments were coming from unbiased users of products; now it is necessary for consumers to think about which posts to trust as unprejudiced.

Privacy Issues for Blogging

Trust is the main privacy issue that someone might have to worry about in regards to blogging. Do consumers care if people are putting up positive advertisements to counteract a negative comment by someone who tried a product and was truly not satisfied? What if the advertisements and promotions by companies are not entirely factual? Once again, technology has preceded law making. As of spring 2007 the Commercial Speech Doctrine had not subjected this type of communication to the same regulations of other forms of advertising, essentially making blogging a current loophole for advertisers to give consumers misleading or biased information (Sprague).

Future Hotel Advertising

Another interesting place advertising technology might be changing is hotels. One possibility would transform hotels into retail showrooms, where a guest could essentially buy anything of interest in their room. Hyatt and Kimpton hotel chains have already implemented a system like this to advertise the products in their rooms. Personalized advertisements could also start showing up on a consumer's hotel television based on any personal information the hotel may have collected about someone upon check-in. If someone puts anything in their hotel closet, their clothing might also subject them to more advertising, with future closets having the ability to read the radio frequency identification tags in clothing and be able to suggest new items and stores for the consumer to visit. One last way advertising might be implemented in someone's hotel room is in the bathroom. The tile floor would be able to take a readout from bare feet and suggest health products, like vitamins and nutrients that a person might be lacking (Frary).

The possibilities are endless, and so are the privacy issues related to this potentially invasive form of advertising. The main privacy issue for hotel advertising is concerned with who has access to this personal information and if hotel guests are worried about this type of knowledge being available to others. This form of advertising could prove detrimental to business for hotels as well because some guests may feel bombarded by additional ads and sales of products in their hotel room, and may choose to take their business elsewhere. With regards to the conveyance of health information in a hotel bathroom, many may not wish to hear a report on their health while on vacation, or traveling for business. Another threat arises if this collected health information could be given to insurance companies who could then use it to judge a consumer's health risks and potential policies. Only time will tell what consumer opinions will be regarding this new hotel advertising and its affects on privacy.

Consumer Privacy Issues

Society is constantly concerned with convenience in one's life; an element that provides ease and simplicity to the consumer experience. Advertising and marketing agencies try to make everyone's life easier in the hopes of subsequently making a profit. But are people willing to enjoy this convenience in exchange for an infringement of their privacy? Is society ready for these new technologies? The pivotal question that needs to be addressed is: will consumers of the world allow marketers, retailers, and advertisers to watch every decision and every move they make in order to provide convenience in the long run? Or do they even have a choice?

Many consumers argue that personalized advertising will not work on them because these new technologies, which create excitement among marketers, will in fact repel the targeted consumer. Instead of people being attracted to a customized shopping experience, they are turning away from it. But why, would it not be great to have every shopping experience tailored to a customer's needs?

In order to address these questions a single question survey was developed. The top of the survey had a short note that read: "Advertisers today are constantly inventing new ways to target specific consumers and get into their heads. As new technologies bring about more convenient shopping methods, consumers will have to give up an increasing amount of personal information." Following this statement was the survey's sole question: "How willing are you to give up personal information in order for the consumer experience to become more convenient?" The respondent was then presented with a scale from one to seven, with one being "ultimate privacy" and seven being "ultimate convenience", to rate their willingness to give up personal information for consumer convenience.

Ultimate Privacy	Some Privacy		Balanced	Some Convenience	Ultimate Convenience	
1	2	3	4	5	6	7

This scale portrayed the trade-off between privacy-convenience. The results of this question provided some interesting conclusions. Of the 50 respondents, 39 (78%) answered on the privacy side of the scale. It is not surprising that most people would like to have their personal information kept private. The other 11 respondents favored convenience, which implies an interest in the development of technology and a more personalized consumer experience. As mentioned previously, there are many techniques and tools that advertisers are using to get consumers to give up their personal information, and some consumers are participating willingly. Once again this creates concern regarding consumers surveyed who in the majority answered that they want to hold on to their privacy, but in actuality are divulging personal information on a daily basis.

Privacy Protection

Some consumers are opposed to the idea of mass consumer databases and implementing new technologies that track customers. In 1999, CASPIAN (Consumers Against Supermarket Privacy Invasion and Numbering) was created in order to educate people about shopper surveillance. CASPIAN stands against the use of member cards in grocery stores that create savings to those that have them, while making those who are not members pay the full price. This group feels that while member cards may appear to benefit the cardholding consumer, they are in fact created to help the retailer. CASPIAN argues that the savings cards will only help the shopper in the short-term and will end up hurting them in the long run by creating a segmented market for many years to come. CASPIAN attempts to inform consumers about these practices through demonstrations, protests, and informing shoppers of local stores that do not track their customers. Although such groups can inform consumers about possible privacy issues, they cannot completely prevent advertisers from continuing to use such technologies. It is difficult to make laws and regulations against this information collection because the shopper is voluntarily giving up their personal information. The consumer is responsible for not divulging personal information to their local retailers if they want to prevent future privacy issues.

Conclusion

Advancements in technology have been growing exponentially for years, and are likely to continue expanding. Is whether the world prepared to take on the new advancements? Will the consumer be ready for the future of advertising and the privacy issues that will surface from advertisers' attempts to become one with the consumer? The truth is best told through the words of Paco Underhill, "one of the poignancies of our era is that our technology has moved at lightning speeds past what our privacy laws are." The goal of this technology and consumer tracking will be to improve the quality of life and it will be interesting to observe what regulations are put into place to protect the consumer of the future. The public can only hope that those with access to the information prevent a Big Brother world, and instead lead consumers into a future of convenience and simplicity without sacrificing security.

Works Cited

Christensen, Bill. "'Minority Report' Ads Are In Your Future." 19 Sep. 2006. 11 Feb. 2007. <http://www.informationliberation.com/?id=15926>.

Frank, Scott. "Minority Report." 16 May 2001. 3 March 2007. <http://home.online.no/~bhundlan/scripts/MinorityReport_frank.txt>.

Frary, Mark. "Eye on the Future." Business Travel World Dec. 2006: 44-47. 09 Mar. 2007.

Scott, Mark. "This Computer May Be Too Smart." Business Week Online 14 July 2006: 10. 09 Mar. 2007.

Sprague, Bobert. "Business Blogs and Commercial Speech: a New Analytical Framework for the 21st Century." American Business Law Journal os 44.1 (2007): 127-159. 09 Mar. 2007.

Steinberg, Brian. "Minding the Blog is the Nest Big Thing in Managing Brand." Wall Street Journal 14 Feb. 2007, Eastern ed. ProQuest. University of Colorado Library. 09 Mar. 2007.

Stone, Gigi. "Advertisers Try New Ways To Get Into Your Head." ABC News. 16 Dec. 2006. 11 Feb. 2007. <http://www.abcnews.go.com/WNT/Business/story?id= 2731799&page=1>.

Tarnowski, Joseph. "Ahold's Shopping Buddy." Convenience Store News. 12 Oct. 2003. 11 Feb. 2007. <http://web.ebscohost.com/bsi/detail?vid=3&hid=3&sid= 5e08300c-3612-492f-95a2d96b62582cac%40sessionmgr3>.

Terdiman, Daniel. "Soon, Marketing Will Follow You." Wired.com. 16 Dec. 2003. 21 Feb. 2007. <http://www.wired.com/news/technology/1,61597-0.html>.

C.A.S.P.I.A.N. Consumers Against Supermarket Privacy Invasion and Numbering. 2004. 18 Feb. 2007. <http://www.nocards.org>.

RFID. Spychips. 2007. 21 Feb. 2007. <http://www.spychips.com>.

"White Noise on Future of Advertising." Advertising Lab. 5 Feb. 2006. 26 Feb. 2007. <http://adverlab.blogspot.com/2006/05/white-noise-on-future-of-advertising.html>

9

Paypal's Phishing Dilemma

Ben Weinbaum and Brett Mencin

In today's world of ecommerce, efficiency seems to come at a price. This price is most prevalent in the online payment and credit industries, where thousands of people in both third world countries as well as more developed nations seek out the financial information of others. While many financial companies are at risk of being hijacked by scammers, the vulnerability of Paypal is widely seen as the biggest risk of all.

What is Paypal?

Paypal is an online ecommerce payment company that was acquired by eBay in 2002. With over 133 million accounts in 103 countries, it is the largest e-payment company in the world. Paypal is unique in that it allows buyers to purchase items using only their email address. Once a consumer registers on Paypal, they can fund their account by transferring money from a personal bank account. Bank information is stored on Paypal and the account can also be directly linked to a credit or debit card. Paypal's simplicity is what makes it so popular and creates an appeal for online shopping. Members do not have to enter their credit card information numerous times at merchant sites, making them able to buy something in a matter of seconds. There are over 42,000 merchant websites that currently accept Paypal as a form of payment, and the company's site's popularity is soaring as major brand names such as Apple, Dell, Walgreen's and many more, join the ranks of those who use Paypal as their form of online payment.

The majority of Paypal's business comes from eBay, where nearly every seller accepts Paypal when purchasing an item. Paypal's global reach and vast customer base makes it a prime target for fraudulent activity, especially phishing.

What is Phishing?

According to the FTC, Phishing is a form of fraud in which Internet users are sent instant-messages, or more commonly emails, claiming to be from a company or organization that a user may deal with on a regular basis. Phishers attempt to fraudulently acquire sensitive information such as passwords, login names, credit card numbers, bank account numbers and other personal information. Paypal and Citibank are currently the most targeted companies in phishing attacks, especially in terms of fraudulent emails. Fraudulent emails from companies such as Paypal request the recipient to "confirm" or "validate" account information. If the recipient does not comply, the email suggests that consequences may arise. The emails then have a link to a bogus website that looks just as legitimate as the original website. The sole purpose of this is to lure email recipients into divulging personal and financial information to the operator in order to gain access to bank account and credit card information. Phishing has become increasingly more prevalent on Paypal than anywhere else on the web.

Advanced Techniques

Phishers need to accomplish three objectives in order to successfully retrieve the personal information they are after. First, the target must read the email. Second, the target must click the link to the fake website embedded in the email. Third, the linked website must be a mirror image of the website they are trying to fraudulently represent.

Phishers use specific techniques to achieve their objective to gain your personal information. The most common technique used is called "link manipulation." A link is disguised as a legitimate website by using misspelled letters in the URL or using a sub domain such as www.paypal.com.security instead of www.paypal.com. If someone were to click on the fraudulent link, they would be directed to a forged website that appears to be legitimate. Websites can be forged by using JavaScript commands to alter the address bar. When someone clicks on the link in the email, the website they are taken to detects what browser they are using; then it suppresses the real address bar and generates a fake one to take its place. The fraudulent browser bar shows the real web address of the website being impersonated rather than the address of the scam site the user is actually visiting.

Another method that phishers use is called "URL Redirection." Anyone who owns a website can re-direct their site to someplace else. This allows phishers to take advantage of website misspellings and re-direct users to a forged website. For example, users type in www.paypal.com hundreds of thousands of times a day. If someone were to type in www.paypol.com or www.paupal.com, they could potentially be re-directed to a forged "Paypal.com" without knowing they misspelled the intended domain name and could be subjected to a phishing attack.

How the Paypal Email Scam Works

The operators of this particular phishing scam involving Paypal have, without a doubt, created one of the most malicious and deceiving scams the Internet community has seen. There are many variations of the Paypal scam, but they usually involve a spoofed email address such as security@paypal.com. The branding and logo of the email look nearly exact when compared to any other email members may receive from Paypal. This is a problem in itself, because Paypal tends to send its members regular emails. The email message may vary from a simple "Please update your account" message to "Please Confirm Your Purchase" to "Notice: Buyer has filed a Claim on Your Recent Transaction." Messages such as these are very threatening because of their specificity. It is not uncommon for a high volume seller to have buyer complaints about wrong merchandise sent or failure to deliver. When a buyer files a claim, Paypal freezes the seller's funds in the amount of the transaction until an investigation is complete or the buyer and seller resolve the issue. Nonetheless, Paypal notifies both parties via email when a claim has been filed and will continue to send emails as deadlines approach for submitting evidence and feedback. Because of the need for Paypal to communicate with members through email, these fraudulent emails can potentially deceive a seller into believing a legitimate claim has been filed and consequently, the member will log in to their account from the sham link in the email.

Recognizing the Threat

Paypal phishers are highly sophisticated in computer language programming. They are always whipping up new methods to attack the oblivious consumer who either lacks attention to detail or is unaware of warning signs that would help to identify a fraudulent email. Fortunately, it is possible to recognize the anatomy of a fake email from Paypal. Here are some of the most common elements that a Paypal user should know in determining the authenticity of the email:

- Paypal will never send an email asking for personal information
- The email has forged headers. This requires looking at the email addresses source by right clicking on it.
- The greeting begins with "Dear Paypal Member" instead of "Dear (user's first name)
- The email is a threat in the form that if not completed the required action there will be a suspension of account.
- The link will not direct the user to a secure page. Secure pages have a "padlock" symbol in the url bar.

Since phishing is based on impersonation, preventing it depends on users having some reliable way to identify the fraudulent sites. For example, some anti-phishing toolbars display the real domain name for the visited website. The petname extension for Firefox lets users type in their own labels for websites, so they can later recognize when they are back at the correct site. If the site is a suspect, the software may note that the website is not trusted or block the site outright.

How Victims are Targeted

It remains unclear as to how people are targeted for phishing attacks. During research with a Paypal security representative, it was determined that Paypal has no knowledge whatsoever as to how people are targeted. This leaves one to speculate that phishers have different ways of acquiring email lists from marketing firms. The most likely scenario is the purchase of email lists from marketing firms. Companies such as Constantcontact.com allow customers to narrow their prospects by many different demographics, such as income, online spending activity, geographic location, age, and other criteria. Phishers can then purchase a list of 1000 or so email addresses that match the criteria "high online purchase rate," under the assumption a Paypal user worth scamming would make frequent purchases.

Damages Incurred By Phishing

Identity theft has affected over 9.3 million Americans since 2005. Damages are estimated at $52.6 billion with 11.6% of instances occurring online. Phishing damages alone have cost consumers and businesses over 2 billion dollars since 2005.

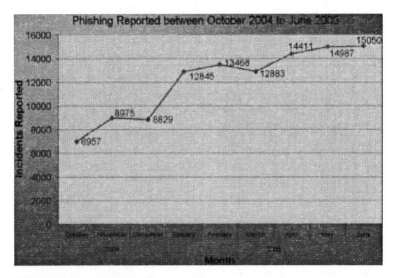

Financial and Legal Recourse

On January 26, 2004, the U.S. Federal Trade Commission filed the first lawsuit against a suspected phisher. The defendant, a Californian teen, allegedly created and used a webpage designed to look like the America Online website, so that he could steal credit card information. Other countries have followed by tracing and arresting phishers. One phishing kingpin, Valdir Paulo de Almeida, was arrested in Brazil for leading one of the largest phishing crime rings, which in two years stole between $18 and $37 million USD. In 2006, eight people were arrested by Japanese police on suspicion of phishing fraud by creating bogus Yahoo! Japan websites, netting themselves 100 million yen ($870 thousand USD). The arrests continued in 2006 when the FBI Operation Cardkeeper detained a gang of sixteen in the U.S. and Europe. On March 1, 2005, United States Senator Patrick Leahy introduced the *Anti-Phishing Act of 2005*. The federal anti-phishing bill proposes that criminals who create fake web sites and spam emails in order to defraud consumers could receive a fine up to $250,000 and receive jail terms of up to five years. The UK strengthened the legal arsenal against phishing with the Fraud Act 2006, which introduces a general offense of fraud that can carry up to a ten year sentence and prohibits writing or possessing phishing kits with intent to commit fraud.

Companies have also joined the effort to crack down on phishing. On March 31, 2005, Microsoft filed 117 federal lawsuits in the U.S. District Court for the Western District of Washington. The lawsuits accuse "John Doe" defendants of using various methods to obtain passwords and confidential information. March 2005 also saw Microsoft partner with the Australian government to teach law enforcement officials how to combat various cyber crimes, including phishing. AOL also reinforced its efforts against phishing in early 2006 with 3 lawsuits seeking a total of $18 million USD under the 2005 amendments to the Virginia Computer Crimes Act, and EarthLink joined in by helping to identify six men subsequently charged with phishing fraud in Connecticut.

In January 2007, Jeffrey Brett Goodin of California became the first defendant convicted by a jury under the provisions of the CAN-SPAM Act of 2003. The CAN-SPAM act was the first piece of legislation that prosecuted illegal spam within the United States. He was found guilty of sending thousands of e-mails to America Online users while posing as AOL's billing department, which prompted customers to send personal credit card information. He faces 101 years in prison for the CAN-SPAM violation and ten other counts including wire fraud, unauthorized use of credit cards, and misusing AOL's trademark.

Improving Security Measures

In February of this year, Paypal released its latest fraud protection technology. Paypal users now have the option of purchasing a five dollar security token that fits inside a pocket that randomly generates a six-digit code every 30 seconds. Every time a Paypal member logs into their account, they will have to enter the most recently generated

number in order to gain access to their financial information. While this is the most proactive step Paypal has ever made, the five dollar cost may deter members from taking advantage of it. Currently, only Paypal Business Members are waived the five dollar charge for the token. The security device also signals how passwords, which were originally devised for user convenience, might one day be obsolete and replaced by the online equivalent to a combination lock. It will be very interesting to see in the next five years how many Paypal members will embrace this new device.

Another recent security measure Paypal has taken is its partnership with Equifax Credit Reporting Agency. This free service allows Paypal members to sign up and receive early warning emails from Paypal when new accounts are opened that may affect their credit file. In the event that identity theft actually occurs, users may call a 1-800 hotline offered through Equifax to report fraudulent activity and receive dedicated phone support from security specialists who will help track down the source of the theft.

What Actions Need to Be Taken

Paypal is aware of this situation and strives to take every measure currently available to protect the security of its members. Even though Paypal provides guidelines that it recommends its users follow to ensure identity protection, the threat is real, and millions of not so savvy Internet users are at risk. In the event of an account hijacking, recourse is minimal, especially due to conflicting international laws with phishers in third world countries where Internet crimes are hardily punished without the intervention of US Federal agencies pressing foreign governments.

Our Research

Out of the 125 people surveyed, 90% were familiar with Paypal's service. Only 40% were registered members, and 16% had an understanding of online phishing. 100% responded saying they have received an email, yet only 25% had some degree of skepticism before opening the mail. No one responded positive to having been a victim of identity theft or knowing anyone who did. Nearly half responded positively to sending personal financial information to confirm an online transaction. Only 30% would actually carry the security token if it meant their identity would not be compromised (See Appendix A).

These results were not surprising, because no one surveyed actually lost their identity or knew someone who had. That could indicate why only 30% would consider purchasing the token. It would be expected that the percentage would increase in the event of a survey respondent having a friend who had his identity stolen or the respondent himself having had his identity stolen. This would raise the awareness level and cause a proactive approach in the future in terms of protecting identities. The most interesting result of the survey was that 25% had some degree of skepticism before opening an email, yet only 16% had an understanding of what phishing was. This result was puzzling because it was expected that the 16% pool would have been greater than the 25% pool of skeptic respondents. Perhaps the 25% could indicate that a majority were skeptic for reasons other than phishing. Possibly, they were skeptic of obtaining spy-ware or ad-ware. This theory makes sense, because 40% had Paypal accounts and 100% received emails from Paypal. So this means that 100% of respondents who did not have a Paypal account received an email from Paypal which could only be fake because Paypal does not send emails to non-members.

Conclusion

Phishers are always one step ahead of the game. Paypal along with Internet security companies have to be diligent in preventing new attacks, dedicating financial resources, and protecting their members. Phishers only have to be right once. One stolen identity can do immeasurable damage to a person. In the future, expect there to be a breaking point in the amount of online attacks and they will then be reduced to a minimal number. Steps such as issuing the new Paypal token provide the assurance of safety. But the double edged sword still remains; if people want more protection, they may have to sacrifice leisure and convenience.

Work Cited

Dinev, Tamara." Why spoofing is Serious Internet Fraud."
   Communications of the ACM. 49 Oct. (2006): No. 10
"Phishing is Catching on." Communication News. 44 Jan. (2007): No.1
"Phishing Trip: A Majic Bullet Becomes the Crooks' New Weapon."
   Bank Technology News. 20 Jan (2007): No. 1.
"The Latest in Phishing schemes uses dual authentication sign-ups to
   scam Bank. Customers." Bank Technology News. 20 Jan (2007):
   No. 1.
Jakobsson, Markus. "Privacy & Security of Customers Information '07."
   The Human Factor of Phishing. Retrieved on February 2, 2007.
Tan, Koon. Phishing and Spamming via IM (SPIM). Internet Storm
   Center. Retrieved on Dec 5, 2006.Skoudis, Ed. "Phone phishing:
   The role of VOIP in phishing attacks", searchSecurity, June 13, 2006

Appendix A

A recent survey was administered to 125 people to find out their knowledge and behavior in online security theft pertaining to Paypal. Please answer the following question to the best of your knowledge. This research is completely confidential and will be used to comprise an academic paper.

1. Are you familiar with the Paypal payment service?
    a. yes
    b. no

2. Do you currently or have you ever had a Paypal membership?
    a. yes
    b. no

3. If you answered yes to #2, how much do you value Paypal for your online shopping capability? (Please circle your response)

    NOT IMPORTANT   VERY IMPORTANT
                1 2 3 4 5 6 7 8 9 10
4. Do you know what the term Phishing means?
    a. yes
    b. no

5. Whether or not you are a Paypal member have you ever received an email (notification) from them?
    a. yes
    b. no

6. If Yes to #5, were you skeptical before opening the mail?

a. yes
b. no

7. Have you ever experienced any level of credit card theft?
   a. yes
   b. no

8. Are you comfortable giving your banking information via e-mail, to secure or confirm an online transaction?
   a. yes
   b. no
   c. no, but do it anyway to avoid any hassle with my purchase

9. Would you pay $5 for a palm-sized token that generated you a new password every 30 seconds if it guaranteed your account would be safe?
   a. yes
   b. no

10. Do you know someone who had their identity stolen?
    a. yes
    b. no

10

Are Marketers Crossing the Line with Online Tracking?

Kimberly Miller and Mari Gottlieb

Introduction

How would you feel if a complete stranger followed you around with a video camera while you shopped, documenting your every move? At first thought it may not seem too harmful. So what if people know what groceries you buy or what car you are looking to purchase? Consider a different scenario--how would you feel if that stranger followed you into the adult section of the local video store? While marketers cannot follow customers' every move in the real world, they can on the Internet—and they do. Marketers track online behavior to customize their advertising to specific users. It may not seem harmful for marketers to know what consumers buy but there is the issue of consumers' privacy.

Consumers have three primary concerns with online tracking. One concern regarding consumer privacy is the lack of understanding the numerous ways companies can track online consumer behavior. Even though recent litigation requires companies to make their tracking activities and privacy policies more visible, there is still a general lack of knowledge about online tracking. Thus, the less knowledgeable people are on the topic, the easier it is for marketers to take advantage of them. The second concern is how marketing companies use this information. The third concern is that there are no current laws that strictly regulate online tracking companies.   Where should the line be drawn between privacy and online habit tracking?

How Do Marketers Track Our Online Behavior?

Spyware is one of the most prevalent ways that marketers track consumers online. It is software that is usually bundled with freeware (free copyrighted software) or shareware (copyrighted software for sale) designed to gain access to a computer. Spyware gathers information from a computer, many times without the users' knowledge, while it monitors keystrokes, browsing history, chat programs, and scans files on the hard drive (Eschelbeck). Three types of propagation techniques for advanced spyware include: Internet browser exploits, site redirects or misleading browser pop-ups, and piggybacking. A browser exploit is a short piece of code that attaches itself to a computer's browser and exploits a software bug. It then causes the browser to do something unexpected, such as crash or install spyware onto the computer. Site redirects and misleading browser pop-ups occur when a user accidentally mistypes a website domain name or clicks on a window that suddenly opens in their screen, redirecting them to a site which automatically installs spyware onto the the computer. Finally, piggybacking occurs when a company attaches spyware to a particular software download option.   Thus, consumers believe they have downloaded an innocent program, when they have actually downloaded spyware.   The consumers give up their privacy by involuntarily allowing companies to track their online activity. When tracking consumer behavior, companies find out how close a consumer is to making purchases, and send out advertisements and special promotions to that person to further entice them to buy their product. Spyware producers earn revenue by offering marketing companies the data that was collected, which provides the opportunity to display these tailored ads.

One specific form of spyware is cookies. A cookie is a small piece of data that is sent to a web browser, such as Internet Explorer, from a web server[1]. This allows for easy and systematic tracking of a computer's IP address, brand of browser used, operating system, and URLs visited. When a specific browser revisits the server, it passes the cookie back allowing the server to identify that particular browser. Cookies were originally developed to allow web pages to store user specific information allowing computers to remember login names and provide quicker Internet usage (Stein 2007) but are now used for more malicious purposes.

Today, marketers use third party cookies, or "tracking cookies," to trace online behavior. Marketing firms contract with client sites, such as Sony, to advertise on their pages. The client sites then place tags on these advertisements containing the URL of the marketer's advertisement server and the URL of the client's page. When a browser opens the client's web page, the ad displayed comes directly from the

---

[1] A web server is a computer that manages and shares web based applications, and stores HTML documents that are retrievable by any web browser.

marketer's site. At that point, the browser receives a cookie. The next time the browser views any page with one of the marketing company's ads, the cookie is sent back to the company. This enables the marketing company to track a person's browsing path or click-stream and see the pages visited and the frequency of the visits. Over time, data is collected, and companies infer consumers' habits and interests.

Marketers use this information to tailor their advertising to specific browsers. For example, when someone fills out a form online specifying that his or her favorite color is green, the server sends that information to the browser in the form of a cookie. The next time the user visits the site, the browser sends the cookie back to the server, and it alters its background color to green to please the consumer (Stein). For consumers, a privacy issue arises when they fill out a form and provide their name. The marketing company can associate their IP address with their name; therefore, not only is the company tracking their behavior, they can now link their behavior to their name. For example, "John Smith" would most likely not like his porn browsing history linked to his name and kept on record, readily available for distribution to other companies.

Are Consumers Concerned About Online Habit Tracking?

A survey was conducted among 100 random University of Colorado students in Boulder, Colorado, to find out their feelings about online tracking and their privacy. According to the survey, 87% of the students shop online and are concerned about personal information being held and sold to other companies. An overwhelming 93% of students are bothered by the thought of someone seeing every site they visit while surfing the Internet. Interestingly, the 7% that answered "no" were men, showing that women are more concerned with their personal privacy online. This corresponds to the question, "does it bother you if a marketing company could link your name to your tracking history?" to which 87% of students answered "yes." Furthermore, a much smaller 73% responded yes when asked if they were "bothered if marketers could get a hold of the sites you look at and use it to tailor their online marketing." This result is likely due to the fact that people are more concerned with their personal information and privacy. Most believe it is more acceptable for companies to use browsing history for marketing reasons rather than to discover their particular name and use it to send targeted e-mails and direct mail. Because the lists of names and e-mail addresses are often sold to other companies, the students revealed further concern about the availability of their personal information to marketing companies.

To further investigate this topic, a larger sample size is ideal to obtain a better representation of the total population's concerns with online tracking. The sample included only University of Colorado at Boulder students, whereas a more diversified sample would be preferable. Time constraints were also an issue that hindered the results.

The Legalities of Internet Advertising Companies

In the U.S., Internet based companies are self-regulated with little government oversight. Because of this, the current laws fail to address the concerns expressed in the research. A common misconception is that Title II of the Electronic Communications Privacy Act (the Stored Communications Act) protects users from spyware and cookies (Khan). The act actually prevents hackers from tampering with electronic communications and provides sanctions for "any person who gains unauthorized access to communications facilities and thereby accesses electronic communications stored incident to their transmissions" (H.R. 229-109th Congress). This act is intended to guard information stored on computers, but it is important to note that the act does not regulate the use of spyware or cookies, which is one of the primary concerns of consumers.

Government officials attempted to address consumer concerns regarding online tracking by creating bills to regulate the use of spyware, but all failed to become laws. Individual states let companies regulate themselves. Two examples of bills written to govern spyware are H.R.29 [109th]: Spy Act and H.R.29 [109th]: I-Spy Act (Khan). The purpose of the Spy Act is, "to protect users of the Internet from unknowing transmission of their personally identifiable information through spyware programs and for other purposes" (H.R. 229-109th Congress). The Spy Act also "prohibits use of spyware to collect personal information and to monitor the behavior of computer user's without user's consent." It states consumers must receive a "clear and conspicuous" notice prior to the downloading of software, but the act gives numerous exceptions to downloading disclosure. It punishes violators for modifying a browser's home page, or disabling antivirus software without proper authorization. The Spy Act attempted to set boundaries for software that transmits information across the Internet, where The Federal Trade Commission would regulate, and fine violators up to $3 million. This bill passed in the House of Representatives but did not become a law. An amendment added to the Spy Act made cookies, including third-party cookies, exempt from any spyware legislation that passes in the House of Representatives. This further limits consumer protection against online tracking.

The I-Spy Act differs from the Spy Act in that it focuses on punishment of spyware abusers instead of the protection of consumers (Khan). It amends the criminal code as follows:

> To prohibit intentionally accessing a protected computer without authorization, or exceeding authorized access, by causing a computer program or code to be copied onto the protected computer and intentionally using that program or code: (1) in furtherance of another federal criminal offense; (2) to obtain or transmit personal information (including a Social Security number or other government-issued identification number, a bank or credit card number, or an associated password or access code) with intent to defraud or injure a person or cause damage to a protected computer; or (3) to

impair the security protection of that computer" (H.R. 229-109th Congress).

The House of Representatives passed this bill in 2005, but it was not ratified.

The growing number of privacy suits is further evidence to consumers' concern about online tracking. Recent litigation has required advertising companies and ad serving companies to update and make their privacy policies about online tracking more detailed. DoubleClick is an example of one company that dealt with numerous privacy complaints. In 2001, a dozen cases were filed against DoubleClick in the state of New York. The Southern District of New York consolidated these cases in *In re DoubleClick Inc., Privacy Litigation* (Khan). The plaintiffs challenged the company's online tracking techniques, arguing that the use of cookies invaded privacy and unjustly enriched DoubleClick. The court dismissed both claims against DoubleClick for failure to state a claim on which relief can be granted. This decision implies that the use of cookies for internal business purposes does not violate any current federal statutes. This case is extremely important because it set a precedent for all other cases involving user information over the Internet.

Additionally, in 2002 DoubleClick settled with the Attorney Generals of 10 states after being investigated for 2 years. The investigation examined the company's methods of and practices for collecting user data. DoubleClick agreed to pay $450,000 to meet new privacy standards. These standards required the company to "make its tracking activities more visible and to give consumers access to their online profiles" (Khan). DoubleClick now posts a privacy policy explicitly disclosing its practices. They also offer a first-party website notice requiring their clients to follow certain guidelines about the disclosure of users' information. DoubleClick "will not share user data obtained on behalf of one of its clients with any person other than that client or as told by the client" (Khan 2). Finally, DoubleClick is required to take collected data offline after three months.

In 2005, another public case accused the New York based company, Intermix Media, Inc. of alleged illegal use of spyware (Livingston). The attorney general, Eliot Spitzer, claimed the company's use of spyware software went against New York state law. Intermix put hidden spyware on users' computers creating pop-up ads. Spitzer's suit against the company claimed Intermix used deceptive acts and practices, false advertising, and trespasses to chattels[2]. It was deceptive because adware was secretly installed when users downloaded screensavers. Additionally, it was hard to remove. Intermix also falsely advertised the software as "Free from Spyware." New York law prohibits the "intentional intermeddling with a chattel" that results in "the deprivation of the chattel or impairment of the condition, quality, or usefulness of the chattel." The software Intermix used caused the computer system to slow down, and therefore, violated this law as long as the user did not give consent to the spyware. In the end, Intermix Media Inc. agreed to pay the state of New York $7.5 million over three

---

[2] Chattel is someone's movable personal property.

years as a settlement. This case shows that even without specific laws governing spyware, it is possible to make a case with existing laws. "Spitzer is saying he doesn't need a state anti-spyware law to take action against spyware promoters" (Livingston). As long as it is regulated with existing law, the government sees little need to create new laws. However, the level of consumer concern about online tracking implies that the laws are not sufficient in protecting privacy.

What Do Internet Advertising Companies Do With Users' Information?

According to research, a major concern consumers have is what advertising companies do with the information that is collected. When companies track Internet users, they are able to find out an abundant amount of information about a particular person. Companies understand a person's tastes by observing what kinds of sites the person visits, and what the person types in search engines. For example, if a company started tracking "Katie" through spyware, and she types "discount trips and vacation get-a-ways" into Google search engine, the marketing company could instantly begin displaying ads for a discount flight to California rather than an extravagant trip to Fiji, based on her interests in a discount vacation.

Sybase, a global enterprise software company specializing in data management and mobile security, is an example of a company benefiting from tracking customers by finding out the most advantageous marketing techniques. An interview conducted with a marketing associate of Sybase explained that sending out e-mails to potential leads or people registered to receive information regarding the company's web seminars, and inviting them to attend an upcoming seminar offers a source to gain tracking rewards (Rogers). Sybase sends e-mails through an e-mail generator called Eloqua, which is linked and sent to leads through SalesForce.com, a sales management tool. Sybase finds the most influential wording in the subject line, the most dominant way to enter the registration page, and which presentation style of e-mails should be used again through SalesForce.com. Via their registration page, they find the best target markets by asking the registrant their company and position title, enabling them to target similar positions of other comparable companies. Sybase easily finds out information for developing a target market, potential leads, and perfect e-mail marketing techniques by tracking their e-mails and registration page. These opportunities increase companies' interest in online tracking.

Due to the use of emerging technology, companies often struggle to keep their websites updated. The online tracking company, Omniture, offers a solution. Omniture is a company specializing in offering online business optimization services. It helps companies answer questions such as "how to increase revenue from their homepage, how to decrease customer acquisition costs, and how to evaluate and optimize the efficiency of keyword buys" (Omniture). The company's offering consists SiteCatalyst, Data Warehouse, Discover, and SearchCenter. The four facets of Omniture offer the ability to transform a website to make it more lucrative. They find the most profitable paths through a company's website, examine how different types of visitors interact throughout the website, generate re-marketing lists, track click-stream history, understand cost-effective content placement and site navigation, and determine beneficial search engine marketing. Omniture is an effective company known for providing solutions to prominent companies such as DaimlerChrysler, Microsoft, Visa, Pepsi, Ebay, and The New York Times. Omniture analyst Brian Haven commented,

> As the number of broadband users grow and digital content distribution takes hold, tracking users' behavior on a Web site will be critical for tracking site performance and customizing content, marketing, and services. Use of these tools will become a core competency for any media company, driving marketing and product development (Omniture).

This statement is evidence of the importance and value of online tracking for companies who advertise online.

Online ad serving and management technology companies, such as DoubleClick, sell their software to numerous advertising agencies and media companies. DoubleClick developed the software called DART, which uses tracking cookies to target, track, and analyze the promotions on their clients' sites. DART allows a server to send cookies with specific identification numbers, simplifying the tracking process (Stein). Because they contract with a large number of companies, they collect large amounts of information about consumers online. Each time a user visits a site that does business with DoubleClick, every article they read and every ad they click will be tracked. This allows companies to find out where users travel on their sites, improve their online merchandising strategies, adjust their offers and ad placements, analyze users' purchasing and drop off behavior patterns, and tweak many other marketing techniques. Over time, DoubleClick creates profiles of a person's interests and selects ads they think that person might find appealing.

With this wealth of information, they have the potential to collect personal information as well, such as names, e-mail addresses, home addresses, and phone numbers. DoubleClick states that, "the personal information collected is used only for the purpose for which it is requested" (Stein). While this may be true, the company still legally gives click-stream information to its member websites to use for audience profiles and to judge rating effectiveness of advertising. Contractually, DoubleClick's clients say they will not use information that "could recognize as either sensitive or personally identifiable" (Stein). DoubleClick's opt-out policies are clearly stated, and their cookies are easy to identify; however, inexperienced users rarely know how to view these options.

Another company that tracks consumers is Genius.com Inc. This leading Web analytics company created a program that alerts a sales representative when their client is online. This program allows the rep to not only see what their client is doing in real time, but to also record the client's Web session for later viewing (Goldman). With real-time viewing ability, the sales rep sends e-mail and Web advertisements to correlate with what the client is currently viewing. In addition, the sales force receives updated reports on the main activities a specific client performed online. The implications of this technology for marketers are substantial. They observe and predict the behavior of their customers much faster and more precisely. They know exactly how much time and energy a user expends on certain sites (including their competitor's sites) and can see exactly how long it takes to get a customer response to customer communication (ads). In the marketing world, this is hitting the jackpot. However, this growing technology further interferes with our privacy, and consumers show a great deal of concern.

Ethical Issues

The ethicality of behavioral marketing and online tracking is a difficult issue because when contemplating the consumer side, there are both positive and negative outcomes. The consumer receives targeted ads from the marketers based on his or her tracking history and interests, which are either convenient or bothersome, depending on the consumer. Often, the marketers keep the users' information on file and can use it for re-marketing material years later. For the consumer, this is also seen as either convenient or bothersome. An example is if a user types, "study abroad programs" into the Google search engine, a marketer continually sends out advertisements for their particular program for years, long after the consumer considers the trip. Another issue is the idea of stored personal information. Privacy policies are put into place to put Internet users at ease, but the extent to which the information is guarded is often uncertain. Some consumers do not want their information stored; however, by offering their personal information online, their privacy instantly becomes an issue. Therefore, people's privacy is measured against a convenience factor, and it is hard to say where the line is drawn in an ethical sense because so much depends on the individual. As research shows, people are aggravated with online tracking and take steps to battle against the loss of privacy that comes with it.

Marketers, on the other hand, only gain through the use of online tracking. They receive more information to help define their target markets, implement product strategies, and send targeted advertisements. Although it is expensive to implement the tracking devices, it is extremely profitable and valuable. Therefore, to ensure consumers are not taken advantage of, it is necessary to put restrictions on marketing companies' use of online tracking.

Conclusion

Online tracking is a critical issue on the Web. It has many implications for users' privacy and for advertising companies. As the research demonstrated, marketers use people's personal information and tracking history to make profit. The information helps them solidify their online merchandising strategies, using tracking to adjust offers and ad placements, implement more profitable paths through a company's website, and provide beneficial search engine marketing. For marketers, online tracking is a dream come true, as it holds the key to consumers' thoughts with a reduction in time, costs, and efforts. While this is beneficial to marketers, research shows that consumers are not comfortable with the current protection of their privacy. As long as Internet users express a high level of concern about online tracking, there will be no shortage in lawsuits against advertising companies. In order to alleviate concerns, the government should begin regulating online tracking more closely.

Research shows an overwhelming 93% of students in the survey were bothered by the thought of someone seeing every site they visit. A smaller, but still significant percentage of 73%, agreed that the idea of marketers using their browsing history to tailor their advertisements is bothersome. Consumers are concerned with their personal information being used and stored by marketing companies. The respondents are not in favor of companies watching their every move. Nonetheless, they welcome the idea of targeted ads, because they are convenient and helpful. Each consumer is different in how much privacy they are willing to give up in order to gain an easier Internet experience. The personal attitudes of individual consumers make it difficult to draw the line between convenience and privacy.

Works Cited

Andrews, Walter J. Berk, Lon A. Winston, Frank Jr. "Cookies Remain Intact While Plaintiffs' Claims Crumble." Shaw Pittman Newsletter (April 2001).

Eschelbeck, Gerhard. "Webroot: Anti-Spyware." University of Colorado. Boulder. 15 Feb. 2007.

Goldman, Larry. "Customer Intelligence." DM Review Magazine Oct. 2006. 23 Feb. 2007 <http://www.dmreview.com/article_sub.cfm?articleId=1064638>.

H.R. 29-109th Congress (2005): "Securely Protect Yourself Against Cyber Trespass Act" and "Internet Spyware Prevention Act." Accessed March 11, 2007. <http://www.govtrack.us/congress/bill.xpd?bill=h109-29>.

Khan, Mickey Alam. "DoubleClick Settles With States on Privacy Standards for Online Tracking." D.M. News (2002).

Livingston, Brian. "Is spyware Illegal Under Existing Laws?" JupiterMedia: Datamation.24 May 2005. <http://itmanagement earthweb.com/columns/executive_tech/article.php/3507261>.

"Omniture Home Page." Omniture. 2007. 10 Mar. 2007 <http://www.omniture.com/>.

Rogers, Makenzie. Personal interview. 3 Mar. 2007.

Stein, Lincoln, and John Stewart. "FAQ." 26 Feb. 2007. World Wide Web Consortium. 23 Feb. 2007 <www.w3.org/security.html>.

III

SOCIAL
NETWORKS
AND PRIVACY

11

Can Your Friends Make or Break You?
The Analysis of How Friends Portray Each Other

Joy A. Eagle and Kyle R. Momii

Introduction

Picture yourself sitting in your favorite coffee shop when a person you have never seen before asks if it is true that you are a liberal Christian from California, graduating in 2008. This person does not looks familiar, but you must have met him somewhere if he knows all of these things about you. You are even surprised he was able to track you down at your favorite place to study. He asks if you would like to go to dinner at The Cheesecake Factory, your favorite restaurant, and tells you he can pick you up at Bear Creek Apartments, your current residency. You sit there stunned, asking yourself, "How does he know all of this information about me?" He proceeds to inform you that you are in the same chemistry class and he searched you on Facebook, but was unable to view your profile. He was, however, able to view the profiles of your friends to gather these facts about you.

Although this particular situation is fictitious, it *is* possible. Chapters 4 and 12 explored the some of the privacy issues related Facebook and determined that this social network is a powerful search engine that employers have no problem utilizing for business purposes.

For the purposes of this chapter, social networks will be explored further, particularly Facebook, but with a different point of view. The research will be narrowed down to the information that can be obtained through a blocked profile in a social network. The purpose of this research is to determine if it is possible to gather enough information about a person to categorize them without actually looking at their profile, but through gathering their friend's information. Further, the paper will investigate the average Facebook user's thoughts about whether their reputation can be harmed based on their *friends'* interests and the information that their *friends* disclose.

Background Information

Social networking technology began with online games, bulletin boards, mailing lists and dating services (Mitrano). Classmates.com is one leader in online social networking that began in the late 1990's. It connects millions of members with friends from school, work and the military. In 2002, Friendster.com became another popular social networking tool to search for old friends and meet new people through friends. Today, there are over two hundred social networking sites (Hawkins). Myspace.com and Facebook.com are two sites that are most frequently featured in the media. Facebook was originally created for college and university students, but has now opened to other networks such as companies or regions. Facebook only requires an email address to become a member. The majority of university and college students are members of this site, so Facebook has been chosen as the focus of this research.

Social networks give people the opportunity to branch out of their small communities and make connections around the world based on shared interests (Mitrano). All social networks share the following elements: they are usually free to join, the user creates a "profile" page, which includes a picture and personal information, and users link their profile page to the profiles of their "friends" (OS Weekly). This last criterion is important when exploring the possibility of learning about a person from her friends' disclosed information. Gathering information on how users are connected to other users in their network is one of the first steps in the research process.

Facebook was created in February 2004 and is one of the most significant social networks relating to higher education because it was originally created for the college/university market (Mitrano). Over seven million students from 2,600 colleges and universities use the website (Hawkins). In September 2005, 85% of students attending a college or university had a Facebook profile. 60% of users log in daily, 85% log in at least weekly, and 93% log in at least once a month (Hawkins). According to the website, "Facebook is a social utility that connects you with the people around you" (Zuckerberg).

Although Facebook is a successful social network that generates millions of dollars, many issues are raised, such as personal safety, monitoring for content and the new generation's expectations of privacy. Facebook can include contact information such as email, instant messenger screen names, physical address and phone number.

It also often includes more personal information, such as interests, photos and lists of friends (Hawkins).

Hypothesis

It is important to note that Facebook users may not be aware that their friends' profiles can harm their reputation. However, the authors hypothesize that by examining only a person's friends, an accurate profile of that person's social category may be derived. The information gathered will help to determine the political views, religion, favorite music and college major of the person being investigated. Then, the person will be defined in terms of socialization categories, based on their friends.

Method

To test the hypothesis, a multi-method approach is employed. The three different methods include: the use of surveys, the use of interviews and a study examining numerous Facebook profiles.

Survey

The first part of the research consisted of surveying university students to obtain the opinions of students that have a Facebook profile. This survey was used to determine whether people block their profiles and if people think their friends' profiles can harm their reputation. The survey was distributed to University of Colorado-Boulder students, and the results provide an initial understanding of attitudes and beliefs regarding information available through Facebook. The survey is available in Appendix A.

Sociology Expert

The next step in the research involved interviewing a sociology expert, a professor from the University of Colorado, to get her position on Facebook. She was able to guide us in the categorization of Facebook users.

Field Study

The main component of the research was the field study. A template was compiled to gather data for the study to ensure consistent results. The template consisted of the types of information that can be found on a typical Facebook profile. The control groups are to test if the method proves the theory. Author 1 chose 10 of Author 2's Facebook friends, filled out the template, then tried to decide what that person was like and what social category they fall into. The experimental group consists of filling out the template for persons with no relationship to the authors.

Putting it all together

All of the methods are dependent on one another. Once results were obtained for both the study and the surveys, they were combined into a two way matrix. Below is the matrix that was used:

	Field Study Results		
		yes	no
Survey Results	yes	A	B
	no	C	D

If the results had fallen into Box A, the field study proved that it is possible to categorize a person based on their friends' information, and the survey indicated that the majority of the sample believes friends' profiles can affect reputations. Therefore, students are aware that is it possible to learn about someone based on their friends, while also conscious of the risks involved. Box B means that the study proved that is not possible to categorize a person based on their friends, but the survey indicates that the majority of students believe that friends can affect their reputation. Therefore, students are overcautious of Facebook profiles. Box C is the opposite of Box B, the study results are yes, but the survey results are no. Therefore, students are not aware of a privacy issue that has been proven to exist. If the results fall into this Box, the hypothesis is proven correct. Finally, Box D means that the study proved it not possible to categorize people based on their friends, and the survey reveals that the friends' profiles cannot affect reputation and a great amount of information cannot be gathered. Therefore, students believe that Facebook is only used for legitimate social purposes and a blocked profile is safe.

Results

Survey
Surveys were distributed among 87 University of Colorado students. 88.5% indicated they had Facebook profiles. Of these students, 61% check their Facebook accounts on a daily basis. 49% block their profile. Of the Facebook members surveyed, only one member believed that his or her Facebook friends are dissimilar. Finally, only 39% believe that their friends' profiles can harm their reputation. Hence, many Facebook users are not aware that their friends can harm their reputation. This piece of data narrows down the ending results of the two way matrix into Box C and D; surveyed students do not think it is possible to gather information about a person through their friends' profiles.

Sociology Expert Findings
Dr. Glenda Walden, a sociology professor at the University of Colorado, explained that it is possible to notice patterns through the arrangement of online social networks. She felt that we would be able to identify individuals based on ethnic backgrounds, religious participation, political affiliation and extra curricular activities. However, it would be difficult to identify a person based on their social traits, such as an introvert or extrovert, and further, she did not think it was necessary to try to categorize individuals in broad social categories (Walden).

Professor Walden helped narrow the focus to specific categories, such as political views, religious views, activities, music/movie interests and other evidently repetitive specific factors. Through determining the patterns of the subjects' friends from these categories, an idea of the subjects' interests and views could be formulated; therefore, learning more information about the subject than was initially disclosed.

The Field Study

Based on the control group, it was possible to define a majority of the subjects' interests, political and religious views, and involvement in certain clubs. At times, it was surprising how much was able to be discovered from friends when the only directly available information from the user, in most cases, was the name, major, year and photo. However, other cases revealed that it was more difficult to determine certain characteristics about the subject, such as political views because friends had a wide variety of beliefs. A few cases failed to disclose information for certain characteristics, such as religious views, but it was still possible to make assumptions through the little information revealed. The majority of the cases revealed it was possible to find a pattern with a few similar traits.

Another tool discovered through research was the way in which Facebook organizes their networks. For example, a few cases revealed where the individuals went to high school because Facebook organized those friends into a high school network. Another case revealed that there were over 100 friends that go to school in a particular area. Through this, we were able to target the home town of the individual.

Facebook also has a "Groups" page in which anyone can join and view. The groups helped us determine the types of extra curricular activities individuals are involved in. For example, in one case, the majority of an individual's friends were part of a business fraternity. To ensure that she was in the fraternity, a search was done for that group and in the group members section, her name appeared.

Another interesting factor was that finding out information on females seemed to be a lot easier than collecting information on males. When placing individuals into specific categories, there was less certainty with male candidates then with female.

Overall, the study revealed that much information can be gathered on a subject with a blocked Facebook profile by looking through their friends with unblocked profiles. By drawing conclusions from their friends, enough information was gathered to determine a general perspective of the person. Therefore, in the two-way matrix, the results were closer to Box C rather than to Box D, signifying that students are not aware that their information can be exposed to others even with a blocked profile.

Implications of Research

Upon gathering data, there were a few noticed implications to the research. First of all, the survey only gathered data from a small sample of college-aged students from the University of Colorado.

Next, while filling out the templates, it was only possible to view friends of people that also attend the University of Colorado. There is no access to students in networks in which the viewer does not belong to. Therefore, only friends that did not block their profile from the University of Colorado could be viewed. However, since our subjects are at school for the majority of the year, they tend to be around the people from their college network more often than friends from other networks, allowing for better conclusions to be drawn from those friends in their college network.

Only state agencies are able to view blocked profiles, and this limited the research. In addition to a blocked profile, there is another privacy setting that takes away the ability to view friends. Some people are aware of this, but the surveys showed that most people are not. Therefore, while conducting the study, it was necessary to ensure the subjects' friends could be viewed.

Further Analysis

The survey indicates that the majority of the participants are upperclassmen, junior level or above. At this point in college, students are usually looking for internships and even entry-level jobs for after graduation. Therefore, it is ironic that the majority of Facebook users surveyed do not block their profiles and do not believe their friend's profiles can affect them.

Another feature that was noticed after searching through the profiles is that some people post false information in their profiles, such as relationship status, that are obviously untrue. This skewed the actual data collection, but it also exposed a new problem for the individual's profile. If someone tries to search for information, but does not necessarily know that such information is false, it can still be taken seriously and can hurt one's reputation in the future.

It is also necessary to point out that even by having a Facebook profile, whether it is blocked to users out of the network or not, the information is usually available. Using the example from another chapter of employers or any person of a high power using information from Facebook, these individuals can look up information that is linked to potential employees and use it against them in any way they please. Because people are linked through networks of friends, employers can make potentially untrue assumptions about individuals. Anything disclosed online, can come back to haunt people in the future.

Parts of the hypothesis have been proven correct, but there was one major difference. The biggest misconception uncovered during data gathering, particularly after speaking with Professor Walden, was that people were not able to be placed into a specific social category. It was not possible to objectively narrow down the types of categories to place people in. Therefore, it was impossible to decide what specific category a person can be placed in based on the profiles of their friends. However, the patterns of specific traits were used to accurately configure the subject's religious views, social groups and hobbies. It was also discovered that more information could be found through the labeling of specific networks that Facebook.com provides. For example, when looking at the subjects friends, they were organized by the different networks, essentially categorizing how people knew each other. Through this process, it was easy to determine how old the subject was and what high school and hometown they could have possibly grown up in. Furthermore, this freshly discovered tool could be used to find out what other social groups the subject was a part of on campus. The accuracy of the findings proved that a substantial amount of information could be discovered about a person even though their profile was blocked.

Conclusion

Many new concepts of social networking were uncovered during the extensive field study. The research recognized that many students are not aware of a problem that has been proven to exist. If a person has a Facebook account and does not strictly filter the information given out, his or her privacy is compromised. This study is not meant to persuade students out of using a social network, such as Facebook, but is intended only to share the valuable information that was acquired through our research. We were able to decipher characteristics and views of students who had restricted their information to share amongst friends only. If someone was motivated enough, using our method, a lot of information can be uncovered. For those students, faculty and alumni who do use Facebook, MySpace or any other social network, understand that there should always be a privacy option and take the time to see how to filter private information. Cyber networking is a new concept that many are still trying to understand. This study is intended to provide awareness to help someone safely navigate the new world of social networking, but also enjoy what it has to offer.

Works Cited

Hawkins, Brian L. and Oblinger, Diana G. "The Myth about Putting Information Online: No One Cares What You Say Online." *EDUCAUSE Review.* Vol. 41, no. 5. September/October 2006. Page 14-15.

Mitrano, Tracy. "A Wider World: Youth, Privacy, and Social Networking Technologies." EDUCAUSE Review. November/December 2006: 7 pages.

Osweekly.com. <http://www.osweekly.com/index.php?option=com_content&task=view&id=2227&Itemid=468>. 13 March 2007.

"Positive Behavior Support Glossary." Online Academy. 3 February 2007. <http://rrtcpbs.fmhi.usf.edu/rrtcpbsweb/glossary.htm#A>.

Zuckerberg, Mark. Facebook. 2007. Facebook. 3 February 2007. <http://www.facebook.com/>.

Appendix A

Facebook Survey   Age:_____ Class:_____
Circle or write in the best answer.
1. Do you have Facebook?

     Yes   No

2. How often do you go on Facebook?

     hourly   daily   weekly   monthly   other_____

3. Is your profile blocked so that only your friends can see it?

     Yes   No

4. If yes, why do you block your profile? If no, why don't you block it?

_____

5. Has your Facebook profile gotten you in trouble in any way? (ie with parents, employers, etc.)

     Yes   No   Explain, if yes:_____

6. Are your friends on Facebook similar to you?

     Yes   No   A mixture

7. Do you think that your friends' profiles can harm *your* reputation?

     Yes   No

8. Why do you think yes or no?

_____

9. Other Comments about Facebook?

_____

12

Social Networking Privacy and Its Effects on Employment Opportunities

Nicole Kennedy and Matt Macko

Prologue to Social Networking Overview

Imagine entering your final semester in college. Throughout the previous four years you have made it a goal to be involved with extracurricular activities at the university, to volunteer in the local community, to maintain a high grade point average and to receive recommendation letters from several well-known professors at the university. You are ready for your first interview, and have no doubt that you can land that dream job you have been working towards for the last four years. That is until the interviewer refers to direct quotes from your online social network profile and begins asking about your listed interests such as partying, drinking with friends, going to bars, and even your political views. You begin to wonder if they can use this information against you, and ask yourself the question: when did my online social life become a factor in my future professional life?

Unfortunately, this situation is not unrealistic. Currently, no regulations exist to protect job candidates from harassment of this sort. Government agencies work to resolve on the job issues with regards to fair hiring practices but the U.S. does not regulate an employers' search for incriminating information. This threat will remain a possibility as long as the world of social networking continues to expand and social profile privacy issues remain unresolved.

Overview of Social Networking

Social networking on the Internet began with a desire for people to quickly and conveniently share information with their friends and family. This form of communication blossomed rapidly and started competing in popularity with e-mail and text messaging. Entrepreneurs harnessed this technology and created various Internet sites, including Facebook and MySpace, designed to allow users to create a profile containing information about themselves that others can view. These sites also allow users to build social networks with hundreds or even thousands of people. Previously, the use of these websites posed little known threat to personal privacy and users' comfort levels changed. They started by displaying the necessary information to construct an online persona. But the reality is, some information on these sites is very private and not something a person would share with their family at a reunion, a stranger on the street, and certainly not with a professional hiring manager.

As the world of social networking became more popular, Facebook increased the availability of its product, opening doors to new networks and members. What began with restricted access to students with valid university-issued e-mail addresses, spread to allow high school and corporate networks as well as users without verified e-mail addresses. These users can create profiles, and gain access to information on other members of the site (Facebook Opens Site to Everyone). College-aged students are beginning to see the mistake of providing private information on the Internet as more employers gain access to Facebook and use the information they find as a factor in hiring decisions. According to a July 2006 survey by the U.S. National Association of Colleges and Employers, "27% of employers have Googled their job candidates or checked their profiles on social networking sites" (George). These privacy issues are important to consider when creating a profile and interviewing for jobs. This chapter will shed light into the questions: Is it ethical for employers to use social profile information as a factor in hiring decisions? Are they currently using this information for decision-making? How do students feel about this "invasion of privacy?" What is happening today and what does the future hold for the confidentiality of social networking?

Facebook's Claim to Privacy Security

According to Facebook's Privacy Policy:

> Facebook is about sharing information with others — friends and people in your networks — while providing you with controls that restrict other third parties from accessing your information. We allow you to choose the information you provide to friends and networks through Facebook. Our network architecture and your privacy settings allow you to make informed choices about who has access to your

information. We do not provide contact information to third party marketers without your permission. We share your information with third parties only in limited circumstances where we believe such sharing is 1) reasonably necessary to offer the service, 2) legally required or, 3) permitted by you (Facebook).

At first glance, this privacy policy appears all encompassing. It protects personal privacy rights, but under the auspices of the privacy clause listed on the Facebook website, the default account settings allow for anyone in a shared network to view a user's entire profile. In conjunction with the use of the Facebook Development Platform, third parties who agree to abide by the Platform's Terms of Service, including restrictions on access, storage and use of such data, are given limited rights to view members' personal information. "We have undertaken contractual and technical steps to restrict possible misuse of such information by such third parties, but of course cannot and do not guarantee that all third parties will abide by such agreements" (Facebook).

Essentially Facebook states they will attempt to protect their user's information, but do not guarantee protection and refuse to take responsibility for certain breaches of protection. "Dan Hornig, a senior recruiting manager for Novo Recruiting, spends more than one-third of his day researching clients - and yes, that includes looking for information about them online" (Lupsa). This recruiting manager is an example of the third party who agreed to the Facebook Development Platform terms of service and now accesses thousands of college students' social profiles using that information however he pleases. All the while, Facebook escapes responsibility. Several cases in the past few years dictate the lack of privacy encompassed by the Facebook Privacy Policy.

Previous Case Involving the Threat of Social Networking Information

"A survey by CareerBuilder.com found that one in four hiring managers used search engines to screen candidates. One in ten also checked candidates' profiles on social networking sites such as MySpace or Facebook" (Lupsa). This is precisely what happened to an unsuspecting Louisiana State University student while interviewing for a job in 2006. He was a member of Facebook for over two years and maintained an "all-inclusive" online profile with pictures, quotes, and more. While interviewing for internship positions, he followed the advice of his mother as well as school advisors choosing to make his profile "private," so only his friends could see his information; or so he thought. Surprisingly, this security measure was not enough to protect his information from discovery.

During the interview, something he was not prepared for happened. The interviewer began asking specific questions about the content on his Facebook.com listing and the situation became very awkward and uncomfortable. The student had thought that only those he allowed to access his profile would be able to do so. The interviewer explained that as a state agency, recruiters accessed his Facebook account under the auspices of the Patriot Act (LSUS Career Services).

This is one example of the unpredictability of current privacy controls and the misconception that only a member's friends can see their profile when they select "private" on Facebook. The consequences shocked the student. A seemingly innocent social networking site crushed his chances for the job and the company disappointed him with how far they went to unearth his private information. Extreme as this case may be, it accurately depicts privacy issues presented with social networking on the World Wide Web.

The Ethics Related to Social Networking Privacy:

The general definition of ethics is "a system of moral principles governing the appropriate conduct for an individual or group" (Encarta Dictionary). How does this theory of ethics apply to the study of social networks and employers' use of them? Research of peoples' opinions on the ethics of employers using online information, especially that stemming from social profiles in a hiring or recruiting decision, shows continued controversy over this highly debatable topic. Current research finds one-third of students feel the practice of Facebook research is "unethical" (George). Students' worry employers will take information out of context and the purpose or rationale behind their social profiles will be misunderstood. In further research, "42% of students said that for companies to make hiring decisions using Facebook is a violation of privacy ... whereas ... only 21% of employers thought the same" (George). According to Philadelphia attorney Jonathan Segal, "the question is what employers do with the information they find on the Internet," (Segal). Clearly differences in opinion exist, but where should society draw the line between employer due diligence and applicant/prospective employee privacy?

Why Employers Are Researching Job Candidates Online

Due diligence is defined as "the degree of care that a prudent person would exercise, and a legally relevant standard for establishing liability" (Encarta Dictionary). Insurance companies conduct extensive research compiling information to value a policy and the inherent risks of a client. Companies now initiate the same techniques with background checks in an effort to acquire outside information regarding potential job candidates. Companies perform these necessary tasks to protect themselves and their organization by mitigating risks through due diligence and exercising a distinguished degree of care when evaluating job candidates and clients.

Is it reasonable to expect a corporation not to conduct proper background checks on job applicants? They limit their liability of choosing the wrong candidate and the majority of people agree to a background check when requested during the job application process.

Can students and future professionals expect prospective companies to disregard information they willingly place on the Internet when being evaluated for possible careers and considerable responsibility within the company? Countless companies argue they simply perform due diligence when evaluating applicants based on personal information, including that found within their online social profiles. Others agree, believing people who voluntarily and knowingly place private and personal information on public networking sites should recognize the likelihood employers will access the information and use it to their discretion.

Chris Wiley, the study's other author, predicts that the debate over the increasingly blurred line between personal and professional life on the Web will eventually be settled in the legal system: Facebook is just a small part of the bigger issue of privacy on the internet. In the meantime, until members of the Facebook generation become bosses, keep your profile private, or don't put anything on there that you wouldn't want your mom to see (George 2007).

Keeping one's profile completely private may seem unnecessary, but as the information revolution progresses, and privacy becomes increasingly more important, private profiles may be the only safety net available to the next generation of social networking clientele. In order to determine the use of this "privacy" function among current business students, the following research was conducted.

Survey and Statistical Research

This chapter's research looked to discover differences in students' as well as employers' opinions regarding online profile privacy. The student surveys asked questions to see what students felt was important to their privacy in regards to social networks as well as what they thought might affect them in a hiring decision. The employer surveys were very similar and were used to compare differences in student and employer opinions regarding social network privacy. The goal was to discover whether a difference exists in these opinions between male and female students, as well as any differences between students and employers. In the quest for employer diversity, opinions were sought from human resource departments at an engineering firm, several accounting firms, as well as a local bank. The surveys were distributed and returned by over 100 students and 14 employers before data analysis began.

The survey data was compiled and analyzed by employing several techniques to determine if the results were indicative of the general business student population. Due to the nature of the survey questions, median testing was required to properly examine the data. This is the result of using a small number of discrete variables (1-10: strongly disagree - strongly agree) as opposed to a continuous number format. The Mann-Whitney Test was employed, which specifically tests medians and assumes equal variances between numbers, and can be used where normality in data is not required; all of which pertained to the collected data. "The Mann-Whitney Test is a nonparametric test to compare two populations, utilizing only the ranks of the data from two independent samples" (Seward 706). A hypothesis test was also applied to compare two proportions. "A hypothesis test is a decision between two competing, mutually exclusive, and collectively exhaustive hypotheses about the value of a population parameter" (Seward 350). This test was primarily used to compare the original pre-conceived notions (null hypotheses) of the business student and employer population with survey sample results. These tests helped gain insight into how the business student population feels about their social network privacy as well as into how employers feel about this relatively new and powerful tool.

Survey and Statistical Research Results

The analytical research results confirmed several pre-conceived notions regarding opinions on social network privacy, but also proved interesting in various unexpected facets. The Mann-Whitney Test was applied assuming women would rank a majority of the following: address, phone number, e-mail address, birth date, relationship status, class schedule, etc., as being more important to their personal privacy than men. The test showed a significant difference between women and men across the population for information such as address, phone, e-mail address, current employment, and class schedule, each having P-values of .05 or lower. This means female business students rank this information as more important to their personal privacy than male students, which confirmed expectations.

A hypothesis test then determined whether there was a difference in the population of men and women business students with regards to their profiles being classified as private. The null hypothesis stated that the proportion of women with private profiles was equal to the proportion of men with private profiles. This analysis went against previous assumptions that more women would have private profiles than men, thus a one-tailed test of the alternative hypothesis was used for verification of these results. The one-tailed hypothesis test resulted in a P-value of .04, which signifies a substantially greater proportion of women business students than men business students who have made their profiles private.

Earlier literature research quoted, "42% of students said that for companies to make hiring decisions using Facebook is a violation of privacy … whereas … only 21% of employers thought the same" (George), which set expectations for various survey outcomes, yet further analysis yielded surprising results. 41% of the 100 students surveyed actually found it ethical for employers to use social networking sites in hiring decisions, and 57% of employers thought the same. Further analysis using a hypothesis test determined the difference between men and women's feelings regarding the ethics of social networking privacy in hiring situations. Respondents were asked, "Do you think it is ethical for hiring managers to use information obtained from your social profile when making hiring decisions?" A two-tailed hypothesis test resulted in a P-value of .63, and produced the null hypothesis that women and men feel the same in regards to the ethics of using social networking sites in the hiring process. The survey data did not show a statistical difference between men and women's feelings on ethics across the population of business students, so a rejection of the null hypothesis failed. These sample results were surprising based on previous expectations that a difference would exist. Yet, it remained to be determined whether there existed a variation in opinions between students and employers.

Based on previous literature review, a greater percentage of employers view the use of social network sites in the hiring process as an ethical practice. Due to this original hypothesis a one-tailed test was used to determine if surveyed employers would agree, and resulted in

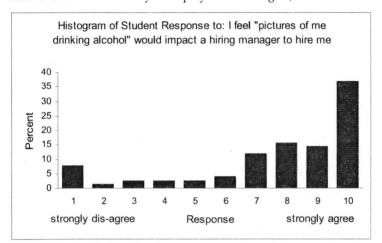

the P-value of .16. This P-value was not small enough to conclude that employers and students feel differently regarding the ethics of using social network sites for hiring decisions. In fact, several prior theories regarding differences between student and employer opinions proved inaccurate. Below are two histograms showing this unexpected difference:

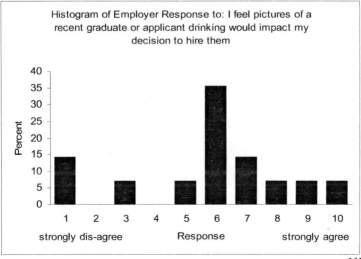

Surprisingly, students were more apprehensive about an employers' viewing pictures of them drinking than the employers surveyed, who in the majority gave a nearly neutral answer on the topic. Although the employer sample was small, the results are unanimous: employers ranked online pictures and videos, drinking and drug paraphernalia pictures, promiscuous behavior pictures, etc., all at a lower importance than students. These results were the most astonishing.

This survey data gathered provides insight into the differences in opinion regarding social network site privacy issues, but certainly does not give a comprehensive picture. Time constraints limited the extent of analysis of the survey data collected. Finding correlations as well as statistical comparisons between categories and between classes (Freshman, Sophomore, Junior, Senior) would be the next step. The Kruskal-Wallis test is recommended for this research as it compares the population medians across multiple categories. In addition, the limited amount of employer respondents was a restriction on conclusive decisions and broadened the possibility of error in statistical results. The students surveyed consisted primarily of a broad population within the Leeds School of Business, and do not accurately depict the opinions of the University of Colorado or scholastic institutions as a whole. Student opinions from the Leeds School of Business may have been altered by classes teaching privacy issues, or from their predispositions regarding business ethics. Tailoring the survey to include a more diverse student sample, acquiring data from more employers, and deciphering the data with a continuous number format to allow more statistical analysis would yield more accurate results for future research. Until that time, it is necessary to explore the current state of affairs regarding these rising privacy issues.

What is Being Done: The Present

To resolve these concerns, laws need to be enacted to protect the respective parties and regulate the use of the wealth of online social networking information. The decision to either empower employers by allowing them to use all public Internet information in hiring decisions, or to protect potential employees by restricting the information employers are legally able to use, is imminent in the U.S. However, as of March 2007, no evidence of lawsuits or legal actions against a company that used public Internet information against a job applicant exists.

Very few laws protect applicants and currently we found virtually no statutes in place to restrict discriminatory Internet practices. With the recent escalation in the importance of this topic within corporate America and the news, lawmakers may be forced to address this controversial issue sooner rather than later. With the abundance of public information pouring onto the Internet, laws will be necessary to protect applicants in the future.

New York currently protects applicants by prohibiting employers from "taking adverse action against employees' off-duty, political, or union activities and recreational activities" (Segal). This is by no means a universal law, nor does it protect employees from persecution during the recruitment process; however, it does address a critical issue: the importance of distinguishing work life from an employees' social life outside of work. The question is whether what one chooses to do outside the office should be their private business. Employees tend to characterize their company both at work and at home. Upper level management is certainly expected to maintain a representational responsibility to their company:

> David Perry, an executive recruiter, says a candidate to become a chief financial officer was found to have a gambling problem. We actually found it out and tracked his profile back to an online gambling site on the Web. Now, you have to ask yourself, what's that got to do with his job? Well nothing, probably. But this is a multibillion-dollar corporation that we were putting a chief financial officer into and we just didn't think it was appropriate (NPR).

Where should the line be drawn? Laws will be necessary to determine whether due diligence background research should stop at mid-level management or continue all the way down to the mailroom employees, as is possible today.

Finland is currently the only country progressively handling these Internet privacy issues in a concrete way by passing nationally recognized regulations.

> Finland's Data Protection Ombudsman ruled in a November decision that employers cannot use Internet search engines, such as Google, to obtain background information on job candidates. Ombudsman Reijo Aarnio told BNA the decision was clear-cut. 'According to the [Privacy in Working Life Act], employers can only view personal data provided by their employees, and this includes data about job applicants'. He continues saying 'the act is based on the idea that everyone is in agreement on the kind of data collected' (Segal).

From an employee's standpoint, it may be a relief to see countries taking action to protect their individual privacy rights; however, an entirely different issue regarding the feasibility of monitoring and enforcing these laws will arise in the aftermath of their creation. What policies could stop an employer from searching possible candidates on the Internet, and who would enforce such conventions? When will laws govern these unique situations? Based on current U.S. regulations, the Equal Employment Opportunity Commission could become that governing agency.

Equal Employment Opportunity Commission

Currently, the Equal Employment Opportunity Commission (EEOC) protects employees from discrimination.

The Equal Employment Opportunity Commission is an independent federal agency created by Congress in 1964 to eradicate discrimination in employment. The various statutes enforced by the Commission prohibit employment discrimination on the basis of race, color, sex, national origin, religion, retaliation, age and disability (EEOC).

This commission protects employees from discrimination in the interview process, employment process, and the firing or lay-off process; however, finds difficulty regulating the pre-interview process. Below is a fictitious example of how the Internet and social networking sites may adversely affect an applicant.

A professional hiring manager is prejudiced to certain personal characteristics. He keeps his views secret within the workplace, but exercises these beliefs on a daily basis while reviewing and searching applicants' personal information on the Internet. Upon discovering conflicting information regarding the applicants' religion, racial preferences, or national origin, he simply disregards their résumé. To avoid prosecution, he claims he never received the résumé. This employer undeniably uses the Internet in a discriminatory way and it is likely these practices will not be discovered nor will he see legal action under the current set of laws governing hiring practices. To illustrate the purpose of this example and to understand its high likelihood, consider the following interview with Steven Viscussi explains:

> Interviewer: Does that mean the employer might find out about things they could not ask about in a job interview?
> Steven Viscusi: Absolutely, like your sexuality, which is often on MySpace or Friendster Connection. They can find out about how many kids you have, your family, who your looking for, even what your habits are. and by the way, its no longer a chance that they might find out, many human resources departments are actively pursuing these sites to find out all the questions that they can't legally ask you (NPR).

Hiring departments use the Internet to their discretion in order to narrow the applicant field without seeing repercussions from the EEOC. "Some employers worry that because of the access it gives them to information on race, sexuality, or religious affiliation, using Facebook as a hiring tool may be in violation of equal opportunity standards" (George). As long as this prejudiced screening process occurs before the interview, there is little an applicant can do to argue they should have been hired. While no litigations attributable to these laws and regulations currently exist, the controversy surrounding privacy and the Internet will press courts to address these issues.

Fair Credit Reporting Act

The Fair Credit Reporting Act and Accurate Credit Transactions Act of 2003 (FCRA) regulates third party background screening agencies who conduct comprehensive pre-employment screening, criminal searches and background checks for various corporate clients. Companies specifically contract these agencies to search for and scour information on employees, possible insurance policy purchasers, and an assortment of potential consumers of numerous industries. The FCRA defines a consumer report as:

> Any written, oral or other communication of any information by a consumer reporting agency bearing on a consumer's credit worthiness, credit standing, credit capacity, character, general reputation, personal characteristics or mode of living, which is used or collected in whole or part for the purpose of serving as a factor in establishing the consumer's eligibility for credit or insurance to be used primarily for personal, family or household purposes; employment purposes; or any other permissible purpose authorized under 1681b (Sotto 3).

Invariably, these third party background screeners also use the Internet in their extensive searches. If screening firms find negative information on a candidate, federal law requires them to notify the candidate as well as establish a procedure to verify the information is current and accurate. Unfortunately, these regulated procedures are not always followed. Tena Friery, research director at the nonprofit consumer organization Privacy Rights Clearinghouse in San Diego, said, "screeners often turn up erroneous information by failing to properly match key 'data points,' such as first, middle, and last names; previous names; Social Security numbers; date and place of birth; and previous addresses" (Sotto 3). These laws and regulations cover only a portion of the issues currently confronted in new "ordinary" hiring practices, and the future is guaranteed to bring new opinions and regulations regarding these concerns.

What the Future Holds

If reputation protection is a concern, Claimid.com and a host of other Internet sites assist in this process. Fred Stutzman and Terrel Russell organized an online service to help people track, verify, annotate, and prioritize personal online information. The goal of the service is to provide a representative depiction of yourself when you are searched online (George 2). Other companies such as Naymz and ReputationDefender.com exist for the same purpose. For a small fee starting at about $5 a month, these sites monitor online profiles as well as provide the necessary tools to protect reputations and the accessibility of any negative information.

The goal for many of these sites is search engine flooding, which pushes negative press to the second and third pages of a search where the likelihood of its discovery drastically decreases. They also have the ability to contact the site administrator where they lobby on your behalf to remove any information you choose, especially useful when disputing the accuracy of information. ReputationDefender.com's motto is "search and destroy."

For a small fee, Michael Fertik (ReputationDefender.com's creator) digs through clients' Internet profiles and then shows them how they appear online. If clients see something they do not like, ReputationDefender will contact whoever controls the Web page and urge them to delete the material. If they resist, Fertik -- a Harvard law graduate -- says his company is ready to use attorneys (NPR).

Services such as ReputationDefender.com provide a public relations service to the layman. These sites grow in popularity daily but are still underused and underappreciated. "Perry (creator of Naymz) says that with so many recruiters vetting people on the Internet, job candidates either need to background themselves or hire someone else to do it for them" (NPR). The reality is that more and more employers search the Web and social network sites everyday. Students and job candidates need to protect themselves whenever possible and should consider using one of the aforementioned sites or protect themselves by maintaining a private and "clean" profile that is free of any information that could reflect poorly on their character.

Conclusion

The age of information distribution has arrived and regardless of the varying opinions concerning social networking sites, it is important that individuals are aware of the risks as well as the benefits that these services may inadvertently provide. This chapter focuses on the negative uses of social network information; however, there could be many arguments supporting the use of this information in hiring decisions as well as how these sites could indeed benefit the job applicant or student. Due to time constraints, it was impossible to research and focus on the possible benefits that could be obtained through positively networking oneself on these sites in order to gain contact with a potential employer. Many recruiters use these sites in addition to hiring sites such as Monster.com and Careerbuilder.com to get in touch with possible job candidates, and social networking sites could prove to be a powerful recruiting tool if created and maintained effectively by both students and employers.

In the present situation, regardless of whether someone posted the information or it simply exists in cyberspace, protecting oneself is a serious concern. A majority of people already do so by making their profiles private to outside viewers or by employing reputation defenders, but most do not understand the strict need for protecting an online persona from employers. Employer snooping occurs daily and will occur increasingly in the future; the question is a matter of what people will do about it until laws are created to overcome these obstacles. The goal of this chapter is to create an awareness of the seriousness of this issue and its contested existence. It is expected that the future will bring new laws and regulations regarding the knowledge and the use of this information that is provided so freely through the ever-expanding World Wide Web. Until then, student and job applicants beware, this information has the potential to harm reputations as well as career opportunities.

Works Cited

"Facebook, Myspace, etc. And Getting Hired." Louisiana State University Career Services. <http://www.lsus.edu/career/announcement_details.asp?ID=43>.

David P. Doane, Lori E. Seward. Applied Statistics in Business and Economics., 2007.

Encarta Dictionary. March 7, 2007.

"Facebook Opens Site To Everyone." September 26, 2006. <PCMagazine.com>.

"Facebook Privacy Policy." October 31, 2006. <www.facebook.com>.

George, Alison. "Facebook Follies Can Hurt Your Job Prospects." December 8, 2006. <USNEWS.com>.

George, Alison. "Living Online." New Scientist 2006. February 5, 2007.

Lupsa, Christian. "Do You Need a Web Publicist." Christian Science Monitor November 29, 2006: 13.

"NPR.org." <http://www.npr.org/templates/story/story.php?storyId=6462504>.

"NPR.org." <http://www.npr.org/templates/story/story.php?storyId=5695383>.

Segal, Jonathan. "Vetting Via." Abstract.

Sotto, J. Lisa, and M. Elisabeth McCarthy. "An Employer's Guide to Workplace Privacy Issues." 24.1 (2007)

13

Privacy and Online Dating
Brent McRae and Jessica McKnight

Introduction to Online Dating

Imagine that you are one of the millions of customers who are participating in online dating sites to meet that someone special. Why did you decide to date online in the first place? There are multiple reasons given for why online dating is becoming so popular. Many online daters argue that the dangers associated with online dating are actually the same or less dangerous than those associated with conventional means of dating, such as meeting people at bars and night clubs. Some also argue that being able to preview a person's profile and personal information online makes subsequent physical dates much less stressful. Other benefits to online dating include the sheer number of singles looking for a match, the ability to meet someone from the comfort of your own home, decreased fear of rejection, and the reduction of time constraints on traditional courting. Nonetheless, the fact that online dating occurs in a virtual world does not mean that real world threats do not exist.

Take the case of Polly (name changed to protect privacy), for example. Polly is a 25-year old woman from California who, like millions, turned to Internet dating as a means of increasing her chances of meeting the "one." She began conversing with a young man, George (name changed to protect privacy), after an Internet dating site deemed that the two were compatible. At first, George seemed to really be what

Polly was looking for and the two quickly began conversing online and eventually moved to daily phone calls. Despite how close they became, Polly was still cautious of what information she revealed, contending that she greatly valued her privacy. After a few days of speaking on the phone, Polly's opinion of George suddenly changed. He began disclosing to her stories of narcotics abuse, emotional instability, and an inability to get through the day without speaking to her. When Polly politely ended things between her and George, she had no idea that her nightmare was just about to begin. While asleep in the middle of the night, Polly heard a loud knock at the door. When she asked who it was, the reply was "It's me, George." Polly, shocked and confused, recalled that she had never given him her address, and that the only personal information he did have, her phone number, was unlisted. Although Polly's case did not worsen after George showed up at her house, she did put herself in a position to incur substantial danger. This is just one case of many where a person's life and privacy was put in jeopardy as a result of an online dating site (Online Dating Experiences).

This chapter critically reviews the problems with privacy and online dating, such as the case of Polly above. The research will attempt to answer the following questions: Can certain people be more easily targeted than others? And, what makes someone a more susceptible target of potential online dating scams and predators? Revealing too much information is what makes someone susceptible to online dating problems. If this is the case, then how much information is too much? And who generally reveals an unsafe amount of information?

This chapter also focuses on observed affiliations between categories of people and the amount of information that they reveal. The effects that age, sex, and political affiliation have on a person's susceptibility to online dating calamities can be better understood by analyzing over 800 profiles from the top online dating sites (Match.com, True.com, and Yahoo! Personals).

Background of Online Dating

As early as the 1960's, computers have been used to link people together by their likes, dislikes, hobbies, and turn-ons (Hamilton 83). Computer dating developed into a simpler and cheaper relationship tool in the 1990's. Since, the start of Match.com in 1995, this industry has blossomed along with Internet growth. The latest Neilson/NetRating, conducted in August 2004, indicated that there are over 22 million active members on the top five online dating sites.

Today, it could not be easier to create an account on any of these Internet dating sites. All that is needed is a computer with an Internet connection and a little bit of time. The routine for viewing or joining online dating sites is very similar. On the home page the user can search for the type of man/woman you desire. Members designate ages, location, your gender, and the gender of the desired partner. Once submitted, the dating site will generate a list of profiles meeting your criteria. If your interest happens to be peaked by one of the profiles, an account must be created with this site where you will be asked to provide personal information. The personal information divulged is then used in the matchmaking process, whereas some sites will automatically match compatible profiles. The time it takes to fill out these personal surveys ranges, and common traits amongst surveys from various sites include age, location, income, occupation, education, and can include pictures of the user. Some members disclose this information without regard to privacy, while others restrict their profiles to the basics. Although this process may seem harmless, one must consider the dangers of providing Internet dating sites with such a plethora of personal information.

Privacy and Safety Implications of Online Dating

When participating in online dating, there is significantly more to worry about than just trying to meet that special someone. As with other social networking sites, Internet dating services pose a great deal of threats and privacy concerns. Potential dangers include stalking (both physically and on the Internet), sexual assault, fraud, identity theft, financial losses, security, privacy ploys, and exposure to offensive material, including materials that a user may not know is being stored on their computer such as child pornography or other graphic or illegal materials.

Many Internet dating sites are free and offer no assurance as to the true identity of those using their services. Even the majority of sites that require users to pay a membership fee still do not guarantee that the identities of their users are accurately portrayed. Potential suitors on online dating sites may simply be lying about their hair color or body type while others may be lying about their gender, age, and intentions. Various up and coming online dating sites are beginning to target niche markets providing comfort for specific on-line segments. The niches range anywhere from specific professions, such as teachers or doctors, to particular sexual orientation sites, sites designed for Star Trek fanatics, as well as a site specifically designed for pet lovers. Although these sites are designed to make the user feel more comfortable and safer in meeting their potential suitors, none of these sites offer assurance that those involved in this dating network are truly who they claim to be.

Another major issue with online dating is the availability and accessibility of user information. The majority of sites that require users to pay membership fees allow any interested party to access and review user profiles and information. The range of information given in many user profiles can reveal a great deal about a person. This information includes, but is not limited to: appearance, city of residence, occupation, age, interests, income level, and other personal affects. By analyzing the information provided combined with using other public resources, Internet daters may be revealing more about themselves than they originally intended. For example, without paying for a membership, the authors of this chapter were able to quickly identify and locate people. By conducting a search within Yahoo! Personals, the authors found many profiles listing a great deal of private information. One such subject, John (name changed to protect privacy), commented that he was a junior, sociology major at the University of Colorado. This information was used to locate him on another social networking site, Facebook.com, which revealed his address, phone number, place of employment, in addition to other personal information. The authors stopped their search of information of this matter to avoid possible legal ramifications. However, this is just one case of how easy it is for potential online predators to obtain personal information about someone without their knowledge. It is clear to see that if John's personal information were to fall into the wrong hands, he could be at risk of being stalked, robbed, or worse. With all of these dangers of online dating, safety protections for Internet daters is becoming a pressing issue.

Current Protections for Online Daters

Although the majority of sites are doing nothing to regulate the safety concerns associated with online dating, a few websites have initiated efforts to combat the recognized dangers of Internet dating. Two such sites are True.com and SafeDate.com. True.com offers background checks on complying members. Other members on the site can see that checks have been done, which somewhat alleviates potential online dating risks. SafeDate.com also does background checks and grants users "stamps" which they can put on any online dating site so that other users may see that they have undergone and passed a criminal background check. Although these sites are making progress towards improving the safety of online dating, the majority of the numerous dating sites remain unregulated (Links).

Just as online daters and their respective dating sites are becoming ever more guarded about the risks of Internet dating, so are state governments. Although a debate exists over whether online dating sites should simply be regulated by the websites themselves, more and more states are passing and proposing laws to protect users from criminals or predators who may wish to harm them. Over the last year, New York, California, Florida, Michigan, Ohio, Virginia, and Texas have introduced legislation regarding online dating. Some of these states mandate that criminal background checks be conducted on registered users, while others simply require the website issue a warning stating that they do not require background checks. Although background checks may eliminate some of the risks associated with online dating, the problem with requiring them is that users are giving up the anonymity that made dating sites so popular (Ramastry).

Current Online Dating Research

Internet dating is a relatively new idea, but extensive research has already taken place. While this chapter focuses on the characteristics of people that are more open in disclosing their personal information, additional hypotheses have been researched. Other research projects that look at different aspects of online dating include: "Self-Presentation in Online Personals," by Jennifer Gibbs, Nicole Ellison, and Rebecca Heino; an extensive research project being conducted at Berkley; and the Pew Internet & American Life Project.

The Gibbs, Ellison, and Heino project focuses on the role of anticipated future interaction, self-disclosure, and perceived success in Internet dating. The main hypothesis focuses on how the importance of wanting a long term face-to-face relationship that results from online dating affects honesty in self-disclosure, and how that relates to the aggressiveness and intention of those actions for successful face-to-face meeting (Ellison, et al).

Berkeley has a team of five researchers in the School of Information and the Department of Psychology working together on two tracks regarding online dating. Track one is a quantitative behavioral analysis. This research project's goals are to answer fundamental questions which include, what predicts how many messages a given user will receive and what is the effect of having a photo on communication success? Track two examines perceptions and expectations. Track two follows on the heels of another scientific finding on online dating done by the Berkeley team, which showed that relationship success heavily correlated to actual and perceived similarities between the two parties (Fiore, et al).

The Pew Internet and American Life Project shows the correlations between the use of online dating sites and the users' safety knowledge. The majority of the project is statistical analysis of a survey given to over 15 millions Americans. Through widespread use of online dating and through these other research initiatives, it is becoming clear that online dating is an emerging issue in our increasingly technological society (Pew). The authors of this chapter hope to shed some light on what categories of people are predisposed to revealing too much personal information, thus, making them greater targets of online dating predators. In summary, the research is aimed at proving that certain groups are at higher risk to online dangers than their counter parts.

Method of Data Collection

The process for collection was simple. On dating sites, there are various search criterions that one can chose from when looking at possible profiles. Basic criterions include sex, race, age, location, and so on. For the purpose of this research, the primary targets are age, sex, and political affiliation. In order to run searches on profiles, a randomized search of conservatives and liberals was used. We picked zip codes throughout the country and put in the largest allowable location distance of 500-1000 miles. This search brought up the maximum profiles, which were randomly selected to use as our data population.

After a profile was pulled up, its data was examined, and answers were recorded to the targeted data points. In order to quantify the data, three possible codes for responses were used: 0 points for no response or a response of "I'll tell you later;" 1 point for a simple response to a pull down item menu; and, 2 points for a descriptive answer or a response that is above and beyond the pull down menu options. For example, on Match.com, there is a pull down menu of responses available for different subjects. For an occupation query, Match.com gives about 20 choices such as administrative/secretarial, medical/dental, executive/management, labor/construction, etc. The points for each subject were then totaled and used for analysis.

The three sites used for this research were Match.com, True.com, and Yahoo! Personals. Each site is slightly different but all had the primary profile questions needed for the research. Our target questions included: occupation, education, income, children, living situation, and how many pictures the profile included. We will discuss and analyze these target questions for each subject based on the demographics of sex, age, and political affiliation.

Explanation of Online Dating Sites

Match.com was probably the most useful dating site, returning results with substantial data; and hence, the reason that the majority of the subjects came from this site. The set-up for the profile in Match.com is the most in-depth of the three sites used. There are four sections of each of the profiles that were used for data collection. The preview section; which includes age, race, location, and number of children, was reviewed for this basic information. The second section used was the "More photos of me section", which had the number of extra photos of the subject. Third, "In my own words" is a section to determine if the subject explained more about their occupation and education. This section allows the subject to type their response in sentence form. The last section used for gathering information on research subjects was "About me." This section contains the basic pull down menus from which the following was gathered: education, occupation, income, political affiliation, and living situation.

True.com was a great site for collecting information, except it does not use political affiliation as one of its criterions, which was a large part of this research. Although it does not provide a lot of extra information similar to Match.com, it did provide useful profiles that allowed for easy recording of targeted data. It has occupation, education, and income pull downs, as well as, children, race, age, and sex. It also has a small section for a personal statement that was used to record the '2 point' data.

The last site used in the collection of data was Yahoo! Personals. This site had significant information right up front. The set up of Yahoo! Personals allowed the user to start by personalizing settings in order to view the precise information wanted about each chosen profile. Yahoo! Personals has all the criteria sought, including political affiliation. Yahoo! Personals also has a maximum allowance of five pictures that can be uploaded per profile. The reason for Yahoo! Personals being used less than Match.com was the limited personal response area. While Yahoo! Personals had a basic response box in order to elaborate on yourself, it did not go into as much depth as Match.com.

Results

After the collection and analysis of the data, many interesting results presented themselves in regards to the amount of information revealed based on sex, political affiliation, and age. After interpreting the data amongst sexes, the results indicated that men are more likely to reveal personal information about themselves than women. Of the 839 total subjects, 404 of them are women and 435 are men. In regards to responses about education, occupation, and income, women were more likely to not respond to any of these questions across the three sites.

Overall, when answering questions about their occupation, women did not respond or answered "I'll tell you later" 28.8% of the time, compared to men who answered the same way at a much lower rate of 9.5%. To the education question, 25.6% of women did not respond, whereas only 10.1% of men did not have an answer. The question of income was a little closer between men and women because the responses were only 0 or 1 point, as not one subject expanded on their income. 56.6% of women did not disclose their income level, compared to 43% of men overall. These trends were consistent on all 3 sites. Interestingly, of the men and women who did provide answers to either education and/or occupation, just over one third expanded on the simple answer (see Figures 1.A and 1.B below).

Figure 1.A.

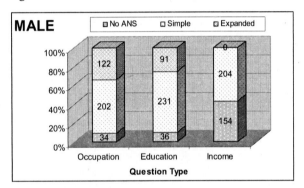

A startling statistic was the amount of subjects that revealed their living situations, especially when it came to women. 75% of women on Match.com put on their profile if they either lived alone or with someone. This number increases to over 95% for profiles on Yahoo! Personals. Of the 268 that answered their living situation on Yahoo!

Figure 1.B.

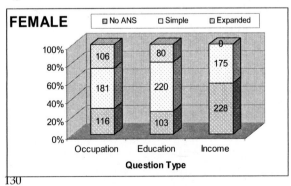

Personals and Match.com, 119 or 44% said they lived alone. The actual number of women living alone is probably higher considering the number of women who live alone and decided not to answer the question. The staggering number of women who reveal to complete strangers that they may live alone has obvious privacy and security issues, considering it is an easy assumption to make a potential link between income and living alone. Those who reveal that they live alone also were more likely to disclose their income and thus could be considered the best targets for criminal activity.

Another issue involved in the research was whether liberals were more likely to divulge information about their personal lives than conservatives. Overall, there was not much discrepancy between the two groups. 17% of both conservatives and liberals did not reveal their occupation. 17% and 18% of conservatives and liberals, respectively, did not reveal their education. The only disparity between conservatives and liberals was income level. 54% of liberals did not respond to the question whereas only 46% of conservatives refrained from answering. When you divide the two political groups by sex, the responses become more revealing. Female conservatives were more willing to give up information on education, income, and occupation (see Figure 2), but less willing to explain their living situation. Only 21% of liberals did not explain their living situations compared to 28% of conservatives that would not mention whether they lived alone or with someone.

Figure 2.

Female Liberals (151)				Female Conservatives (165)		
	Occupation	Education	Income	Occupation	Education	Income
No Reply	29.80%	29.8%	60.9%	23.64%	23.03%	55.2%
Basic	43.71%	47.7%	39.1%	45.45%	.97%	44.8%
Expanded	26.49%	22.5%	n/a	30.91%	.00%	n/a

When looking at the conservative male versus liberal male subjects, a reversal of trends occurred. Male conservatives were less likely to tell people about themselves. 18% of the tested Yahoo! Personals profiles did not give a response for their occupation. Just 9% of liberals within Yahoo! Personals chose not to respond. This remains constant with Match.com with about twice as many conservatives withholding occupation and education. Oddly, male and female percentages switched with regards to income. As conservative males were giving less information about occupation and education, conservative females were more willing to reveal their income level. This occurrence could be explained by the perception that to get a date or find a match, a user must disclose something personal. So, instead of revealing data, after not providing much information on occupation or education, they give their income, which they might feel to be less invasive than the other two topics, or possibly make them believe that their respective income is more appealing to women.

Once gender, political affiliation and the revealing of personal information had been reviewed, a question arose as to whether one's age also plays a factor on how conservative a user is with their information on online data sites. Interestingly, the younger the subject was the more likely to conceal personal data. 33% of subjects under the age of 45 did not reveal their occupation while just 17% of those over 45 years old left their occupation unknown. This trend continues with education and income, but when asked to reveal their living situation, the older age group shied away. 33% of the 45+ subjects did not answer whether they lived alone, with family or with roommates. This was almost four times greater than the younger under 29 year olds (Figure 3).

Figure 3.

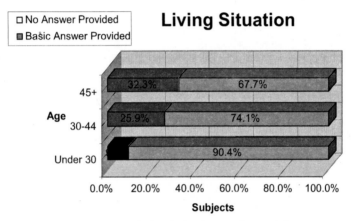

What is the reason behind the inverted trend between income, occupation, and education, when compared to the living situation? One explanation is the different aspects of safety pertinent to the older generation. Since the 45+ generation spent a smaller part of their life with the Internet, its members may be naïve when it comes to security issues on the Internet. They might also be embarrassed to admit living with roommates or family. Alternatively, they may simply be wise enough to know when revealing certain personal information can be dangerous. This could easily be seen as the exact opposite with the Generation Y and Generation X respondents. This age group grew up with computers and the Internet, and was taught beginning in junior high school that what they are looking at on the Web is being monitored. Therefore, this age group may be more reluctant to let someone know where they went to school or their place of employment. However, these respondents are young enough to believe letting someone know you live alone looks impressive and might attract a better match.

Possible Problems with Data Collection

As with most research, flaws exist in the data collection. The first and most important flaw is the subjectivity of the researchers. There has to be a human decision made when deciding if a written response is worth 1 or 2 points. As explained earlier, a 1 point response is a basic answer provided from a pull down response tool. If there is a section that allows users to respond on their answers, this creates a problem for the examiner. For example, a common response found was, "I work in the medical profession and I love helping people." Does this response warrant 1 point, because it does not give more information than just answering the medical/dental field on the pull down choice list, or does satisfy the conditions for a 2 point response? The real dilemma is whether any response above the pull down menu gets 2 points, or should the 2 points be reserved for those that have added something additional to the 1 point pull down menu response?

A solution to this bias may be found by creating a standard method with various levels of responses that go with either category. Also, more response levels could be created. This expansion could be created with a rubric. For example, a 5 point response would be one that reveals an employer name, location, job title, and length of time employed. Each level would be one piece of information lower. So, if they gave just four of the labeled information parts it would be a 4 point response, and so on.

Another problem with the research is the persuasion to provide more information on sites such as Match.com. With Yahoo! Personals and True.com, only one box is provided for a person to tell potential matches more about themselves. However, Match.com provides an almost unlimited amount of space for each profile, including an "about me" section that has space to answer questions like, for fun, my job, my ethnicity, my education, favorite things, etc. With these responses being asked by Match.com the user is enticed to provide additional information about the specific question than they would be in a section entitled "me," like with Yahoo! Personals.

The final obvious problem is the authenticity of the data collected. The researchers had to face the following questions: Was every profile legitimate? Did each person tell the truth about themselves? Or, did the subject lie to make them sound better? This leads to more questions of whether the information provided by subjects is real personal information, or simply fabricated. So, if a person provided extra information on their occupation that was not true, would they have put the truth even if they were not lying? Or knowing they hypothetically had to tell the truth, would they choose then not to answer? The counter-argument for this is the fact that it is a dating site and people inherently go onto these sites to find someone in common with them. This is saying that they would not lie about themselves because they really do want to find someone like themselves, and if they lied, then they are not going to find a compatible match, which is ultimately the goal of online dating.

Conclusion

When it comes to privacy and online dating, it appears that

everyone is at an equal risk of being targeted by online dating predators. Many contradictions became apparent during the analysis of this research. For example, just when the authors came to believe that women might be at less risk to online dating hazards because they revealed less information when it came to occupation, education, and income, it was discovered that they were less reluctant to hold back their living situation. While the younger generation, who should know a great deal about Internet threats, was the front runner for the safest age group using these sites, they too revealed more information in other parts of their profiles. While this research serves as a starting point at identifying what factors may increase or decrease your chances of being targeted by Internet predators, nothing can definitively prevent someone from the threats that exist in using Internet dating sites. While Internet dating sites are gaining popularity and praise, the dangers that exist in using one will be ever present. So the message that this research may point to is that no matter who you are, male, female, old, young, liberal, or conservative, the risks of online dating exist, are not going away soon, and the only measure that might serve as protection from the apparent dangers is self discretion in online dating endeavors.

Works Cited

Online Dating Expiriences: Being Caught Unaware. Online Dating Magazine. 17 Feb. 2007. <http://www.onlinedatingmagazine. com/datingexperiences/04onlinedatingperilsc.html>.

Links Alive: Dating. 2007. Links Alive. Feb 20 2007. <http://linksalive. com/dir.html? category_id=1598>.

Ramastry, A. Legislating Love Online: Should States Mandate That Online Dating Sites Do Criminal Background Checks Of Their Users?. Proquest. Sep. 28, 2006. <http://www.proquest.com>.

Ellison, N., Heino, R., and Gibbs, J. (2006). Managing impressions online: Self-presentation processes in the online dating environment. *Journal of Computer-Mediated Communication, 11*(2), article 2. 11 Feb. 2007. <http://jcmc.indiana.edu/vol11/issue2 /ellison.html>.

Fiore, A. T., Marti Hearst, Coye Cheshire, Lindsay Taylor, and G. A. Mendelsohn. *Online Dating Research at Berkeley*. 2007. University of California-Berkeley. 13 Feb. 2007. <http://www.ischool.berkeley .edu/~atf/dating/>.

Hamilton, A. "The Smarter Dater." Time. Feb 9, 2004. Vol. 163, Iss. 6, p. 83.

Pew Internet: Online Dating. 5 Mar. 2006. Pew Internet and American Life Project. 12 Feb. 2007. <http://www.pewinternet.org/PPF/r/177 /report_display.asp>.

14

How does Cyworld and Personal Networking Communities Effect People's Communication and Relationships?

Minji Park and Jihye Kim

Cyworld Background

Have you ever wanted an online homepage that you could design and decorate and could also use as a social networking site? Cyworld fulfills those needs by allowing users to very simply design and decorate a personal webpage. While building a webpage may require coding in addition to the purchase of a web hosting service and a domain name. Cyworld makes everything easier by facilitating the creation of personal homepages.

Cyworld opened in 1999 and is operated by SK Communication in South Korea. In Korean, "Cy" (pronounced 'Sa-e') means relationship. Hence, in English, Cyworld translates to "relationship world," or in other words, social networking world. This service is very similar to well-known networking sites in the US, such as Facebook and MySpace, but Cyworld has many more features. Cyworld uses a personal recognition program which identifies Korean citizens with their resident registration numbers obtained at birth (a Korean version of the U.S. social security number). The recognition feature makes it so a user cannot misrepresent their identity and/or create duplicate accounts. The user base of Cyworld is mostly segmented to people in their late teens and twenties. Currently, Cyworld is heavily targeting the pre and early teen population, since they will be the future customers. The latest report said that 90% of South Koreans in their twenties use Cyworld. Additionally, as of September 2005, 25% of the total South Korean population is registered users of Cyworld.

Features

Membership on Cyworld is free along with an unlimited number of file uploads. However, homepage personalization is paid for with credits that can be purchased on the site. Cyworld calls these credits "do-to-ri" (or acorn in English). One acorn is worth 100 Won (0.10 USD), with a minimum of ten acorns being purchased at a time. Users can use the acorns to buy music, banners, games, skins, fonts, and other items that they need to decorate their mini-rooms, mini-homepages, or clubs.

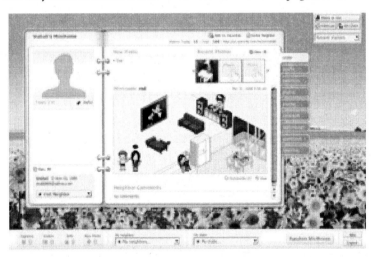

Figure 1: Mini Homepage (U.S) with avatars in the mini-room

Cyworld's main feature is the mini-homepage. This feature includes photo galleries, personal profiles, message boards, guest books, videos, personal bulletin boards, favorites, paper collections, music boxes, and diaries. Cyworld's mini-homepage includes a service that alerts the user whenever people leave messages on the bulletin board or comments below uploaded pictures or videos. Also, Cyworld has its own instant messaging system, which helps users network with people who are in their "il-chon", or friends, list.

Trend

Due to the popularity of Cyworld, many new words and phases have been coined. One such word is "Cy-Pe-In", which describes those users who use Cyworld first thing in the morning. Throughout the day, these users check their account every chance they get. "Pe-In" literally means "moral wreck" in Korean. Thus, "Cy-Pe-In" mean people who are dysfunctional without Cyworld. These Cy-Pe-In spend tremendous amounts of time on Cyworld, where they decorate their pages and post pictures and videos to show their Cy-friends. According to the authors' research and personal experience, these users are unable to sleep unless they spend a certain amount of time daily on Cyworld. Another phrase that is commonly used when describing these people is, "they are Cy-Jung-Dok." "Jung-Dok" mean people who are addicted to Cyworld as if they were addicted to illicit drugs. These words are an example of how popular Cyworld is in South Korea, and it shows the enormous impacts that it has on the users' physical and emotional states. Upon considering the present trends and their presentation in Korean language, it is clear that the implied meanings are not postive.

Reasons for Use

People use Cyworld because it is the single largest social networking site in Korea. They also use Cyworld because of its ease of use and many services and features. One heavily used feature is the photo upload. On average, 6.2 million photos are uploaded to Cyworld each day, many coming directly from cell phones. Another feature that is becoming very popular is uploading videos. Like photos, videos are taken with a cell phone and can then be immediately uploaded to Cyworld. Again, uploading of these pictures and videos is simple and easy. Once the photos and videos are uploaded, friends are able to leave messages and comments on homepages. A third and very popular feature offered is a homepage "famous score." This score is basically a page hit counter and increases when another person visits the homepage. The higher the score is, the more popular the person. For this reason, more people want to use services that bring visitors to their site. Lastly, the people search is a very powerful service that is simple to use and is also heavily utilized. Searches can be performed for people such as favorite teachers, friends from camp, school friends, etc. Just by having and using Cyworld, people are able to expand and increase their personal connections. Because of this, more and more people want to use Cyworld.

Issues

One of the main problems that arise within Cyworld is the simplicity of finding the account holder through name, age or email. The moment the account is established, address, phone number, e-mail address, birthday and information on relationship are exposed to the public. Yet, many people are willing to jeopardize personal information because they are unaware of the risks. This paper will thus examine

Cyworld's privacy policies, the company's efforts to protect the users, and the privacy issues that the site has caused.

Every user must accept the Personal Information Protection Policy prior to joining Cyworld. The policy outlines the safety and security tenets under which Cyworld operates. Users violating the policy can be punished by law. However, the question of how Cyworld keeps in action to find the criminal and protect the account holders remains. Additionally, it is unclear how many account holders know the rights that they have and can realize when these rights are being violated.

Research

Due to the popularity of Cyworld, several problems have started to surface and have been mentioned by a variety of media sources. The common crimes/incidents that are reported and well known to average Cyworld users are career interference, stalking, stealing, kidnapping, underage use, defamation and even death.

The most commonly known privacy invasion today affects career choices. Without legal permission, any information can be obtained from websites/homepages including the ones that are not in your permanent records such as what you did last weekend or who you have dated in the past. Just on like Facebook.com and MySpace.com, there are many issues with how employers interpret and use the information found on Cyworld.

Another issue is the stalking, stealing, and kidnapping problems that stem from peoples' addictions and desires to show off their Cyworld homepage to the public. Open information has given an easier way for the stalkers to find victims information. The information given, such as address, phone number, and e-mail addresses, not only may physical stalking evolve, but a victim may experience abusive or excessive phone calls and threatening e-mails. There is no guarantee that the stalker will never show up to the given address. Not only can criminals access the basic information that is updated on the homepage profile, but they can also view users' diaries that expose daily routines. Knowing where the specific person may be at a certain time gives a thief or kidnapper a better chance for completing what they aimed to do.

Another issue is that children who are underage illegally use their parents' credit cards or phones on Cyworld to buy advanced services and features to decorate their homepages. Since there is no restriction with children signing up to be the account holder, there is also no restriction on what they can purchase or how they purchase it.

Lastly, users can get revenge on others by defaming them on the site, leaving an individual's reputation is a risk. This is partly a result of there being no restriction of what kind of information is posted. Personal photos and descriptions can be obtained from other homepages and can be used to disparage targeted users. Some users have even humiliated individuals who have passed away – a action found to be particularly uncouth in South Korean culture.

Experiment/Collected data

College students were targeted for the experiment, they were asked series of questions about their knowledge of and attitudes towards online privacy. The respondents were also asked about their knowledge related to online crime.

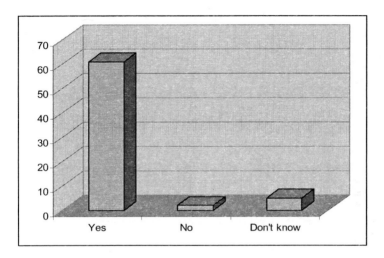

Figure 2: Users who have experienced privacy invasion with Cyworld

- 90% of users agreed that a company gaining personal information through Cyworld can be a major problem.
- 88% of users were aware of unprotected privacy and its exposure.
- 88% of users said that it is a company's responsibility to protect account holders.
- 60% of users also said that people are responsible for their own protection
- 60% of users said that they have tried to gain other people's information using Cyworld.

A high percentage of account holders and users were aware of the unprotected privacy when using Cyworld, but at the same time, they also blamed the company for the problem. Not many users are taking actions to protect themselves. Under the personal information protection policy, exchange of personal information must be trusted between the company and the account holder. It also states that it is both parties responsibility to take action in protecting each other.

Conclusions

Cyworld is only one of the examples of how privacy online is invaded. It also is a good example that shows the similarities between other countries social networking cites and those in the U.S. such as facebook.com and myspace.com. These websites/homepages do create relationships and friends. Considered a relatively harmless social phenomenon by a young generation including college students, Cyworld has the same effects as Facebook.com and MySpace.com when it comes to threatening a members chance of getting a job after graduation. This creates problems for many users when it comes to affecting their entire work career, because a job offer could be based on people's online information such as profiles and activities. What we can assume right now is that it is not long before these websites and homepages will be used for every decision, not just a job.

Online social networking has become a big part of today's culture and has opened new issues related to publicizing personal information. Social network services have provided closer human relationships compared to what was available in the past with interacting while offline. It has connected people with all different types of interests and helped them to expand their network uses. But on large social networking services, privacy is the number one concern when it comes to Internet use. While the importance of protecting their own personal information is emphasized, privacy still faces threats from both private and public sector intrusions. What the privacy laws practices have failed to provide have caused the need for protection and confusion have created distrust and doubt of using today's advanced technology.

Work Cited

Cyworld's Privacy Usage Interview by Shi-Min-Hang Dong 12/07/2005
http://action.or.kr/home/bbs/board.php?bo_table=inforight_radar&wr_id=32 Jung-Bo-In-Guen-Un-Dong- Cyber Culture Research
Cyworld's Privacy Usage Interview by Shi-Min-Hang Dong 06/07/2005
http://action.or.kr/home/bbs/board.php?bo_table=inforight_news&wr_id=653&page=5 Jung-Bo-In-Guen-Un-Dong- Cyber Culture Research
Cyworld; Massive Korean Social Network CyWorld Launches in US 27/07/2006 By Marshall Kirkpatrick,
http://www.techcrunch.com/2006/07/27/this-is-nuts-cyworld-us-opens-for-use/#comments TechCrunch.com
Cyworld vs. MySpace : Korean's most popular online social network enters the American market. By Jason Hahn
2006-07-28
http://english.ohmynews.com/articleview/article_view.asp?menu=c10400&no=308057&rel_no=1 OhmyNews International Science and Technology
Tech Talk; Cyworld Monday November 20 to 24, 2006 by Rajesh Jain
http://www.emergic.org/collections/tech_talk_cyworld.html Emergic.org Rajesh Jain's Weblog on Emerging Technologies, Enterprises and Markets

IV

CORPORATE PRIVACY

15

Email Regulation of Employers and Implications on the Workplace
Valerie Kirby and Amanda Rick

Introduction

A break in the work day reminds an employee that she still needs to make a doctor's appointment and find concert tickets for a sold out show next week. The employee begins surfing concert broker websites on her company-owned computer, making sure to delete the links from her pull down bar. The employee knows her company has a policy against doing non-work related activities at the workplace, but as long as she gets her work done, the employee believes she is not jeopardizing her career.

Employers are monitoring employee computer activity with surprising frequency and often without express knowledge of their employees. Though employee monitoring is an increasing trend in the workplace, the employee-employer privacy debate remains. Do employees have the right to use company time for personal tasks? How does allowing employees more personal time at work affect productivity? Does the employer have the obligation to inform employees that they are being regulated? Does daily activity influence promotions and salary?

Who is Regulating?

A survey of Fortune 500 companies in 2006 proved that monitoring is prevalent in the workplace. 84% of companies regulate email use, 41% regulate instant messaging programs, 76% monitor web surfing, and 65% use programs that block access to inappropriate or frequently visited personal sites (Email 1). According to the *Washington Internet Daily Release*, 67% of these employers have disciplined or terminated an employee for email or Internet abuse (Morris 4). The argument for this regulation is to prevent employees from visiting gambling, pornographic or hate websites. Additionally, it protects employers from responsibility for racial and/or offensive email forwards sent through the office email system (Morris 4). As the number of companies regulating computer use grows, so does the number of companies who have established policies informing employees of monitoring. Of the companies surveyed, 84% claimed to have a clear policy outlining their monitoring practices (Flynn). The number of employees who cited knowledge of monitoring at their workplace is much lower, causing researchers to question how hard employers are working to make these policies known.

Why Employers Regulate

Employers cite two primary reasons for regulating workplace computers. The primary reason is to evaluate performance, with content control cited as a secondary motive. First, employers regulate the workplace to measure and encourage overall productivity. An increase in time demanded at work has caused workers to feel the need to take care of personal business during work hours. Statistics indicate employers are justified in their concern over worker productivity. Employees spend an average of eight hours a day at the office. During this time, an estimated 2.09 hours a day are spent on personal emailing, phone calls, and web surfing (Malachowski). This personal time costs companies an average of $5,270 per employee per year, a total of $759 billion dollars a year (Malachowski). In 2001, personal instant messaging accounted for 82 million hours of employee time (Morris 4). Most companies do not use popular instant messaging programs such as AOL, in order to avoid employees chatting with friends. Online shopping also peaks during work hours. One online retailer records 65% of its orders between 9:00 am and 5:00 pm on weekdays, with a significant decrease during the weekend (Adam 35). With this massive amount of wasted payroll dollars, it is no surprise that employers are regulating email and Internet activity on company owned computers.

Second, companies are ultimately responsible for the actions of their employees and find that regulations protect the company in sexual harassment suits and discrepancies with outside parties. Prior to email monitoring, companies had a difficult time generating enough evidence to terminate or discipline employees who were sexually harassing others (Adam 35). Approximately 50% of surveyed employees at Fortune 500 companies said they had received a "racist, sexist, pornographic or otherwise inappropriate email at work" (Email 2). Of these Fortune 500 companies, 27% have defended themselves against sexual harassment claims, etc. through email monitoring (Email 2). Records of discriminatory comments are a guaranteed way for harassed employees to seek justice.

The increasingly frequent use of email also creates a casual atmosphere surrounding business transactions. Customer service is easily compromised through email, and employees have the power to forward trade secrets with the click of a button. Of the companies surveyed, 80% said they would fire an employee for a first offense of revealing trade secrets and, therefore, find that monitoring and regulating their employees is crucial (Everett 292). Permanent storage of emails allows a company to retrieve an email to enforce an electronic contract or agreement. Many companies argue for electronic monitoring because of the need to legally defend themselves.

The Rights of Employees/ Legal Issues

In 2005, only ten percent of the 14 million Americans who were monitored online claimed to know of any regulation at their workplace (Malachowski). Though the debate remains about whether employees should have to be informed, courts have generally held that employees should not reasonably expect privacy on company-owned machines (Morris 5). Laws have recently been created in some states requiring employers to create an inclusive policy informing employees of how often and what type of content is being regulated. A survey of employees in 2002 found that 26.9% of employees said their Internet and email use was not monitored. An additional 28.1% were unaware they were being monitored [Everett 294]. This perception is often created by companies who allow users to set up passwords to "lock" their computers from outside intrusion. What these employees do not understand is that the company keeps a record of all sent and received emails as well as each computer's daily Internet activity. Employers do not need access to passwords in order to view activity on the computers their employees use.

The Electronic Communications Privacy Act was enacted in 1986 in response to a lack of privacy protection provided by the United States Constitution. Although e-mail privacy is not expressly mentioned in the act, the intent is to cover the scope of all "electronic communications." Unfortunately, exceptions in this act leave employees with virtually no privacy protection. The "consent" exception permits employers to monitor business-related communications and determines if the scope is acceptable based on the employer's reason for monitoring. This is a "powerful exception because of the ease with which an employer can create and provide a monitoring policy" (Email 2). Though no legislation prohibiting companies from monitoring their employees exists, there is a proposed legislation called the Notice of Electronic Monitoring Act (NEMA) which deals with how often employers must inform employees of electronic monitoring policies. Under last year's version of this bill:

> Employers would be required to tell employees at the time of hire about their electronic monitoring policy, notify workers annually and after a material change in electronic monitoring

practices occurs. The notice would include monitoring scope, frequency, method, and use of the information. Employers would be exempt from giving notice when they reasonably believe that an employee is engaging in 'harmful' or 'illegal' conduct at work (Email 2).

This act is a step in the correct direction, because it would increase employee awareness and clarify what is being regulated.

What Employees Can Do to Protect Themselves

While companies should be clear about their policies by distributing them regularly to employee mailboxes, many are not. The most important thing an employee can do to protect herself is to inquire with one's employer to determine the company guidelines.

Currently, there are few legal protections or rights for employees on company owned computers; therefore, employees need to take it upon themselves to learn and understand company monitoring practices. An article in *Time* magazine cites nine guidelines for smart work practices at a company that monitors an employee's every move. Knowing the company policy tops the list, with other obvious hints, such as surfing the Web sparingly and not downloading pornography at work. Employees often do not think twice when forwarding "funny" forwards to outside friends and co-workers. However, *Time* magazine suggests considering whether a particular forward could be seen as offensive to women, minorities, etc. before forwarding. Any email sent from a specific employee's account reflects her character and could put her job at risk. The article suggests proofreading emails and assuming the boss will see everything sent to others. Finally, the article recommends protecting the computer with passwords so coworkers cannot log-in to the machine; any information viewed, downloaded, or sent from that computer is assumed to be performed by its licensed user (Dell). These tips will help employees make smart decisions about the information they view and send on company-owned computers, because technological privacy is virtually nonexistent in a monitored workplace. The best practice for monitored employees is to assume they are being watched at all times and save personal activity for personal time.

How they do it

Businesses employ different monitoring practices depending on their needs and number of employees. Smaller companies flag emails based on specific words or repetitive domain names. Many of these smaller companies only spend the money to monitor "on an occasional basis in the manner of spot checks rather than constantly or on a regular routine" (Ciocchetti). Even more frequently, smaller companies will not regulate on a daily basis, choosing to only retrieve information from the database in defense of a particular claim (Ciocchetti).

Regulation programs are more sophisticated in larger companies, as these companies have higher occurrences of misuse due to the larger number of employees. A company with full monitoring services can potentially be recording information, such as the email recipient, the email sender, the number of words in an email, the amount of time the employee spent reading and composing the email, the number of attachments, and whether the email was personal or business-related (Ciocchetti).

SpectorPro is a type of software created to monitor employees in the workplace. This program observes every action performed on individual computers, including instant messaging, email, websites visited, pages visited on domains, searches, photos viewed, and programs downloaded. This advanced system not only records what employees do, but also the exact order in which employees perform these functions. For a one-time fee of $99.95 per computer, SpectorPro will provide full monitoring services and can track most independent email programs, including Outlook, MSN, and AOL databases (Spector).

Ethical Issues

Is it ethical to monitor personal activity considering the increased amount of time employees are spending at work?

It is no surprise that Americans are spending more time at work. Longer hours result in less personal and family time, more pressure to perform, and scattered work hours. During the work day, the average employee spends an estimated 45 minutes per day on personal tasks. Younger employees spend more time on personal activities, estimating that those between the ages of 18-34 spend 13 more minutes than 35-65 year-olds and 28 more minutes than those over 65 (Goodman). In response to financial incentives for longer hours, approximately 18.5% of men work an average work week of 50+ hours (Kuhn). As this average continues to increase, employers are considering the ethical implications of allowing a small amount of personal time at work. Employees agree that as long as personal tasks do not interfere with work deadlines and results, taking care of personal issues on company time can actually improve productivity.

The result of increasing technology and longer work weeks is scattered hours, allowing employees to be technologically connected and theoretically available at most times of the day. This constant communication redefines the definition of a "work day." Employees may spend a little under an hour per day between the standard hours of 8am to 5pm work day on personal tasks, but often make up for that by working after hours and on weekends.

An article from *Digital Trends News* cites alternative reasons for cyber shopping during regular business hours. According to CyberSource, online shopping peaks around 4:00 pm Eastern time, or 1:00 pm Pacific time, with the heaviest volume on Monday and Tuesday and the lowest volume on Saturday and Sunday. These statistics are in spite of recent data that 2/3 of American homes have Internet access (Duncan). However, researchers are inferring that employees are using company time to surf the web, but do not take into account recent shifts in normal business hours. Additionally, many companies purchase items online or have employees work on flex-time schedules. Flex-time schedules allow employees to work convenient hours as long as the work gets finished. Companies are becoming more lenient in the structure of the work week, mostly because of technology that makes employees available anywhere.

Employers are generally understanding of the need to address personal tasks during work. The demand for additional hours spent on work tasks creates a need for employers to understand personal needs as long as employees maintain productivity standards and meet the bottom line.

Does monitoring affect productivity?

An increase in the average workday has caused many employees to resort to work hours to complete personal tasks. Researchers argue that strict policies against completing personal tasks may actually slow productivity as workers are stressed and preoccupied with things they need to take care of or simply need a short break to converse with friends. The argument is that if employees feel comfortable with taking work time to complete tasks, they will be more efficient in their work and more agreeable during the day. In fact, over 87% of employees found it permissible to spend 15-30 minutes per day checking personal email or surfing the web. Employers are beginning to agree. Though 51% of employers believe surfing the Internet and sending personal emails decreases productivity, 82% of companies are willing to compromise 15-30 minutes each day in return for improved attitudes and reduced stress levels of their employees (Muhl 38). Though the above number is lower than the current average time employees spend on personal activities during the work day, it makes it clear that employers are willing to compromise as long as the bottom line is met.

Another issue affecting productivity is employee trust and stress related to employee monitoring. Employees tend to feel mistrusted in their ability to do their work when they are being monitored. This loss of confidence in their work can affect performance and overall productivity. According to Alex Fowler, a spokesman for the nonprofit advocacy group Electronic Frontier Foundation, these feelings of mistrust are soothed by employers who maintain an open line of communication. "When companies are open and honest with their workers, they have a high degree of acceptance of their policies," said Fowler (York). An understanding of the reasons policies are put in place as well as an understanding of their scope, will make employees feel more at ease. Being clear about the boundaries and what is permissible on company-owned computers will help dispel rumors and feelings of mistrust.

Should employers have to inform?

Another ethical dilemma is whether employers should be required to notify their employees that they are being monitored. Though courts have often held that employees have no reasonable expectation of privacy, the United States government is trying to introduce a law called Notice of Electronic Monitoring Act, as discussed above, which requires frequent notification of monitoring. As of 2003, two states have enacted legislation requiring sufficient notice of privacy policies to employees (Morris 4). Most companies surveyed have a regulation policy, but making employees aware of such practices helps prevent problems and keeps employers within reasonable boundaries. After cases of employers monitoring employees in private restrooms and tapping into personal email accounts, Kevin Conlon, district counsel for the Communication Workers of America, developed general guidelines to prevent employers from crossing the line into personal privacy breaches. He stated that there should be no monitoring of highly private areas, namely restrooms; that employees should have access to any of the information gathered about them during monitoring; that advance notice should be required; and only information relevant to the workplace should be collected (Pincus and Bucci 14). While few laws have been put in place requiring notification, employers have ethical obligations to inform their employees and not cross the reasonable expectation of workplace privacy.

What are employers looking for and do minor issues affect promotions?

A key factor in monitoring is understanding performance measures in the future. A study at Purdue University said companies were more likely to monitor new or entry-level employees before further promotion, or employees who were performing below the expected level (Alge 381). For this reason, higher level management is not regulated as intensely as lower level workers. Often, they are not regulated at all. Companies want to determine if employees are "dedicated" and "ethical" before increasing their salaries and promoting them for long-term careers. Employees who are performing below the desired level are also intensely monitored to determine if these employees are spending work time on personal tasks. The study concluded minor offenses of web surfing and personal emailing can affect promotion in instances where personal activity is interfering with performance or in cases of competition for a promotion.

When used effectively, "monitoring can serve to enhance productivity, establish and maintain production standards, and to diagnose problems in work flow and job design" (Lund 198). Many employers couple workplace monitoring with incentive pay or bonus structures. Companies who have clearly outlined promotion programs generally have lower instances of shirking. Shirking is defined as spending company time and resources on personal issues. Employees who feel valued in the workplace and understand the career path have lower instances of shirking and therefore, decrease the need for workplace monitoring. Employees who understand that their daily performance is monitored and will affect their future record have been shown to lower instances of personal activity during the work day (Lund 198).

Case Studies

To more closely examine the effects monitoring has on employees' productivity, interviews were conducted at three companies in the Boulder area over a two week period. At the request of one of the companies, the names and interview subjects have been removed to protect company practices. Company A currently monitors their employees' Internet activity, but does not have a clearly stated policy regarding their regulation. Company B also monitors their employees but has a policy that employees must sign their first day of employment, and Company C does not monitor their employees' Internet activity. Company A and B are mid-sized companies with 75+ employees each, while Company C only employs 13 people.

A survey was developed and distributed to employees at the three test companies. The survey consisted of 7 questions and asked current employees' opinions pertaining to whether they thought it was acceptable for their employers to monitor their actions. The survey continued by questioning what level of monitoring was acceptable, answered on a number rating scale. Additionally, the survey asked the employees if they were aware of their companies monitoring policies. The survey concluded with five questions that allowed insight into how much time the employee spent instant messaging at work, checking and composing personal emails, making personal phone calls, and amount of time spent each day on personal activities in the workplace.

The surveys were distributed to twelve employees at Company A. Currently, Company A uses e-mail monitoring software that monitors emails sent and received from their work addresses only. Company A has no clearly stated policy informing employees of this regulation. In an interview with the Executive Human Resource Director at Company A, she stated that "because the regulation only pertains to our employees' work email, they should know better than to send personal emails through their work address." After analyzing the survey results from Company A, it was found that an overwhelming 9 out of 12 employees did not believe their employer was currently monitoring their Internet activity. The results also showed employees used 1.65 hours of the workday performing personal tasks, most of which was spent on personal emails.

The results from the surveys distributed to fifteen employees at Company B differed from Company A's results. Presently, Company B monitors their employees using SpectorPro, the software described earlier. Company B uses this software to monitor all employees' Internet activity including, but not limited to, instant messaging, emails and web surfing activity. Company B also informs employees of their policy upon hiring. The following is part of their policy: "misuse of company computers, as outlined in the following policy, may result in suspension or termination of employment, and/or possible legal consequences. [Company B's] procedure is to deal with each net-abuse case on an individual basis, taking into consideration the severity of the case." From the survey it was found that 93% of Company B's employees were aware that their employer was monitoring their Internet activity, and 6 of 15 employees surveyed felt it was acceptable for the company to do so. Additionally, the average amount of total time spent at work conducting personal activities was 35 minutes, leading to the conclusion that awareness of monitoring drastically limits the employee use of company time for personal tasks.

The results from Company C were even more predictable. An interview was conducted with an Executive Account Representative, who outlined the reasons behind the company's decision not to monitor the workplace, "We do not monitor our employees because we feel our 10 hour workdays provide very limited time for employees to conduct personal tasks. With that said, if we feel an employee is abusing company time, they will be dismissed." 6 out of 13 employees were surveyed at Company C. The results revealed only one employee believed his/her daily activity was monitored. The average amount of time spent instant messaging was 45 minutes per day, and overall time spent performing personal tasks averaged 2.16 hours. The results lead to the belief that the majority of the employees were aware they were not being monitored and abused this knowledge. The employees at Company C spent the more time than both Company A and B performing personal tasks while on the job.

Conclusion

Workplace monitoring is an increasing trend, especially among recent college graduates. It is crucial for employees to be acutely aware of the monitoring policies at the company they work for, as well as understanding how this monitoring affects promotion. While this essay explored ethical issues in workplace privacy, it is important to understand that individual workplaces have separate standards and that employees have extremely limited legal defenses against workplace monitoring. The best practice for employees is to use caution when sending and checking emails, making phone calls, and surfing the Web on company owned technology. Monitoring is an increasing trend and can potentially make all the difference in that promotion or salary increase.

Works Cited

Adams, Hall, Suzanne Scheuing, and Stacey Feeley. "E-Mail Monitoring in the Workplace: the Good, the Bad and the Ugly." Defense Counsel Journal 67 (2000): 32-47.

Alge, Bradley, Gary Ballinger, and Stephen Green. "Remote Control." Personnel Psychology 52 (2004): 377-410.

Ciocchetti, Corey A. "Monitoring Employee E-Mail: Efficient Workplaces Vs. Employee Privacy." Duke Law and Technology Review. 14 Mar. 2007.

Dell, Kristina. "How You Can Stay Out of Trouble." Time Canada 11 Sept. 2006.

Duncan, Geoff. "U.S. Likes Cybershopping During Work Hours." Digital Trends (2006). 18 Mar. 2007.

Goodman, Abby. "On 'Borrowed' Time: Employees Spend Three Work Hours a Week on Personal Tasks, Survey Shows." Office Team. 16 Feb. 2007.

Email Can Make Big Business Act Like Big Brother. The Urban League of Greater Kansas City. Kansas City: Blue Symphony LLC, 2006. 1-2. 14 Mar. 2007 <www.ulkc.org>.

Everett, Andre, Yim-Yu Wong, and John Paynter. "Balancing Employee and Employer Rights: an International Comparison of E-Mail

Privacy in the Workplace." <u>Individual Employment Rights</u> 11 (2004): 291-308.

Flynn, Nancy. "2005 Electronic Monitoring & Surveillance Survey: Many Companies Monitoring, Recording, Videotaping—and Firing—Employees." <u>American Management Association</u>. 18 May 2005.

Kuhn, Peter, and Fernando Lozano. "The Expanding Workweek? Understanding Trends in Long Work Hours Among U.S. Men." <u>National Bureau of Economic Research</u> (2005). 18 Mar. 2007 <www.nber.org>.

Lund, John. "Computerized Work Performance Monitoring and Production Standards: a Review of Labor Law Issues." <u>Labor Law Journal</u> 42 (1991): 195-203.

Malachowski, Dan. "Wasted Time At Work Costing Companies Billions." <u>SFGate.Com</u>. 11 July 2005. 25 Feb. 2007 <www.sfgate.com>.

Morris, Jr., Frank. "The Electronic Platform: Email and Other Privacy Issues in the Workplace." <u>The Computer and Internet Lawyer</u> 20 (2003): 1-8.

Muhl, Charles J. "Workplace E-Mail and Internet Use:Employees and Employers Beware." <u>Monthly Labor Review</u> (2003): 36-45.

Pincus Hartman, Laura, and Gabriella Bucci. "The Economic and Ethical Implications of New Technology on Privacy in the Workplace." <u>Business and Society Review</u> (1998): 1-24.

"Spector Professional - Internet Activity and Email Surveillance Software." <u>Netbus.Org</u>. 14 Mar. 2007 <www.netbus.org>.

York, Thomas. "Invasion of Privacy? E-Mail Monitoring is on the Rise." Information Week. 21 Feb. 2000.

16

Celebrity CEOs and Privacy Issues
Anna Kaufman and Yael Wolf

Introduction to Celebrity CEOs and Privacy Issues

Celebrity CEOs are executives at the largest and most well-known organizations in the U.S. These CEOs find themselves at the center of attention inside the corporations they work for and in the public eye as representatives of the corporation. Celebrity CEOs appear regularly in countless newspapers, magazines, and company press releases. The leadership role and measure of fame that high-profile CEOs find themselves in is unavoidable and often unstoppable. Celebrity CEOs are public figures and are therefore constantly in the spotlight.

Included in the list of Celebrity CEOs are the biggest names in the business world, such Warren Buffett, Kenneth Lay, Michael Eisner, Charles Schwab, Bill Gates, Steve Jobs, Sumner Redstone, Michael Funk, John Thompson, Eli Broad, John Tyson, William Ford, and Lillian Vernon. The companies these executives work for make them attractive media targets.

This paper's research about high-profile CEOs focused on answering the question: What private information is released to the public regarding Standard & Poor's 1500 (S&P 1500) CEOs and how does it affect them and the companies they work for? The question was answered by using a databse to look through a large-sample archival database about S&P 1500 firms and the CEOs that work at them. The database included newspaper articles, magazine articles, and press releases dated from 1980 to 2006. This comprehensive database of media attention was used to find the most important and prevalent privacy issues facing celebrity CEOs.

Media Sources Archived in the Database

Where information comes from is a crucial factor in deciding its validity and trustworthiness as a source. The vast selection of reputable media sources and company released information available in the S&P 1500 database allowed for a dependable array of information. The newspapers and news magazines that were archived in the database are all national media sources that millions of Americans read on a daily basis.

The database we worked with provided thousands of articles from reputable newspapers and magazines. Along with these media outlets, companies' public relations newswires and press releases are archived in the database but are not mentioned in the table due to the extensive list of companies mentioned. In Table 1 you can see a full list of these news sources.

Table 1: Media Sources Archived in Database

Newspapers

Washington Post	USA Today
San Francisco Chronicle	International Herald Tribune
Los Angeles Times	Daily News
Chicago Tribune	The Independent
New York Times	State Journal Register
Boston Globe	The Guardian
Wall Street Journal	Denver Post
Rocky Mountain News	Atlanta Journal
St. Louis Post Dispatch	Houston Chronicle

Magazines

Forbes	Business Week
Maclean's	The Economist
Fortune	Multinational Monitor

Celebrity CEOs are mentioned in the most reputable newspapers and magazines in the U.S. Their personal and business lives are scrutinized every day by avid readers and journalists who are interested in the successes and failures, trials and tribulations, and other sensitive information about them. Because the articles found in the database are from trustworthy press outlets, most people tend to believe what they read, hoping that all sides of a story have been covered and the article is free of any biases. This may be a downside for high-status CEOs, because once the media's opinion is out and into the minds of the public, it is hard to change their view of the situation. On the other hand, it is important for celebrity CEOs to be featured in trustworthy news sources so they are able to build on the fame and status. Celebrity CEOs are expected to bring attention to the companies they work for and therefore, it is very important that whatever information is released ends up in a respectable newspaper or magazine. This spotlight on S&P 1500 firms is important for their continued success and prominence in the public eye.

An important consideration is the reason companies give out information about their CEOs? Do companies release information about CEOs to help build the company image? Do they release information to give the public a go-to face for the company? Is it all just a branding scheme? Do companies release sensitive information about CEOs to distract the public from something else going on inside the company? Do companies release information to media outlets under the idea that any publicity is good publicity? Do they just release information so they can get out a story before the media investigates it and makes the company look bad? Is honesty really the best policy? If a company releases information about their executives, should the private information still be considered protected information?

Privacy Laws

The Federal Trade Commission (FTC) has created numerous federal laws to protect the public from disclosure of nonpublic personal information. Even with these laws, however, a lot of details in articles are disclosed anyway. Some of these laws include the Drug and Alcoholism Abuse Confidentiality Statutes (21 U.S.C. § 1175; 42 U.S.C. § 290dd-3) that prohibit the disclosure of information about people's drug and alcohol abuse and their rehabilitation, except in cases of medical emergency or court order. The Health Research Data Statute (42 U.S.C. § 242m) prohibits the disclosure of health records that identify a person in any way. The Privacy Act (5 U.S.C. § 552a) prohibits the collection and disclosure of information about an individual's use of First Amendment rights (Gramm-Leach-Bliley Act).

Some state laws have also been adopted to protect personal information. One such law is the Common Law remedies, which provides compensation for invasions of privacy, including defamation, disclosure of privacy facts, and breach of duty of confidentiality. These remedies provide for money damages and, in some cases, special or punitive damages (Privacy Laws). These laws, however, are not enacted in every state. For example, while Bank Record Statutes, which prohibit financial institutions from disclosing employee and customer financial records, are ratified under U.S. Federal Law, less than half of the U.S. states have ratified the law and therefore, protected citizens against this crime (Smith).

One important question to ask is how do these editorials about celebrity CEOs get around the laws and provide the public with private information about CEOs? Though it is impossible to know for sure, it is possible that these S&P 1500 companies compensate their CEOs in advance in order to be able to disclose their personal information to the media. This again brings up the issue of whether any press coverage is good coverage for companies. A possibility is that companies are willing to pay their CEOs extra money in exchange for extra exposure. This is probably not done explicitly although it is obvious that CEOs do, at least metaphorically, sign away their privacy rights for fame and fortune.

After analyzing the available data, a framework of celebrity CEO privacy disclosures was developed. This framework covers six categories of disclosure as seen in Table 2.

Table 2: Categories of Privacy Invasion

Disclosure Category	Description
Donations, contributions, and philanthropy	Charity contributions are made every day but some can either help or damage companies' reputations. It is hard to keep large donations quiet.
Real estate and personal possessions	People with a lot of money will buy expensive things but whose business is it to know how much people spend on their personal possessions?
Religion	Religion has always been a sensitive issue which will often lead people to either hide their true beliefs, or sometimes publicize them to help their image. Whose business is it to know what faith others follow?
Substance abuse	It is always more interesting to hear about how people mess up rather than how they succeeded. Thus, if a CEO has abused a substance in his past, it will be written about.
Sex scandals	People's personal lives are always interesting to the public no matter what form they are presented in. The negative aspects, however, are always more prominent.
Private family information	Most people in the public eye want to protect their family from being scrutinized for every move they make, but it is not possible to keep them hidden. Thus, information about the most interesting family members are usually revealed.

Donations, Contributions, and Philanthropy

The contributions to society made by Bill Gates, Warren Buffet, Eli Broad, and Mel Karmazin reflect well on them and the S&P 1500 companies they run. Many of these CEOs have a "you have it, you share it" mentality to donating their hard-earned money (Goldberg).

Eli Broad, CEO of Sun America and well known philanthropist and art collector, donated $20 million to establish the Eli Broad College of Business and the Eli Broad Graduate School of Management at his alma mater. Broad donated 2.5 million frequent-flier miles to CalArts for student travel and also established the Eli Broad Family Foundation to share his art collection with the world (Haithman). These contributions helped to improve his image and that of the company he works for. Although it is important to donate money, is it necessary to write about it in editorials and showcase it to the world? Some people want their donations to society to be kept quiet, but with such large donations, it is hard to keep such a monumental philanthropic moment quiet for long.

For Bill Gates, CEO of Microsoft, his billion dollar donations to the Bill and Melinda Gates Foundation has improved his public image that had been previously damaged by the Justice Department investigation (Klinkenborg). Gates' contributions to educational advancements improves his image and therefore, the image of his company. One issue with disclosing donation information in news sources is that philanthropy can be dehumanized and can become just a competition to see who gets on the media's top philanthropist lists. Gates and many other philanthropists want to support education which was "their own key to success" and, by doing so, encourage people to "transition into the information age" (Klinkenborg). Microsoft and Gates see an important opportunity to show the world they are interested in educating the leaders and customers of tomorrow.

Although Mel Karmazin, CEO of CBS Radio, donated $1.7 million to the federal government, he had a reason behind the philanthropic contribution. Due to Howard Stern, "radio's outrageous bad [boy]," and his repeated charges of indecency with the Federal Communications Commission, Karmazin was faced with charges against CBS Radio. In return for the record clearance of Infinity Broadcasting Co., a division of CBS Radio, Karmazin voluntarily contributed the small fortune (Gunther). Although this contribution helped the public, the reason behind it could be viewed as shady to some and the article may make Karmazin's contribution reflect poorly on the company and damage the company's, as well as his own reputation according to the public. This example shows that not all contributions are free of purpose and given from the goodness of one's heart. These CEOs are business people and many will do anything they can to protect the companies they represent, as well as their fortunes.

In 2003, Berkshire Hathaway announced an end to its charitable giving program where Class A shareholders holding physical certificates could pick which charitable organization to donate to. Although a good idea, Warren Buffett, Berkshire Hathaway's CEO, controlled over half of the Class A shareholder votes for where contributions should be made. Millions of company dollars were donated each year to The Buffett Foundation due to invested interests by Buffett. This development was controversial, because The Buffett Foundation donates to population control, family planning, and helps to finance trials of the abortion pill RU-486 (Weekend Journal). This seemingly good deed turned bad due to the controversy of Buffett pushing his ideals and agenda onto other shareholders.

Real Estate and Personal Possessions

In a fame and fortune-obsessed world, the public is interested in public figures' wealth and ownership. High-profile CEOs often live in luxurious homes and own extravagant things that many can only imagine.

Michael Funk, United Natural Food's CEO, is building a solar-powered house out of wood, which will be cut in environmentally correct ways, in Nevada City, California. The article this was in, titled *Health Food Seller Is Back to Health* was totally unrelated to Funk's private life and yet the mention of his home made its way into the article (Murphy).

Lew Frankfort, CEO of Coach Inc., lives in a 100-year-old house in a fashionable New Jersey suburb and has a weekend place in the Hamptons. In 2004, he purchased a $160,000 Aston Martin (Berner). This information may make Frankfort look bad, because it shows his outrageous wealth that he acquired from Coach, and it leaves the public wondering how well everyone else at Coach is doing. People may wonder if they and company employees are being taken advantage of while the CEO makes off with all the big money.

In 2000, *Washington Post* published an article describing home and possessions of Lillian Vernon, CEO of direct mail giant Lillian Vernon. Vernon's home is complete with rabbit decorations, Christmas lights hanging from umbrellas, and fountains in her garden. She has glass walls and a huge skylight in her living room. This description of her home is contiguous with her company since it sells home and garden items. The article goes on to describe her "rust-colored linen suit and soft backless moccasins," which is clearly an unnecessary issuance of private information (Woman Who Has Everthing).

John W. Snow, CEO of CSX Corporation, owns the Commonwealth Club of Richmond, which only in the past 20 years has allowed African American people to join the country club (Snow Discloses). This article makes Snow look like a racist man who only recently adopted American values of freedom and equality.

Eli Broad of SunAmerica paid $2.5 million for a Roy Lichtenstein painting at Sotheby's on his American Express credit card. The upside to this for him was that he also got 2.5 million frequent-flier miles (Purdum)! Again, this information is private and not necessarily important information in building his image in the public eye.

Univision's CEO, A. Perenchio owns a 243 foot long British custom-made yacht, called Eco that cost an estimated $45 million (James)! This is unnecessary information that is being released to the public by the *Los Angeles Times*. This information may make people uncomfortable about the amount of money this CEO is making and therefore, this media attention could negatively affect the company and the CEO.

Symantec's CEO, John Thompson, has been in the media spotlight due to the company's recent success in the AntiVirus software industry. Thompson owns a 1949 convertible Chrysler Woody and lives in a $10.2 million house in Silicon Valley. He also owns a private jet and a wedding ring from Tiffany's. A USA Today article describes Thompson as seeming a "little embarrassed about his wealth," even mentioning that his private jet was rented on occasion (Kessler). The image that Thompson attempts to uphold is one of the common American. He does not want to be looked at like a wealth and high-class individual. He likes looking humble, and these descriptions about his extravagant possessions disrupt that image.

Religion

The First Amendment to the U.S. Constitution prohibits the federal legislature from making laws that establish a state religion or prefer a certain religion, and prohibit free exercise of religion, among other things (U.S. Constitution). Although this law exists, it does not protect public figures from having their religious beliefs and backgrounds put on display for the world to see.

In adjacency with Dean Foods Co.'s principles of environmentalism and organic foods, Gregg Engles learned some Buddhist principles that he carried over to his management practices (Adamy). This *Wall Street Journal* article had a positive affect on the image of Engles and Dean Foods Co. since Engles was able to align company ideals with customer ideals.

A *San Francisco Chronicle* article revealed a previously hidden identity of Sumner Redstone, the CEO of Viacom. Redstone's family is Jewish and his father changed the family last name in the 1940s to help Americanize the family. Unfortunately for Redstone, this name change has been a source of embarrassment (Sumner Redstone). The family's name may have been changed to help mask their Jewish identity at the time when anti-Semitism was widespread and could have hindered the family's success. Differing religions will always upset someone, and knowing this information may lead people to judge Redstone for his decisions.

For Lillian Vernon, her life was in danger due to her Jewish identity and as a result, she legally changed her name from Lilly Menashe to the more Americanized version she keeps today. Because Vernon decided to change her name, it was easier for her to merge her identity with the company's identity (Woman Who Has Everthing). This is another example of a name change that was made to mask a past identity that is now coming to light again because of media interest in Vernon's life and business.

Substance Abuse

There have been many biographical articles written about important people, celebrities, CEOs, and other public figures. However, information in these articles is generally taken half from interviews with the subject and half from research and interviews with their friends, families, and coworkers. Though it is not always clear that the subject of the article did not give some information willingly, a lot of the negative information is not commented on by the subject. This makes it seem as though it either did not come up in the interview or the subject chose not to comment on it.

In a biographical article about John Tyson, the CEO of Tyson Foods, written in Fortune magazine, Tyson told a story about his first summer working at Tyson Foods where he did not pay attention to the instructions given to him and spilled excrement from a chicken coop all over himself. Although unrelated, the journalist of the article took this opportunity to relate the story to Tyson's troubles later in his life. The next part of the article talks about how "John descended...into a haze of alcohol and cocaine addiction that frayed his relationship with his father and pushed him to the periphery of the business." The only introduction to this story was a mere "John's youthful follies lasted well into adulthood." (Stein) It is not an important part of the editorial since most of the article spoke about how John turned the company around since his inception as CEO, but it is an interesting piece of information that would make him a more unlikely hero.

Another article, written in the New York Times, said, "While [Tyson] was addicted to drugs and alcohol, he was named to the board of Tyson Foods" as if it is not a big deal (Barboza). In this article, however, Tyson does go on to talk about how he now goes to schools and prisons and talks about his substance addiction and life troubles. This move may have been done to alleviate the severity of his past mistakes. If people are going to ask about it and write about it, he might as well make light of it. Community service always looks positive in the eyes of investors and so does mending past mistakes.

Another example is a 1992 article about King World Productions Inc., the nation's dominant seller of game, talk, and magazine shows, and why their stock is not as high as expected. The article says a potential cause is that one of the King brothers, Roger, the CEO, was arrested in 1987 for auto theft, cocaine possession, and robbery after a fight with a cab driver. This incident, which happened five years earlier, could not possibly be the cause of the falling stock; however, the fact is still stated – apparently for no reason. The article recognizes the lack of connection later after relating it to another arrest that happened a year before the article was written, where earnings rose 7% in the coming year (Fabrikant). As stated in the Privacy Laws section of this chapter, it is illegal to discuss people's alcohol and drug abuse problems and arrests. However, the articles still mention these problems even when they are not pertinent to the article. Substance abuse instances can hurt the credibility of an executive and the company they work for.

Sex Scandals

Sex and infidelity have always been interesting issues to people whether the news is about a high-profile CEO, a celebrity, or a neighbor. It is not surprising when reputable media sources take personal information about sex scandals and expose them to the public. The media exposes sex scandals because the public is interested in what CEOs have done in their personal lives that may help or hurt them in their jobs. Unfortunately, sex scandals sell in the media and are therefore over exposed, leaving the victims' private lives are completely destroyed after the stories are dissected. A sex scandal creates a situation where the media will then delve deep into any other issue that has ever occurred in the person's life, thus making the situation even worse and making the media coverage last even longer. Although this is a federal criminal offense and therefore not a protected private act, the explosion of media attention for sex scandals can ruin careers and damage the reputation of a company.

An example of this is at the detriment of Sumner Redstone, CEO of Viacom, during his divorce battle. Even when Redstone explicitly asked for his divorce court papers to be sealed, at least six articles were written in USA Today, The Wall Street Journal, New York Times, and the Boston Globe about the details of the mess. Three articles state that Sumner's wife, Phyllis Redstone, is seeking $3 billion in the case and accusing her husband of adultery and cruelty. The other three articles say that she dropped the suit against her husband. One article even states that Redstone asked to seal the details, and in the next section talks about what his wife is suing him for (Graham).

In 2005, Robert Johnson, CEO of Newsday, was indicted for downloading child pornography onto his office computer and then trying to destroy it upon learning that his company was being investigated. The next day New York Times wrote an exposé revealing every fact of the case and what Johnson had done (Preston). It is obvious that Johnson would not want this information revealed to the public and he would never talk about these intimate details with the press or family, friends, and colleagues. There is an act, however, that protects media sources so that authors do not have to reveal where they receive the information (Privacy Laws). Although there are laws preventing legal and personal information from being leaked, whether it was legal to write this article is still up for debate.

A last example is the several articles written about Henry Nicholas, former CEO of Broadcom, a company that makes chips used in cable modems, set-top boxes, and other devices. For Nicholas's 40th birthday, he ordered the MTV band Orgy to play at his party. After a miscommunication, a porn star showed up at the party – this was in the newspapers the next day and the news even reached his mother in a nearby state. As if this was not bad enough for Nicholas' reputation as a credible and reliable executive leader, throughout the next few years, articles written about the company talking about technology mentioned the incident in completely unrelated ways (Holson). This unfortunate mistake has cost Nicholas, his family, and Broadcom their reliable reputations and the incident has severely tainted his public image.

Private Family Information

Although most CEOs are willing to give up vast amounts of privacy for a large paycheck and fame, when does the media go too far in freely providing sensitive family history information?

Family information has been written about Millard Drexler, Lew Frankfort, Mel Karmazin, David Moore, Jerry Fiddler, Gerald Levin, Jeffrey Swartz, Eli Broad, Edward Whitacre, Paul Fireman, David Overton, William Ford, Edgar Bronfman, and many other celebrity CEOs.

For David Moore, an article published about him referenced his ability to understand how hard it is to succeed. The article described Moore's 20-year military career and paralleled that experience to Moore's ability to succeed and understand the meaning of calculated risk. This article shows that Moore has a lot of experience dealing with risk and the experiences he had earlier in his life helped him be the successful businessman he is today. The article also described an event during his military career in which he kept his men alive despite hostile conditions in Vietnam. This shows Moore's ability to take control of an ever deteriorating situation and save the day (Kroll).

This family information, although highlights the family and brings them into the spotlight, not everyone in these CEOs' extended family may want to be showcased to the world. Some may live quiet lives that have been interrupted by a distant relative's fame and fortune. Other stories describe harsh backgrounds and rags to riches stories that encourage news readers that follow CEO articles to believe that their own dreams may become reality.

Conclusions

Just like any other celebrity, celebrity CEOs live their lives in the public eye, and thus their whole lives are scrutinized by the rest of the world. However, unlike Hollywood celebrities, everything that happens in these people's personal lives reflects not only their reputation, but also on that of their company. As in the previous example of Roger King, CEO of King World Productions Inc., his previous drug problem was one of the possible explanations for the falling stock of the company. No matter how preposterous the claim is that something that happened so long ago was the cause of a newly developed problem, it will always be a stain on his character. People will always look at him and wonder whether he will ever be capable of making crucial decisions. Many times the CEO is not only the one being talked about, but his or her family members are used as publicity pawns. For example, the mere mention of Peggy Broad and Eli Broad's being married for 43 years is used to translate his commitment to marriage into the commitment he has for the company he works for (Haithman).

Not all publicity, however, is bad publicity, and certain information published about CEOs can be for the benefit of the company. A good example of this is the Gates foundation and the Eli Broad's contributions to establish a business and graduate school. If the CEO is giving money to such good causes, more of his or her mistakes are forgiven. Also, sometimes what seem like unnecessary details about people's possessions can be important facets to a company. For example, in the article describing Lillian Vernon's house, one can gather that she is proud of her company and the things it sells. It also shows that Vernon not only endorses the products but also uses them. If the CEO of the company uses her own products, people will be more likely to buy the product

Weaknesses and Future Research

A weakness in the research is a lack of time to fully research more articles and delve deeper into the issues of privacy related matters of celebrity CEOs. If there was more time to examine these issues it would be good to research more articles and highlight more key privacy issues. Because the database is so large, it is very hard to go through every article and find every privacy issue relating to S&P 1500 CEOs in the time given to research and write this chapter. If time persisted, more research would lead to new revelations and more in-depth conclusions, making the argument stronger.

Another issue is that neither the time nor resources were available to truly understand the impact these privacy breaches have on S&P 1500 companies. It would require direct interviews with the companies and CEOs to really know whether the articles have had a positive or negative affect on the company, or any impact at all. Personal interviews with the newspapers and journals would also help immensely because one could gain understanding of the media's point of view and figure out how they are getting around the legal issues of publishing private facts.

In order to understand these issues fully, it would also help to research more in-depth the privacy laws and court cases that have been brought against media sources regarding public figures' privacy released to public. Knowing previous cases would either help or hurt our argument, but it would make the paper stronger and more reputable.

Works Cited

"A Review of Federal and State Privacy Laws." BBBOnLine, Inc. 2006. Council of Better Business Bureaus, Inc. 21 Feb. 2007 http://www.bbbonline.org/UnderstandingPrivacy/library/fed_state PrivLaws.pdf.

Adamy, Janey. "Nature's Way -- Behind a Food Giant's Success: an Unlikely Soy-Milk Alliance; At Dean Foods, CEO, Buddhist Team Up to Sell Silk Brand; and Gain Clout in Organics; Mr. Engles's Lesson on 'Sukha'" Wall Street Journal All Edition 1 Feb. 2005. 3 Mar. 2007. 786989481

Barboza, David. "Why is He on Top? He's a Tyson, for One." New York Times 4 Mar. 2001. 69209982

Berner, Robert. "Coach's Driver Picks Up the Pace; CEO Frankfort's Overhaul Has Doubled Revenues and Sent the Stock Up 900%." Business Week 29 Mar. 2004. 645321941

Fabrikant, Geraldine. "The Rise and Rise of the Brothers King." New York Times 26 July 1992. 964905071

Haithman, Diane. "Intense (in Tens') Adj. 1. Very Strong 2. Zealous 3. Having or Showing Firm Purpose 4. Eli Broad." Los Angeles Times 19 Oct. 1997. 19110967

Holson, Laura M. "'Anti-Silicon Valley' Broadcom Chief Rules in the Wired World." New York Times 26 June 2000. 55480381

Goldberg, Carey. "Computer Age Millionaires Redefine Philanthropy." New York Times 6 July 1997. 12805244

Graham, Bob. "Sumner Redstone's Wife Files for Divorce." USA Today 20 Sept. 1999. 45004354

"Gramm-Leach-Bliley Act: Subchapter I: Disclosure of Nonpublic Personal Information." Federal Trade Commission. 5 Apr. 2007. US Government. 3 Mar. 2007 <http://www.ftc.gov/privacy/glbact/glbsub1.htm#6801>.

Gunther, Marc. "King of All Radio." Fortune 14 Apr. 1997. 11319118

James, Meg. "The Old Versus El Nuevo; the Young Leader of Spanish Media Giant Grupo Televisa Has His Sights on Univision, But the L.a. Billionaird in Charge Isn'T Budging." Los Angeles Times 10 Mar. 2005. 805468401

Kessler, Michelle. "Symantec CEO Turns Flying Blind Into Profit ; Thompson Spent Three Decades Behind Scenes." <u>USA Today</u> 25 Oct. 2004. 723579881

Klinkenborg, Verlyn. "The Man At Microsoft; or How High the Moon." <u>New York Times</u> 4 Sept. 1999. 44428515

Kroll, Luisa. "One Tough Lesson Plan." <u>Forbes</u> 28 Oct. 2002. 209354831

Murphy, K. "Health Food Seller is Back to Health." <u>New York Times</u> 31 Dec. 2000. 65884759

Preston, Julia. "Newsday Ex-Chief Indicted in Child Pornography Case." <u>New York Times</u> 29 June 2005. 860213031

Purdum, Todd S. "Moving Heaven and Earth for the City of Angels." <u>New York Times</u> 12 Aug. 2000. 57858814

Smith, Robert Ellis, and Privacy Journal. "Privacy Laws by State." <u>Electronic Privacy Information Center (EPIC)</u>. 1997. 23 Mar. 2007 <http://www.epic.org/privacy/consumer/states.html>.

"Snow Discloses His Assets, Pay; Treasury Nominee Lists Holdings of Up to $295 Million, and Club Perks." <u>The Washington Post</u> 23 Jan. 2003. 279718651

Stein, Nicholas. "Son of a Chicken Man." <u>Fortune</u> 13 May 2002. 118167115.

"Sumner Redstone / Media Honcho Redstone Proud of His 'Passion to Win'" <u>San Francisco Chronicle</u> 5 Jul. 2001. 74972949.

"The United States Constitution." <u>The U.S. Constitution Online</u>. Apr. 1997. U.S. Government. 17 Mar. 2007

"The Woman Who Has Everything; for Lillian Vernon, a Business Empire Made to Order." <u>The Washington Post</u> 22 Apr. 2000. 58457881

"Weekend Journal; Taste: Giving Until It Hurts." <u>Wall Street Journal All Edition</u> 1 Aug. 2003. 378145211

17

A Balancing Act:
Privacy, Regulation, and Innovation in Hedge Funds

Thomas Van De Bogart and Justin Blincoe

*Selected definitions and terminology available in Appendix at the end of the chapter.

Introduction

In a world where individuals and institutions try to diversify away systematic risk, collective investment schemes provide a way to hedge risks and to share the costs of doing so with others. Hedge funds are unregulated, private and exclusive collective investment schemes. Hedge funds are only available to 'accredited investors,' meaning individuals with a net worth in excess of one million dollars or a previous and expected future salary in excess of $200,000 per year. Thus, investing in hedge funds has traditionally been limited to the wealthy. Currently, the assets that hedge funds hold under management are estimated to be well over one trillion dollars (Labaton). A few major components separate hedge funds from other types of collective investment pools such as mutual funds, pension funds and insurance companies. First, limitations on participants and minimum investments work to ensure hedge funds are not available to the general public. Second, most other collective investment vehicles are highly regulated by limiting which types of securities they can hold (i.e. only technology stocks or bonds). Regulated investment firms also face strict borrowing and leveraging restrictions. Additionally, registered investment companies, like mutual funds, are prohibited from charging performance or incentive fees, a component of hedge funds that magnifies the lucrative returns these funds are associated with.

Because hedge funds are not registered with the Securities and Exchange Commission (SEC) or the National Association of Securities Dealers (NASD), hedge funds cannot be regulated by these agencies. Only the terms of the contract and the bankers who loan the money can regulate positions taken by the fund manager. Without regulation, and with performance incentives rewarding high risk, hedge fund managers have strong incentives to employ severe leverage as well as incredibly complex uses of derivative markets – and they are free to do so without disclosing the positions they have taken (Labaton). This lack of hedge fund regulation has many implications. It creates the potential for hedge funds to make, and potentially lose, extravagant amounts of money. Without proper controls, this could have consequences that disrupt the larger, public, financial markets. Recently, major hedge fund collapses have lead to increased media attention and more scrutiny from governing bodies. Even so, hedge funds are still an accredited investment vehicle that, when managed correctly, have a proven history of offsetting risk and earning solid returns. With both harsh critics and vehement supporters, the future of hedge fund regulation is centered on a balance between efficiency and privacy, control and protection.

Research Methods

Few people have much experience or knowledge of hedge funds. In order to overcome this naïveté, several financial experts were interviewed. To gain a perspective of how those in the private investment sector view hedge funds, an interview was conducted with both a managing director and a senior associate in a prominent private equity fund. To achieve the academic aspect of the hedge fund industry, Finance professors David M. Gross, Ph.D., and Tom C. Nelson, Ph.D. at the University of Colorado - Boulder were interviewed. The objective of these interviews was to gather insights from people with different perspectives in order to maintain a balanced view on how hedge funds operate and what their impacts are. In an attempt to get an idea of how the ordinary consumer thinks about hedge funds, a survey was given to a group of 32 students at the University of Colorado. Due to the fact that students generally do not have a vast knowledge of the industry, we geared the questions towards finding out how much they knew, trusted, or cared about how a company manages their retirement fund. By combining research, interviews with experts and a survey pertaining to the ordinary consumer's perceptions of the issue, the paper will explore the future of regulation and innovation in the hedge fund world, as well as 'what it means to the ordinary consumer.'

Why Does Hedge Fund Regulation Matter?

"After observing lavish salaries hedge fund managers pay themselves, these funds are no more than a compensation package dressed as an industry."
— Warren Buffet

A common belief towards hedge funds is that 'people who are not actively involved in hedge funds are not affected by them.' Hedge funds are private, highly sophisticated investment tools that only wealthy, 'market savvy' investors are supposed to be involved in. This begs the natural question: Why does it matter if hedge funds are regulated or if the extremely wealthy lose a ton of money? Considering the number of financial problems that people deal with on a day-to-day basis, is there a reason to waste time being concerned with these obscure funds? In the past, one could easily argue that hedge funds have no effect on the average American. Hedge funds were hidden away from the public eye and very few people had stakes in them. However, with the innovation of the 'fund of funds,' access to hedge funds is not as restrictive as it used to be. Similar to mutual funds for single investors, a fund of funds is commonly setup by a group of investors who combine their money to invest in something that they otherwise would not have been able to. This means that investors without significant wealth can pool their money and be exposed to hedge funds. With the recent development of this 'fund of funds' concept, it is much easier for people without high net worth to invest in a hedge fund. For example, to reach the million dollar mark needed to invest in a hedge fund, only 20 people would need to pool $50,000 a piece in order to invest. $50,000 is a far more manageable amount of money than the original one million dollar requirement, and thus, potential investors encompass a far greater percentage of the population. The use of 'fund of funds' has progressed hedge funds from an entirely exclusive private investment mechanism along the spectrum towards the public.

As hedge funds become available to more people, a number of new concerns have cropped up. More people have become very concerned with their financial plan for retirement. With Social Security faltering and companies changing the structure in which their employees' retirements are funded, there is great concern over whether retirees will have enough saved to last for as long a period as necessary. Although the current trend is toward defined contribution retirement plans (where the employee manages their pension), there are still many employers that hire money managers to control and invest the funds of money the company has set aside for its retiring employees. These retirement plans, classified as defined benefit plans, require that the company manage its money to have a certain amount to pay out when employees retire. Money managers employed by companies with defined benefit plans may control exceptionally large pools of money. After many companies' pension funds took major hits in 2001, even those with diversified portfolios, the need for higher future returns to make up for these setbacks became pressing for many pension managers. Even competently managed pension funds invested in companies like Enron and WorldCom, whose collapse greatly hurt the pension funds invested in them. If a pension fund does not meet requirements to pay off the required pensions, the company must look for taxpayers to bail them out or to cut retiree benefits (Steffy). Obviously, each of these moves is undesirable for the company and detrimental to the pension fund manager's career. One way to escape these suffering pension funds is to invest in hedge funds, where the possibility of high returns grant enough leeway to easily cover prior losses. Thus, falling markets and dropping pension funds, combined with ever-increasing numbers of retirees, meant that pension managers had strong incentives to take any action necessary to ensure sufficient funds once employees began retiring.

One example of this risky pension fund management can be found in the company 3M, a San Diego based company responsible for making such products as Scotch tape and Post-It notes. Facing a situation very similar to the one described in the prior paragraph, the pension fund manager at 3M decided to use hedge funds as a way to increase the performance of their pension fund. The professional fund manager invested a sizable amount of money into a hedge fund called Amaranth. When Amaranth lost most of the money invested in a matter of weeks, an already struggling pension fund suffered the loss of all that was invested in Amaranth. The employees at 3M took a huge hit in their retirement packages. The fund manager at 3M lost most of the $175 million dollars it had invested in Amaranth (Strasburg). Additionally, companies that Amaranth invested in, such as Toronto-based Counsel Corp., took huge hits in their own stock prices when positions were liquidated. As a component of many pension or benefits packages of companies, the stock price loss of 14% at Counsel Corp. would have been hugely detrimental to the employees (Strasburg). Just as the thousands of employees at Enron or WorldCom were affected by the poor decisions of their executives, so too can the average consumer be affected by the mismanagement of hedge funds.

Survey Results

One of the most direct impacts hedge funds can have on ordinary consumers is through pension funds. A survey was administered addressing these concerns most pertinent to this chapter. Asked if they currently trusted or would trust their pension plan to their employer, 52% of the respondents mentioned that they had not even considered it. 37.5% said that they would trust their employer. Interestingly, 91% of those questioned mentioned that the safety of their retirement plan was 'very important' to their career. Similarly, we asked if the students worried that some or most of their pension could be lost. Not surprisingly, most of the respondents mentioned that they either "didn't know it could happen," or "had not thought about it." Lastly, we asked if the students thought that a company should have to disclose risky pension investments to its employees. While 16% of the respondents mentioned that they do not care, 78% noted that they should, leaving just 6% of those questioned who think that taking risky positions without disclosure should be allowed. These trends give insight into how the younger generation feels about investing and its affect on their money.

Brief History

Hedge funds date back to 1949 when a Harvard graduate named Alfred Winslow Jones, a sociologist, tested a new investment strategy of buying stocks long while simultaneously selling similar stocks short (McWhinney). By having equally invested amounts in long and short positions, volatility in the market would be counteracted and have limited effect on portfolio value. By eliminating this market risk, Jones was able to narrow his risk to whether or not he had chosen the correct side of the straddle (i.e. long positions went up in value while short positions went down). Alfred Winslow Jones, known as the father of the hedge fund, "altered the structure of this investment vehicle, converting it from a general partnership to a limited partnership and adding a 20% incentive fee as compensation for the managing partner" (McWhinney). The two biggest innovations that came from Jones were his fee structure, as well as this new approach to managing and manipulating exposure to risk. With these new financial tactics that Jones developed, he was much better able to choose which risks he wanted to take, as well as those which he wished to neutralize.

In 1966, the media trumpeted hedge funds for substantially outperforming every mutual fund and their popularity skyrocketed. Within two years, there were about 140 hedge funds in operation. New strategies started to develop, spurred by these new players. Instead of always trying to hedge risk, strategies were developed in an effort to take on more risk. Because the return levels in some of these funds shot out the lights, this style started to become more prevalent. In the market downturn of the 1970's, this led to many fund closures. The industry was relatively quiet until a 1986 article told of an investment that was making consistently higher returns than any other. Alluring strategies kept advancing, and the hedge fund industry grew rapidly until the late 1990's/ early 2000's when the stock market was corrected and many high-profile funds failed (McWhinney). These events lead us to the current debate of hedge fund regulation and disclosure.

Secrecy and Privacy in the Hedge Fund World

Scarcity of regulation has great significance in the financial world. Hedge fund managers defend this privacy and secrecy they need by explaining that many of their strategies are highly proprietary and that performance and efficiency are compromised by public disclosure. Most observers understand this position, but still believe investors need a better way to judge their risk profile. With the recent massive growth of hedge funds, it is no wonder that many in the investment world are wondering if hedge funds may be overhyped and that a substantial sell-off is on the horizon. During an interview, Dr. Tom C. Nelson discussed the present state of the hedge fund industry. Dr. Nelson argues that when hedge funds are run correctly (to hedge risk), they are designed to foster lower but more stable returns. In opposition to their inherent nature of decreasing risk, hedge fund managers (like those at Amaranth) use a lack of regulation to take severely leveraged positions that are not 'hedged' at all (Nelson). The hope of these managers is to see huge returns and capitalize on performance fees. However, as evidenced by Amaranth's $6 billion loss, a lack of disclosure and regulation allows for irresponsible investing and the potential for major losses. Dr. Nelson concluded his interview by warning of a potential burst in the hedge fund bubble, a prediction that could have grave ramifications. With the current size and growth of hedge funds, a collapse could, in fact, negatively pressure the entire capital market.

How Hedge Funds are Affected by Technology

In the past two decades, some significant technological advances have helped fuel financial innovation. The main catalyst behind many of these innovations is the computing revolution which broke its way into societal mainstream. This has caused the spread of information to be much cheaper and easier. It is now feasible to disseminate information to a much broader range of people instantaneously. Using the power of the Internet, anyone with a computer can access financial information, whereas 10 years ago only professionals (large brokerage houses) could acquire this information. Technology has also affected the speed of the financial world. Trades are now done the exact instant a mouse is clicked. Before the Internet connected the entire financial world, trades had to be done on trading floors where only brokers had access.

Hedge funds are on the forefront of financial technological innovation. Because of the complex trading strategies they pursue, as well as their creativity in managing risk, they are mandated to stay ahead of other investment firms. As the number of entities chasing the same returns increases, software and computing power that is capable of locating, processing and finding mispriced assets is a necessity for hedge fund success. As Dr. Nelson summarized, there were lots of opportunities to capitalize on mispricing when the hedge fund market was relatively small. However, with the massive explosion of the market in the last decade, the ability to capture value is becoming far more difficult and requires extremely sophisticated methodology. Additionally, he explained that, as little as five years ago, hedge funds were adept at capturing inefficient niches in the market and exploiting them. This added to market efficiency by correcting the previously incorrect market prices (Nelson).

What Kind of Regulation would be Affective?

"Although markets tend toward rational positions in the long run, markets can stay irrational longer than you can stay solvent."
- John Maynard Keynes

Hedge funds are organized to cater to a much different, higher wealth clientele who care deeply about their privacy and also have the means to lobby to keep their privacy intact. To get around this, attempts have been made to regulate the banks that supply the credit necessary for hedge funds to leverage their positions heavily. Regulators are trying to require the disclosure of risks by the bank and its clients. This involves giving up a level of privacy they have enjoyed until now. Also,

169

by requiring the use of risk controls that force hedge funds to sell assets when their bets experience falling prices, regulators are trying to enact downside protection. These regulations are at the forefront of controversy as they are being introduced in international legislation, through the Basel Capital Accord, or Basel II. During an interview, the Managing Director at a private equity firm explained that one of the main modern, as well as future, movements in finance is the consolidation of regulations internationally by moving to introduce international accounting standards (Private Equity). Avinash D. Persaud, the London-based Managing Director of Global Research for Boston's State Street Bank, is a critic of Basel II. Persaud believes attempting to supervise hedge funds through their lenders could backfire. He agrees some disclosure is essential, but that too much can be dangerous. This could be harmful when a hedge fund needs to sell assets quickly. When this occurs, and this information becomes known to other owners of the same asset, they will try to sell first, driving prices down further (Coy). Such illiquidity is one of the many factors that kept LTCM from remaining afloat when its bets turned sour. Persaud believes disclosure would be less damaging if positions were disclosed only once a month or so, and stated, "Disclosure... must not be a religion" (Coy). Dr. Nelson believes that disclosure is not much of a problem. He believes that these funds already know what positions their competitors are in, so compelling them to disclose publicly would have very little affect on trading styles. These opposing views by sophisticated members of the financial community expose the fundamental disagreements on how hedge funds should operate and how much privacy they should have. Some of the most intelligent individuals in the financial world admit they don't really understand the intricacies of how hedge funds operate. Due to this fundamental ignorance regarding hedge funds, even the regulatory bodies such as the SEC and New York Federal Reserve Bank stated that they don't have the knowledge or experience necessary to effectively regulate hedge funds (Private Equity).

Persaud thinks 'value-at-risk' systems are more damaging. They automatically force funds to sell assets when too much of a funds asset base is at a risk of loss. This strategy could work if one fund engaged in it, but when everyone uses this autopilot form of risk management, the consequences can be undesirable. When a large sell-off occurs, prices go way below their true economic value (Coy). The Asian financial crisis of 1997 is an example of a market downturn that was intensified by these value-at-risk philosophies. One essential reason value-at-risk doesn't always work is that hedge funds actively try to take contrary positions. Many hedge funds take positions inverse to other players in the market, such as buying when everyone else is selling. Hedge funds cannot carry out this opposing strategy if banks shrink loan levels right when they are most needed. The result of this value-at-risk system is that it leads to banks over-lending when the market is rising and overly drastic measures when values become depressed. Although infinite in complexity, these issues all boil down to a main point. Hedge funds may have a riskier probability of causing economic damage, but as is the first rule of medicine, the important thing is making sure the cure is not worse than the disease.

Regulating Hedge Funds in a New Economy

Regulatory bodies are having an exceedingly difficult time trying to regulate hedge funds since they are designed to operate with strong levels of privacy and highly innovative financial strategies. This dilemma is one that the newly appointed President and CEO of the Federal Reserve Bank of New York, Timothy Geithner, has been dealing extensively with since coming to the Federal Reserve in 2003. During a speech in Hong Kong, Mr. Geithner remarked:

> The fundamental challenge for policy is how to achieve the appropriate balance between efficiency and financial resilience... Some vulnerability to crisis is a necessary and unavoidable feature of a dynamic and efficient financial system where asset prices need to be able to adjust to changes in fundamentals. The consequences of trying to induce regulated financial institutions to self-assure against all conceivable potential risks would do substantial damage to the level and efficiency of economic activity and cause the same risks to migrate to other institutions (Geithner 2).

When technology and privacy become entangled, there is always debate about what better serves society's interests. In many cases, increased regulation on technology means additional privacy for those involved. This is the opposite case with hedge funds. Additional regulation means hedge funds would have less privacy in carrying out their investment strategies without the world learning of their unique investment methods.

Geithner went on to discuss how innovation in trading technology and hedge funds has affected how financial markets should be regulated. He stated: "Among the most notable of these changes has been the rapid growth and innovation in derivatives and the greater relative importance of private leverages financial institutions such as hedge funds" (Geithner 2). Because hedge funds have such low levels of regulation and have come under recent media scrutiny, regulatory agencies and central banks are trying to come up with ways in which they can effectively reduce risks these funds pose. Although hedge funds still only control a small percentage of assets under management, their relative share has recently increased significantly and their potential impact on financial market conditions is magnified by their ability to take on substantial leverage and risk.

One of the problems with these new regulations is the unintentional consequences. Regulators certainly have honorable intentions in trying to stabilize the markets, but some believe the effect could be the opposite. Many critics argue that these risk management systems are not as infallible as they appear on the surface. It is suggested that when the market is put under pressure, these regulatory systems will not provide much protection to investors. Along with the untested nature of new regulation comes the idea of regulation inefficiency. In an interview conducted with the Managing Director of a well-respected private equity firm, he warned against the inefficiencies that overregulation can create. He pointed out that Hong Kong has extremely low financial regulation, yet one of the highest growth rates in the world. While this is attributable to many factors, the point that overregulation creates inefficiencies does not fall on deaf ears. The United States is one of the least financially regulated sophisticated markets; and for a long time, the U.S. has experienced higher growth rates economically than most countries in similar situations (Private Equity).

Arguments countering the libertarian idea of unregulated free markets are made by many experts in finance. Dr. Gross points out that while arguments for less regulation always reference the inefficiencies regulations can create. Perhaps, it is really the short versus the long-term effects that matter more. Dr. Gross agrees that regulation inevitably creates inefficiency. In a social sense, paying police officers to protect our streets against crime can be considered inefficient. Police cost resources that could otherwise be allocated to a more productive means for the economy. Large corporations paying one of the Big Four accounting firms to audit all of their financial statements uses money that could otherwise be distributed to the shareholders. Does this mean police stations should be shut down? Can we trust corporations to report accurately without oversight? Some forms of inefficiency can actually be efficient in the long run by serving the function of offering a necessary form of protection (Gross).

Financial markets can be looked at in the same light. Confidence is one of the main reasons capitalism has been such a successful system of equity distribution. In the United States, people trust that effective property rights ensure their property will not be seized by the government without probable cause. Conversely, a lack of protected property rights is at the root of many underdeveloped nations' inability to grow and expand their economies. Finance in the U.S. is no different. Protection and regulation allow for U.S. citizens to feel safe when investing their money. If this sentiment was not widespread, people would be hesitant to invest their money in such markets, thus making the free market economy inefficient and growth limited. Regulation acts to both prevent and punish fraud ensures investor confidence. Average investors are free to invest their money wherever their risk tolerance allows (Gross).

Concluding Remarks

With more time to do primary research, it would be crucial to examine how people closer to retirement viewed their pension. Doing so would give a better idea of sentiments by those currently working towards their retirement, and how safe they believe their money is. We would also like to observe and interview hedge fund managers directly to obtain a better grasp of how those directly involved in the industry feel.

In conclusion, technology has changed the financial world drastically over the past few decades. When interviewees were asked about technology, the first thing out of their mouth was that the Internet has changed absolutely everything in finance. Amidst this technological backdrop, hedge funds have been forced to create innovation as well as learn the ramifications of its use. While major collapses have earned a large portion of the media attention, proper hedge fund management remains a successful and reliable trading strategy. Additionally, although huge performance fees have created some misaligned incentives for managers, it still remains that hedge funds are one of the most efficient forms of investing and can actually work to correct market inefficiencies. Moreover, while regulation serves to protect, the privacy and lack of disclosure hedge funds enjoy is part of what has made them so successful in the past. Considering the risks inherent in hedge funds, it is advisable to do careful research before investing in such a fund. Similarly, those who cannot or do not invest in hedge funds should be equally cautious and observant of the safety of their pension. The key to the future is balancing how privacy, technology, regulation and efficiency interact in the hedge fund industry. A successful combination of regulation and privacy towards hedge funds will result in controlled risk as well as a more efficient and stable economy.

Works Cited

Coy, Peter. "Commentary: the Wrong Way to Regulate Hedge Funds." Business Week. 26 Feb. 2001. 12 Mar. 2007.
    <http://www.businessweek.com/2001/01_09/b3721013.htm>.
Geithner, Timothy F. "Hedge Funds and Derivatives and Their Implications for the Financial System." Bank for International Settlements. 14 Sept. 2006. 12 Mar. 2007 <http://www.bis.org/review/r060918b.pdf>.
Gross, David M. Ph.D. Instructor of Finance, Leeds School of Business. Personal interview. 21 Mar. 2007.
Labaton, Stephen. "Current Hedge Fund Rules Work, Regulators Say." The New York Times. 23 Feb. 2007. 25 Feb. 2007. <http://www.nytimes.com/2007/02/23/business/23hedgeweb.html?ex=1329886800&en=355bfe65e1e1507f&ei=5090&partner=rssuserland&emc=rss>.
McWhinney, Jim. "A Brief History of the Hedge Fund." Investopedia. 8 Nov. 2005. 14 Feb. 2007. <http://www.investopedia.com/articles/mutualfund/05/HedgeFundHist.asp>.
Nelson, Tom C. Ph.D. Senior Instructor of Finance, Leeds School of Business. Personal interview. 20 Mar. 2007.
Senior Associate & Managing Director. Private Equity Firm. Prefer Anonymity. Personal interview. 14 Mar. 2007.
Rogoff, Kenneth. "The Hedge Fund Hegemon." Project Syndicate. 2007. 25 Feb. 2007 <http://www.projectsyndicate.org/commentary/rogoff28>.

Steffy, Loren. "Amaranth Illustrates the Risks of Hedge Funds." Houston Chronicle. 4 Oct. 2006. 25 Feb. 2007. <http://www.chron.com/disp/story.mpl/business/steffy/4234583.html>.
Strasburg, Jenny. "Amaranth Hedge-Fund Losses Hit 3M." Bloomberg. 21 Sept. 2006. 25 Feb. 2007. <http://www.bloomberg.com/apps/news?pid=20601087&sid=aOvmPEFXPizs&refer=home>.

Appendix/Definitions

The below definitions are simple explanations of some of the financial vocabulary used in our chapter. Including these definitions allow people who are not well-versed in financial vocabulary to understand the ideas and concepts behind this paper.

Hedge: Using an investment to reduce or cancel out the risk in another investment.

Leverage: Money borrowed in order to increase the potential return of an investment.

Market risk: Also known as systematic risk, it is risk inherent to the entire market.

Long position: Owning an asset (expectation for price appreciation).

Short Position: Borrowing an asset along with a contract to sell it in the future.

Risk-adjusted return: A measure of how much risk a fund takes on to earn its returns.

Liquidity: The ability to transfer an asset to cash.

V

EMERGING TECHNOLOGY AND PRIVACY IMPLICATIONS

18

Wireless Location Tracking
Adam Barreras and Amit Mathur

Introduction

The Fourth Amendment in the U.S. Constitution states:

> The right of the people to be secure in their persons, houses, papers, and effects, against unreasonable searches and seizures, shall not be violated, and no Warrants shall issue, but upon probable cause, supported by Oath or affirmation, and particularly describing the place to be searched, and the persons or things to be seized

More often than not, the use of wireless location tracking has been utilized by law enforcement to track those suspected of criminal acts or those thought to be involved in criminal activities. Although law enforcement is able to receive a warrant from the Justice Department granting them the right to track wireless devices, advancements in mobile technology have opened the door to seemingly endless opportunities and threats concerning cell phone location tracking.

Cell phones no longer have to be in use in order to be traceable. Furthermore, cell phone users may not be aware that their location can be, and may be, tracked and recorded by cell phone providers or providers of location tracking services. Emerging technology is making wireless location tracking a more viable option, not only for law enforcement, but also for anyone interested in the capabilities. This new ability raises many concerns as to how much these capabilities are infringing on citizens' rights to privacy. It is important to explore the uses of cell phone tracking technology, the advantages and disadvantages of the increase in technology, and the future implications that these services provide in order to ensure that users' privacy can remain assured. If the location tracking services become unregulated, the government, tracking service companies, and those interested in various cell users' location histories will have free reign over cell users' privacy.

How Cell Phone Tracking Works

Wireless location tracking is a technology that enables a device, such as a cell phone, to be traced to its current location, as long as the phone is turned on. In order for cell users to have service that allows them to make phone calls, their phones must be able to connect to a cellular network of cell site base stations, such as Verizon Wireless, Cingular, Sprint, or any other service provider. These devices constantly search for the strongest signal emitted from base stations closest to that user and will connect to the nearest and strongest transmitting site. As the user moves around to various locations, the mobile device switches to various cell sites during calls or while waiting (idle), in order to ensure the phone has the strongest signal (Cell Phone Tracking). As this is being done, information is being stored on which mobile device is using certain cell sites. This allows cellular companies to see exactly where each cell phone user has been.

Cell phones can be tracked in two ways: (1) through triangulation and (2) through a Global Positioning System (GPS) chip that is embedded in users' cell phones. For phones that are not GPS equipped, cell phone service providers can use triangulation, the pinpointing of a location through comparing of signal strength from at least three cell sites, in order to determine a general location of the mobile device. Other cell phones that are equipped with GPS chips can be located through satellite connections, thus allowing for a much more accurate location determination, usually within 10-50 meters (Budden).

At the end of 2005, the U.S. Federal Communications Commission (FCC) established a mandate requiring all cell phones to contain either GPS or some other ability to track the location of a cell phone call, so that the cell phone carriers can trace calls to a location within 100 meters or less (Frenzel). The idea behind these mandates is to ensure that the police can trace an emergency cell phone call. What started merely as a safety precaution has turned into a new cell phone craze, making wireless location tracking a part of everyday use.

Location Tracking Databases

New mobile device technologies ensure more accurate location tracking, whether from the addition of cell sites that gain a more accurate location through triangulation, or GPS equipped phones for even more accurate pinpointing. Essentially, through GPS tracking, satellite signals are continuously being sent, so the location and every move that a wireless device user makes could constantly be recorded (PittsburghChannel). Wireless service providers disclose that phone call histories are stored in databases; however, many are very reluctant to admit that they store location histories.

T-Mobile discloses in their Privacy Policy, that they may collect personal information, which includes: "calling information, and the services you use and how and where you use them" (T-Mobile). Other service providers are more discrete about the utilization of location history databases; however, all wireless companies store such data. Nathan Eagle, co-founder of the MIT/Harvard Center for Large-Scale Network Analysis, sat as an expert witness on an undisclosed court case in late 2006, dealing with information about possible locations of a cell phone retrieved from cellular tower IDs from various base stations. He commented that, though the information had to be subpoenaed from Verizon as part of the litigation, it proves that these wireless service providers do have databases of location histories (Eagle).

Wireless service providers are very discrete about their practices of storing mobile device users' location histories; however, it is necessary to understand that it is occurring today. Mr. Eagle (2006) had no difficulties in getting information about his call log history from T-Mobile, yet he was unable to obtain location history. This brings up the issue about who owns mobile device users' location history and what the benefits that this information provides for the cell phone companies or interested third party companies. New technology that allows for the real-time location of mobile device users raises new concerns about who may gain from such information and how much privacy users are forfeiting through the use of tracking technology. This growing technology begs the question of how far companies are willing to leverage location tracking as a competitive advantage. Is location tracking beneficial by ensuring the safety and well being of mobile users and by providing easy tracking and directions to friends and locations? Or is it detrimental to the users' privacy and safety?

Benefits of Location Tracking Technologies

The original intention and benefit of location tracking was to improve the chances of saving a person in an emergency situation, by allowing law enforcement to pinpoint a distressed person's cell phone call within 100 meters. As the technology evolved, and modern advancements allowed for more precise and real-time tracking, wireless service carriers took advantage of the opportunity to provide their customers with new capabilities to make life easier. Such capabilities include turn-by-turn directions and family, friend, and employee locators.

Law Enforcement Application

One way that the police utilize location tracking is through the new "Enhanced 911" (E911) technology. As stated earlier, the FCC has implemented regulations for all cell phone providers to be able to locate any cell phone within 100 meters. E911 seeks to "improve the effectiveness and reliability of wireless 911 service by providing police dispatchers with additional information on wireless 911 calls" (FCC). By using GPS tracking or Triangulation, dispatchers can accurately locate where the 911 call is coming from, for a more detailed dispatch to the police. Moreover, there are many other opportunities this technology provides for law enforcement, such as enabling the police to track and find kidnap victims. Using this technology will enable the police to "hone in on a specific location of that signal and know that there is a body connected to it. This may help save lives that way, where it will help rescuers get to their position quicker" (PittsburghChannel). Law enforcement can use this technology to help capture a criminal or even track down a missing child through cell phone Amber Alerts, which are public notices of missing children.

As Mr. Eagle previously pointed out, the police are able to subpoena location records for a certain mobile unit, and can now receive the real-time location of a user from the wireless service company. This ability can help locate suspects and criminals attempting to evade the law. In 2002, local authorities near San Jose, California, traced a mailbox bomb suspect through triangulation once the suspect activated his cell phone (Wired News). The police were able to contact the cell phone service company to get the locations of the nearest cell towers in contact with the suspect's phone and capture the man within an hour of doing so. The location tracking capabilities are being used by law enforcement to help save lives and serve criminals their justice.

There are other uses of this technology that the police can utilize to further help society, include Amber Alerts. These alerts give citizens information regarding a missing child, where he or she was seen last, and sometimes descriptions of the suspect's car or physical features. Amber Alerts are usually posted on digital roadway signs on major highways so drivers can see this information as they are traveling in the area and can assist law enforcement agents in finding a suspect by providing any helpful information. With location tracking technology, Amber Alerts can be sent as text messages to all cell phones in the general area of the crime. As a result, Amber Alerts would be much more effective as they could reach citizens who are not traveling on a major roadway, which is a set back of the current method.

It is clear that these uses of the location tracking prove beneficial and demonstrate the possible effectiveness as a tool for the police. Other advantages of this technology include family locator plans to ensure the safety of children, or to provide a new tool for enhanced supervision.

Family Tracking

There are many desirable and attractive safety attributes for the use and implementation of location tracking services and GPS-enabled mobile phones. Sprint Nextel, Verizon Wireless, and Disney Mobile offer plans that permit parents to download the Family Locator application onto their phones, giving them the capability to locate up to four cell phones, whether or not they are GPS equipped (Hayhurst). Having the ability to do this would make many parents more comfortable with their children being away from home.

Guardian Angel Technology is similar software that further ensures the safety and knowledge of the whereabouts of family members. This technology has two parts: (1) the cell phone with the software loaded onto it and (2) the tracking website. Once the software has been installed on the child's phone, the parents will be able to monitor and track the movements of their child through a secure website. This software will allow parents to constantly check their child's movements, as it is continually updated every seven seconds and can be accessed an unlimited number of times. This capability will allow parents to check the path a child has taken 30 days ago and monitor how fast they got there (MacMillan). Knowing that this information is available could prevent young kids from speeding, thus making them safer drivers.

User Convenience Tracking

Location tracking technologies are not used merely to keep tabs on children or to stop or prevent crime. Many other uses are intended to make life easier for mobile device users to communicate with others and to get where they desire in an expeditious manner. For example, Verizon Wireless, Sprint Nextel, Boost Mobile, and Disney Mobile are all carriers of GPS enabled phones that allow users to sign up with various location tracking companies such as Loopt, Dodgeball, and Groundspeak's Geocaching (Reardon 2006). These companies saw tremendous opportunities to take advantage of location tracking technologies to benefit their consumers. Through these service providers, users are able to share their location automatically, find events and places, as well as find and connect with their friends on a detailed map (Loopt).

The purpose of these services is to "offer a mix of social networking and so-called location-based services" (Reardon). These location tracking companies offer a service where you can see the precise position of your friends. This eliminates the need to call or text message specific buddies, because their whereabouts will be recorded on a map on their friend's wireless device with the touch of a button. Not to mention, the users gain the ability to get directions to a specific site by using GPS to receive step-by-step directions to where other friends and locations are, saving time on asking for directions. This capability also eliminates the need to waste time calling someone if it is clear that they are not in a position to answer the call or meet up, such as sitting in a meeting or in class. The location tracking technology not only keeps family and friends in touch, but also allows for a company to ensure efficient utilization of time and employees to maximize resources, time, and profit.

Employee Monitoring

Small companies with mobile units, such as ambulances, can also benefit from the rapidly growing technologies in cell phone location tracking. Equipping employees with GPS-enabled mobile phones gives supervisors access to real-time data about their fleet, ensuring that employees are in appropriate locations and are efficiently managing their time (Hayhurst). Matt O'Connell, operations manager of Waste

Connections Inc., a solid waste company, has benefited immensely from the distribution of GPS enabled cell phones to employees. Operations run much smoother and efficiently as 5,000 new homes are being reached in the same amount of time that it took one home to be reached in previous years. The tracking helps ensure that trucks are not overlapping in areas and are utilizing the most time-efficient routes to hit more houses in the same amount of time (Hayhurst).

Location tracking through GPS enabled phones requires no extra hardware for companies to place in trucks or at the home station. All that is needed is a computer to run the software, and employees to carry their phones with them throughout the day. As a result, companies can pull up real-time displays of what is going on outside of the company building, to ensure maximum efficiency to help increase revenues.

Not only can these capabilities be very valuable as safety measures to track children or to be used in case of emergencies, but they can also be used to help make the lives of these location tracking users much easier by connecting people and employees in ways that never thought possible a few years ago. However, as technology increases and these services expand, users of these services continually forfeit their privacy.

Disadvantages of Location Tracking Technologies

Location tracking technology has strayed far from its original roots, as it was first implemented for safety reasons. As just explored, there are many advantages to the use of wireless location tracking for police, everyday users, and employers. While technology advances, privacy issues are arising and creating a dilemma between how much privacy users of this technology are willing to sacrifice for the sake of protection and convenience. A common, everyday cell phone can now be used as a constant location chip attached to any user.

Law Enforcement Abuses

The use of wireless location tracking can put cell phone users' minds at ease knowing that, in case of an emergency, they can use their E911 application on their phone to notify the police the location of an emergency issue. It has also been discovered that the police can track suspects of a crime in order to find and detain suspects. Such occasions are clear instances of when it is beneficial and acceptable for the police to use location-tracking technology, but it is hard to determine if law enforcement crosses the line of privacy rights when using the location tracking technology for other means. For example, if there was probable cause, or even if the government deemed it important, the police could subpoena a caller's record of, not only who they were contacting, but also where they have been. This ability could be beneficial for anti-terrorism and other crime prevention efforts. Although these capabilities prove useful, it causes much uncertainty as to how much the police can and will use this technology.

Through ambiguities of the Patriot Act and due to lack of regulation of location history databases and tracking, law enforcement agencies can have free access to such information from wireless service providers. Robin Gross, an attorney of the Electronic Frontier

Foundation (EFF), a nonprofit group that works to protect fundamental rights regarding technology, notes that it is "inappropriate to be tracking people under some kind of assumption that they might do something illegal . . . it is ripe for abuse by law enforcement and by government" (Wired News). Law enforcement is not the only entity that abuses the wireless location tracking history as friends, family, and employers also take advantage of these capabilities and manipulate the intended use of this tracking.

User Abuse

New technology, allowing for constantly updated GPS positions of cell phone users, can be as disadvantageous as it is useful for family members, friends, and employees. A once convenient way to ensure the safety of family members can turn into a trust issue and unnecessary surveillance. Children will have the inclination to turn off their cell phones or leave them at home in order to ensure that their parents are not tracking their every move. As a result, the wireless location tracking ends up being counterproductive, leaving children with no ability to make a call in the case of a real emergency.

The same issues occur with friends and employee/employer relations. A Boost Mobile user, for example, may not want to allow their network friends to locate them through the Loopt wireless location tracking service and constantly know their whereabouts. Although the application allows for users to disable their tracking, friends, such as boyfriends and girlfriends may become suspicious if the program is turned off. Furthermore, under Loopt's privacy notice, they disclose: "This location tracking may occur even when the loopt application is not actively running on your mobile device" (Loopt), which means that a user may have a false sense of privacy when disabling the application on his or her phone.

Employers who are utilizing this tool to improve workplace efficiency can certainly abuse the GPS cell phone tracking capabilities, resulting in a decline in employee morale, as the employees feel their privacy rights being infringed upon. The most important objective for an employee is to ensure that they accomplish the tasks required by their job. As long as this is being done, there should be no reason for employers to use a "Big Brother" approach and track every move. By doing this, employees feel like they are being micromanaged and may be uncomfortable knowing that their employer is constantly watching, thus resulting in decreased productivity. Additionally, employees cannot opt to turn off their cell phones because they may be fired for doing so.

There are many promising features for the use of this technology, but the tracking ability also raises many questions as to how far and how much the capabilities will be used and abused by police, service providers, and anyone concerned with such information about product users. It is important to explore what the future has in store for the growing wireless tracking capabilities.

What is in Store for Wireless Tracking Technology?

As wireless tracking technology expands to provide consumers with the newest and most accurate capabilities and as more people begin to utilize this technology, a lot of information is being collected that can be extremely useful to various people and third party companies.

Unwanted Trackers

As Loopt's privacy notices informs users: "Your real-time location information is subject to abuse, misuse, and over-monitoring by others" (Loopt). The data kept by cell phone companies and wireless tracking service providers is not as secure and private as many users of such services believe. Clearly, this can cause safety and protection concerns. As spyware exponentially increases in today's cyber world, people are gaining access to, once believed, secure web sites. Wireless location tracking technology allows for cell phones to be monitored on a service provider's web site. A person with malicious intentions can gain access to a database and constantly track specific individuals, with the intent to stalk, rob, or kidnap. Robin Gross of EFF warned, "cell phone tracking could be used to follow the movements of political dissenters or politicians and other people in power" (Wired News), not only for criminal uses.

Safety and privacy concerns are a looming issue for users, especially for politicians or top business executives whose tracking can provide insight on future deals that a campaign or company may undertake. For example, someone could have tracked the CEO of Sprint and the CEO of Nextel for months before the announcement of their merger. Anyone with common sense could see they were meeting frequently, thus giving rise to suspicion that a possible business deal could be underway that could increase the stocks of these two companies. This type of information can thus be financially advantageous.

Mobile Phone Advertising

Another way of gaining financials advantage via mobile tracking is by using cell phones as the newest accurate advertising medium. Wireless location tracking makes real time locations a highly sought-after advertising advantage for retail companies trying to reach customers in new and innovative ways. Wireless service companies have an enormous opportunity to sell wireless location information to other parties that want to advertise based on location of a mobile device user. The cell phone could become the biggest and most successful advertising medium since television (Halper) – "the ultimate, targeted, personal marketing machine" (Halper). Advertisers desire to utilize the demographic and location data of cell phone carrier users in order to mold campaigns aimed at specific age, gender, income, and lifestyle segments (Halper). Essentially, wireless companies will sell the sensitive information and capabilities for commercial use and profit to these companies.

"Market research firm Informa forecasts an $11.4 billion mobile advertising market by 2011, up from an expected $1.5 billion this year" (Halper). As more companies begin to tap this advertising opportunity, consumers' locations and data will become widely available to third party companies, which might be perceived as an infringement on consumer privacy. Retailers are gaining the technology to receive information about which cell phones are close to their store or product. The retailer could then send a text message to these cell phones with a coupon trying to lure them into their store. Tom Daly, Coca Cola's manager of global interactive marketing, views mobile advertising messages as a way of "getting intertwined with the life of the consumer," as Coke can send an alert to drive a consumer to the nearest location where Coke is available (Halper). In the future, consumers could be bombarded by advertisements from various retail stores attempting to offer coupons to solicit business. Currently in London, a small start up company called iProx is focusing on supplying location-based services (LBS) infrastructure to wireless providers (Picard). Companies like iProx, and others, are working hard to make the text message coupon services a common and effective means of advertising.

There are many positive and negative aspects to the increasing ability of using mobile devices as an advertising medium. Positive aspects associated with this future technology will be the ability to have the latest information on store products, along with receiving coupons on a shopping trip. Customers will not have to walk up and down a mall to find out the best price because the ability to compare text message alerts would let them know who has the best deal. However, this creates a whole new form of "spam" as consumers may get annoyed of receiving countless text message alerts on products. Without regulation, consumers will be at the mercy of their cell phone service providers and advertisers sending them numerous cell phone messages.

Public Knowledge and Concern

The research done on the topic of wireless tracking technology was supplemented by a survey conducted to find out what information about this technology was known by general cell phone users as well as find out sentiment about the implications of the technology. The surveys were completed by 68 students at the University of Colorado at Boulder, ranging from 18 to 24 years of age, by handing the surveys out in freshman level to senior level classes.

The analysis of the information provided staggering and eye-opening results. 78% of all individuals surveyed were unaware that any cell phone that was turned on could be traced within 100 meters. This information demonstrates the lack of knowledge about wireless tracking capabilities and proves that the original intended purpose of emergency tracking is not even known by general consumers. 88% of the Sprint-Nextel & Verizon Wireless customers were unaware that their phones were GPS equipped and nearly everyone (93%) responded that they did not think or did not know that their location histories were stored. After learning that location histories were stored, 67% of the respondents believe that this technology is an invasion of their privacy, and 91% of those surveyed said that they did not want their location histories stored. This information implies that the respondents do not feel that there is a need for such histories to be recorded or known by anyone but themselves. Finally, 62% would not want to receive advertisements from companies/retailers. As marketing executives learn about the tremendous opportunities presented by mobile advertising, it is important for them to weigh the consumer perceived invasion of privacy of such practices before too much money is invested in a campaign that could prove to be disastrous.

Conclusion

Rising technology makes wireless location-tracking easier and more precise. Often times, concerning technology, users of products fear how much their privacy and identity is being protected. Location tracking definitely opens a lot of windows of opportunity for product users' privacy to be compromised. The advantages and disadvantages of the increasing technology in wireless location tracking must be weighed in, determining how much consumers are willing to compromise their privacy in order to gain safety and convenience. All of this will depend on how far wireless device users are willing to let their providers store and release location information because there are no formal restrictions on how this data can be used (PittsburghChannel). It may be that consumers will be at the mercy of their cell service providers to allow consumers to agree or disagree to the dissemination of wireless location information to other parties. Otherwise, the only solution may be for consumers to opt to leave their cell phone behind before traveling to a destination; however, in this day in age, it is nearly impossible for people to survive without their cell phone in their pocket or purse.

Works Cited

Budden, R. "Mobile technology takes on new direction: Location-based services can provide detailed maps and track friends at the touch of a button." Financial Times. December 02, 2003, p 7.

"Cell Phone Tracking." Wikipedia. (2007). February 04, 2007, <www.wikipedia.com>.

Eagle, N. "Complexity and social networks blog." (2006) March 06, 2007, <http://www.iq.harvard.edu/blog/netgov/2006/11 /mobile_phone_service_providers.html.> .

FCC. "Enhanced 911- Wireless services." (2006) February 17, 2007, <http://www.fcc.gov/911/enhanced/.>

Frenzel, L. "Location tech. gives us the world." Electronic Design, 54/27, (2006), p 40-42.

Halper, M.. "Advertising goes mobile." Fortune Magazine, 155/4, (2007), p 14.

Hayhurst, T. "Hauler lauds GPS mobile phone efficiency." Waste News, 12/9, (2006), p 12.

"What's Loopt?" February 21, 2007, <https://loopt.com/loopt/sess/index .aspx.> .

MacMillan, D. "Location, location, location—Via cell." <u>Business Week Online</u>, 1/04/2007, p 16.

Mount, S. "U.S. constitution- Amendment 4." February 06, 2007, <http://www.usconstitution.net.>

Picard, E. "Wireless: Location tracking will change everything." (2001). March 04, 2007, <http://www.clickz.com/showPage.html?page =844141.>

PittsburgChannel. "Special report: Cell phone tracking technology." (2003). February 10, 2007, <http://www.thepittsburghchannel.com /news/2373061/detail.html>.

Reardon, M. "Mobile phones that track your buddies." (2006). February 20, 2007, <http://news.com.com/Mobile+phones+that+ track+your+buddies/2100-1039_3-6135209.html.> .

T-Mobile. "Privacy policy." March 21, 2007, <www.t-mobile.com.>

Wired News . "Bomb suspect traced by cell phone." <u>Wired News,</u> (2002). March 12, 2007, <http://www.wired.com/news/technology /0,1282,52396,00.html>.

19

The Evolution of Global Positioning Systems

Blair Krause and Ryan Murray

Introduction

Global Positioning Systems (GPS) are evolving and new breakthrough products are constantly emerging on the market. The most recent breakthroughs are now readily available to consumers in the form of vehicle navigation and communication devices, theft protection and global surveillance. These technologies offer many benefits to the common user, but also raise security and privacy issues by permitting a high level of misuse. The monitoring and exploitation of one's driving habits, patterns and history can take place. The invasion of the public's privacy happens every day due to a lack of regulation concerning the access and use of GPS data.

GPS 101

GPS satellites circle the globe, hone in on transmitting devices though a series of signals, and then record data such as driving speed and travel routes. GPS devices work by 'listening" for the radio signals from satellites and calculating how long the signals take to arrive. The result of that calculation provides a highly accurate estimation of latitude and longitude. The information transmitted by the GPS tracking device beams back to a user's computer through the cellular network and records in the company's database. Elaborate individual GPS tracking systems are rapidly becoming a standard part of vehicles' onboard computer systems, along the side of seatbelt usage and which passenger's door is open. This developing technology is quickly changing the way users drive and the future of many industries.

Vehicle Tracking GPS

The most advanced GPS products on the market today are vehicle transmitter systems such as LoJack™, and navigation devices such as OnStar™. These systems are available to consumers for only a few hundred dollars and include online services that can instantly map where a car is in real-time. This provides a great service for anyone protective of their car. The return rate for vehicles with the LoJack™ theft prevention system is 90%, and the car is typically located and returned within two hours (LoJack Homepage). These systems may have many great benefits, but how much privacy do people sacrifice by using GPS?

Private Vehicle Tracking Systems

Vehicle Global Positioning Systems are mainly used for theft prevention, but new functions of the systems open the product to a wide variety of alternative uses and misuses. Systems such as LoJack™ were originally built solely for theft prevention, but have evolved into multi-use systems. As mentioned earlier, the monitoring and recording a driver's location, route, speed, and even seatbelt use can take place. These monitoring functions offer valuable benefits to a growing number of innovative industries. New users of these systems include employers, marketing researchers, insurance companies, and the police. These new GPS users may validate their reasons for using the products, but the question of how much privacy the user of the vehicle sacrifices still remains. Situations involving the new uses of GPS systems on vehicles have been questioned because they raise many personal privacy and security issues.

Company Vehicle Tracking

The new Global Positioning Systems have a high potential for misuse. After installing a GPS product in a vehicle, the device begins tracking and recording everywhere it goes. Depending on who the actual owner of the vehicle is, such as an employer, drivers may not know whether a device is monitoring their movements or not. In a CNBC special, Jim Joyce, the Vice President of Nabet stated, "we were concerned about privacy issues and how this information might be used to monitor the employees in a big brother situation" (Joyce). Many employees do not know a GPS device could be monitoring them throughout the workday. Employers can survey online where their company vehicle is and when it has been dispatched. Information is even available on how long an employee is at each location and how fast they are driving. As a benefit to the employer, "dispatchers can see on the map where the closest technician is out in the field, and they can push a job to that particular employee" (Onley). Many say this is an invasion of privacy, but employers justify it as another productivity management system. Jim Joyce points out that his company's productivity has increased significantly since the installation of GPS on their vehicles (Joyce).

Laws already allow employers to monitor employee's Internet and e-mail usage at a computer related job and other industries are beginning to incorporate this productivity measurement method into their businesses. Employers may encounter ethical issues when using GPS, but the law allows them to do so. For example, state surveillance laws now say, "the only person legally allowed to secretly hide a GPS tracking device in a car is the registered owner of the vehicle" (Bohan). This law encompasses the business that owns the vehicle the employee drives. It is up to the employer whether they want to inform the employee about the tracking device. This may seem deceptive, but recent court cases have made it common law. In California, a state with some of the strictest GPS tracking laws, "informing the driver or passengers about the presence of the device isn't required when the unit is placed there by the car's legal owner" (Bohan). Employees still question the use of GPS as an invasion of their privacy. Many compare it to having a boss hovering over one's shoulder at a desk job. Others see the use of these devices as a trust issue with their employer. Whatever the argument, GPS causes a loss in privacy in the working world, but there are currently no solutions unless a court decision is overturned.

Other vehicle-based companies are starting to install GPS into their cars. The trend is most prevalent in the rental industry. Rental car companies, dissatisfied with the treatment of their vehicles, are taking preventative measures to stop the problem. Rental car companies say they "have used GPS devices since the mid-1990s, installing systems to give drivers directions while they're on the road" (Lemos). However, there are many reasons for installing these systems other than navigation.

There have been numerous cases brought to court about rental companies charging penalty fees to drivers for breaking company policies, which they observed through GPS. For example, in a case that could help set the bar for the amount of privacy drivers of rental cars can expect "a Connecticut man is suing a local rental company, Acme Rent-a-Car, after it used GPS technology to track him and then fined him $450 for speeding three times" (Lemos). The man had no idea a device was monitoring him. The main argument concerns disclosing the use of GPS, even though "the policy is stated in bold at the top of the rental agreement" (Lemos). Currently, there are no recent court decisions defining this policy enforcement as legal or illegal. Presently, "Acme has left the decision in the hands of the Department of Consumer Protection (DCP). The judge in the small claims court case has delayed hearing the claim until the department has issued a ruling" (Lemos). For now, the only solution for car renters is to follow company policies and sacrifice their privacy until the DCP makes a decision.

Malicious Intent

Anyone can buy a vehicle GPS tracker and install it on any car they have access to, making it possible to track anyone without his or her knowledge. GPS raises many personal security issues with the threat of stalking or other malicious intent. For example, "in 2001, a man was arrested in Menlo Park in Oakland for using a GPS monitoring device to stalk a woman" (Bohan). In another case, a man in Colorado was convicted of tracking his wife with a GPS bug after she began divorce proceedings against him (McCullagh). These may be extreme examples, but these systems are becoming more prevalent on the market and many consumers are still unaware of the capabilities GPS products possess.

GPS on vehicles is steadily incorporating itself into everyday life. For example, parents are starting to use GPS to keep tabs on their driving teens. In a recent article, a stepfather installed a GPS in his son's car, unbeknownst to him. The stepfather reported "he was running 60 miles per hour up Concannon Street in a 35 mile an hour zone. Data gathered by the device showed that Corey drove from school to friends' homes, indicating that he was carrying passengers in violation of DMV rules for drivers under 18" (Bohan). After the son was confronted he naturally felt betrayed and thought his privacy had been violated. Having one's parents know of their whereabouts may not matter to some, but the thought of someone else using the device illegally, such as an ex-partner, may seem scarier.

The Government has no restrictions on who can buy these systems and there is little or no registration process for the vehicle to which it is attached. These monitoring systems are very small and can be hidden anywhere in one's vehicle. "The LoJack transponder is about the size of a deck of cards. It's small enough to be hidden in dozens of locations inside a vehicle" (LoJack Homepage). The only way to prevent these types of misuses from continuing is for all companies to implement a vehicle owner verification process. This would help to ensure that the owner of the vehicle is the same person who purchased and installed the GPS. Otherwise, it is up to the government to take action. For example, California legislators determined that "the increasing use of electronic surveillance is eroding personal liberty" and that "electronic tracking without the person's knowledge violates that person's reasonable expectation of privacy" (Bohan). This law is one step in the right direction for privacy advocates. Further Governmental legislation is predicted to take place as the frequency of misuse continues to rise.

Public Perception Survey

One group of Americans that are greatly affected by the advances in GPS vehicle navigation tracking are school aged children and young adults. This demographic is often tracked by their parents with or without their knowledge. To test the awareness level regarding GPS vehicle tracking we administered a survey to high school students in the Midwestern US. After reviewing the responses to the questions, we broke the students down into three groups. Depending on which and how many questions they answered correctly, the respondents were placed in with either the Genuine Knowledge Group, General Knowledge Group, or Little or No Knowledge Group. Of 67 surveys returned, only 13% possessed genuine knowledge with regard to GPS tracking capabilities. Of the remaining 87%, only 32% possessed general knowledge of the tracking capabilities of GPS tracking systems, leaving an astounding 40 people, or 60%, with little or no knowledge of their vulnerability. We must also take into consideration the possibility that the respondents did not take the survey seriously, although the numbers were so skewed towards the Little or No Knowledge Group, that we do not believe this to be a strong factor. With this demographic being one of the most affected by this type of technology, such a high lack of knowledge leaves this group open to be tracked by their parents or someone with less honorable intentions.

Marketing Research Uses

The data obtained by a vehicle's GPS is stored in the servicing company's database system. So, what could anyone do with the driving records about thousands of random and innocent consumers? Companies pay good money to conduct marketing research about people's driving habits. For example, one company deciding on where to place expensive advertising billboards will find prime exposure locations based on GPS traffic data. Soon, enough relevant data will be mined and prove to be a beneficial research source. Recently, the Department of Transportation tested the research capabilities of GPS data archives. The results show that "GPS technologies are able to better capture variability in travel behavior across multiple days. It also offers detailed route choice, spatial location and travel itinerary information not available in other travel survey data sets" (Measuring). With this high level of accuracy, marketing research companies could identify someone and abstract information, such as the shopping centers or restaurants they frequent. Based on this information, consumers would be directly marketed. This method is very similar to e-mail SPAM received based on the Internet websites visited. Depending on the service provider and its privacy agreement, people may not have a choice whether their data reaches the hands of marketing researchers. Since the data is compiled on the company's system, they legally own it. In order for consumers to protect their privacy, extensive research of the company's privacy of information policy must take place to ensure selling of database records does not occur.

Insurance Uses

The release of GPS driving records to insurance companies containing data on how often one speeds or if they frequent high crime rate areas, could be financially damaging for drivers. There are currently no laws regulating the access of this data by a third party. Insurers are beginning to use the technology and will "offer a discount to LoJack™ owners. In fact, some insurance companies offer up to 35% off the comprehensive portion of your insurance premium for equipping your vehicle with LoJack™ and an alarm" (LoJack Homepage). Insurance companies incur these discounts because of the perceived risk reduction related to auto theft. Now, imagine how much the company's perception of risk would rise if they actually saw all the poor driving habits of many Americans.

Companies are starting to recognize the opportunity for better risk assessment through using GPS. "In fact, one of the largest insurance companies in the United States, Progressive Auto Insurance, has already tested policies in Texas that tied insurance rates to car usage as monitored by global positioning" (Schwart). Insurers could use this data to find reckless drivers. Soon after, insurance rates begin to rise and some drivers might end up paying even more than the initial discount could save them. A Yale University law professor, who is examining the issue, predicts that "within a decade all our car insurance companies will be offering us discounts if we will commit to Acme-like contracts - if we agree not to speed. The use of tracking technology will grow, even if they don't give us a discount" (Schwart). Many feel that policies like these are a direct exploitation of personal privacy and companies are taking on a "big brother" role. Unless the DCP creates a policy banning the use of this information, drivers are at risk for potential insurance rate hikes due to the exploitation of personal GPS data.

Governmental Uses

GPS technology is becoming a valuable asset to police departments across the country. Not only are these systems significantly reducing the rate of auto thefts, but they also aid the authorities in tracking and prosecuting suspects and offenders. Recently:

> A federal judge in New York ruled that police did not need court authorization when tracking from afar. Law enforcement personnel could have conducted a visual surveillance of the vehicle as it traveled on the public highways. The driver had no expectation of privacy in the whereabouts of his vehicle on a public roadway (McCullagh).

The statement "tracking from afar" entails monitoring using GPS. Without the need for a court authorization, police can track any possible suspect for whatever reason. Reports show there is an "increasingly popular law enforcement practice of secretly tagging Americans' vehicles without adhering to the procedural safeguards and judicial oversight that protect the privacy of homes and telephone conversations from police abuses" (McCullagh). U.S. State departments are even misusing GPS products and many feel that this directly violates reasonable expectation of privacy. "I think they should get court orders," said Lee Tien, staff counsel for the Electronic Frontier Foundation. "We're in a world where more and more of our activities can be viewed in public and, perhaps more importantly, be correlated and linked together" (McCullagh). Some could consider this a violation of the Fifth Amendment that addresses self-incrimination. Shouldn't there be at least some type of probable cause for monitoring a driver?

Since laws are not current enough to include GPS technology, police can use it for any type of law enforcement. For example, "police used a GPS tracking device on a suspect's car to track his movements and accumulate evidence against him. The suspect was ultimately convicted of methamphetamine manufacture based on the evidence police discovered by tracking his car. He appealed on Fourth Amendment grounds" (Berkeley Intellectual Property Weblog). The defendant believed GPS tracking violated laws relating to a reasonable search and seizure, since police had little evidence before the tracking began. The court deemed it constitutional and found the defendant guilty. Cases similar to this are beginning to pop up all over the country. Soon, this technology will become an unregulated and frequently used tool of the police. Police departments will have the power to find vehicles in the vicinity of a crime and pursue the owners as possible suspects. This type of mass surveillance will place police in an extreme "big brother" situation unless Government restrictions are put in place. "Mass surveillance could possibly raise a Fourth Amendment issue, but the 7th Circuit Court declined to comment" (Recent). Soon the Government will be forced to make a decision as the frequency of misuses continues to rise.

Even though a small percentage of cars on the road have GPS, the auto industry is considering incorporating these devices into the car manufacturing process. In the future, "one can even imagine a law requiring all new cars to come equipped with the device so that the government can keep track of all vehicular movement in the United States" (Berkeley Intellectual Property Weblog). There are numerous ethical issues with the Government having this much power over privacy. However, "some legal scholars fear that when the U.S. Supreme Court eventually weighs in on GPS tracking, it will side with police over privacy" (McCullagh). Consumers and companies only see the tip of the iceberg with this technology. It possesses many benefits now, but unforeseen privacy risks lie ahead. James E. Hall, a transportation lawyer and former chairman of the National Transportation Safety Board, states, "we are moving toward a kind of automobile that nobody's ever known. It's mostly good news, but there are negative things that we will have to work through" (Schwart). The issue rests on how much privacy consumers are willing to sacrifice for the luxuries of GPS.

GPS Navigation Systems & Privacy

The term "*Privacy Policy*" is usually a misnomer, and its use in the GPS Vehicle Navigation industry is no exception. GPS navigation companies like OnStar and many others provide eager customers with in-car navigation services. These services include, among others, map oriented navigation screens and roadside emergency assistance. Simple navigation devices typically tell the customer where they are, but systems like OnStar offer a variety of services and are much more invasive.

GPS Navigation Privacy

Of the top GPS navigation companies, OnStar's unique customer interaction platform makes their system the most susceptible to privacy problems. Although OnStar's privacy practices are suspect, the company is among the few who have a detailed Privacy Policy available online that outlines the information collected from their customers.

OnStar Overview

OnStar began as an emergency assistance program for General Motors (GM) vehicles that allowed customers to push a button on the dashboard to call for emergency assistance. When a customer pushed the button, the GPS receiver on the car would register the vehicle's location and transmit it to the OnStar call center via wireless cell phone networks. Also, OnStar connects the distressed motorist with a customer assistance representative when the OnStar button is pushed. The OnStar systems today are very similar to the original, and only recently has OnStar expanded their existing services, and ventured into the realm of map oriented navigation screens and turn-by-turn navigation assistance.

OnStar Privacy

OnStar's vehicle navigation and roadside assistance technology is available on 50 GM models, which include vehicle lines such as Chevrolet, GMC, Pontiac, Cadillac, Buick, Saturn, Hummer, and Saab (OnStar Vehicles, GM Vehicle Showroom Online). The noticeable difference between OnStar and other GPS navigation companies is that OnStar establishes direct communication with the customer via a wireless cell signal. This means that customers can contact OnStar personnel at the push of a button at anytime. As we know, information goes both ways, and OnStar's creature comforts are also what make it a potential security and privacy concern.

OnStar differs from other GPS systems in more ways than one. The OnStar system is available from the GM factory, and it often comes preinstalled on vehicles. This means OnStar customers did not make a conscious decision to go out and buy GPS technology, and thus they might not be aware of its capability. In addition, GM often gives car buyers free trials of OnStar as a bonus for purchasing a car. Most customers take this bonus at face value not understanding the implications stemming from such technology (GM Online).

OnStar is in a unique position to collect information from millions of people, and they can easily profit from it by selling their customer's data. In its Privacy Policy, OnStar states:

> Information we collect about you includes: contact information (such as name, mailing address, email address, phone number and language preference); credit card and billing information (such as cardholder name, card number and subscription package and OnStar Hands-Free Calling minute purchases); and other

personal information that helps us customize our services, such as your requests for emergency assistance or driving directions (OnStar Privacy).

This statement allows OnStar to store any of the information described above. To help put their customers at ease, OnStar insists that their information transferring capabilities are not always on, and the system is only active when needed for emergencies (OnStar Privacy). However, there is a small sentence later on the privacy statement that allows OnStar to turn itself on when "… your OnStar equipment calls OnStar with data updates" (OnStar Privacy). This means an OnStar system can call to "update" anytime, and thus transmit information to OnStar anytime.

Once OnStar has a customer's driving habit information, they can use it for approved uses such as, "to perform market research" (OnStar Privacy). Again, this is a broad term allowing OnStar to use a customer's information in any way they please. The Privacy Policy does not specify who is doing the market research, so third party contracting is possible. This policy also mentions that OnStar may share information with the maker of the car, its wholly owned subsidiaries and its suppliers. The above statement is referring to GM, which has thousands of suppliers and hundreds of subsidiaries. The Privacy Policy goes even further, saying OnStar can give your personal and contact information to car dealers, wireless companies, and XM Radio for promotional purposes (OnStar Privacy).

The most blatant lack for customer privacy concern is in the following statement:

> Your contact information, information about your current OnStar services and certain information from your car (i.e., odometer reading) may be shared with our business partners exclusively to conduct joint marketing programs with OnStar or *to confirm eligibility in car insurance discount programs* (our emphasis). We may also share information with our business partners in other circumstances with your permission…" (OnStar. Privacy)

This excerpt illustrates that the Privacy Statement is not really protecting OnStar's customers' privacy, but simply outlines that they have customers' information, and that they are going to use it regardless of the customer's wishes.

Current Government Use

OnStar lists in its privacy statement that if the government serves them with a legal warrant for a person's information, they will turn over personal and car information. This information has been collected many times by police trying to track down criminals who have cars with OnStar. One example is a case in North Carolina where a man had purchased a 2000 Chevrolet Suburban with a fake certified check. The police activated the OnStar system and tracked the man down (McCullagh). This type of use has been permitted by courts several times, and it makes many privacy advocates wonder where the line will be drawn.

Future Government Use

Many fear that OnStar could be manipulated by the government and turned into what is called a roaming bug. The government's use of a roaming bug means that they activate a customer's asset (car or phone) microphone and listen in on conversations that they believe are important. Concerns over the use of roaming bugs are also being raised in reference to other devices like cell phones whose microphones can also be remotely turned on and off. Luckily for current OnStar customers, the roaming bug is not an issue at present time. The 9th Circuit Court ruled that the FBI's use of OnStar in this way is not permitted since it would render OnStar useless in the case of an emergency (McCullagh). It is important to note that this government use was not overturned for privacy reasons, but rather for safety concerns, and this worries many privacy advocates because the government could easily engineer a fix to this problem. If there is a way around the safety issue roaming bugs may soon become a reality.

Using GPS Information: Google Earth

In the past, if someone were to obtain the vehicle information addressed in this chapter, they would have had a hard time getting an up-to-date photo of all the locations that were listed on a person's vehicle location report. Yet, recent technological advances such as Google Earth make such tracking almost elementary. Google Earth allows customers to see up-to-date images of the entire planet, free of charge. Major cities have higher resolution than rural areas, but the quality level in these outlying areas is still high and improving daily. If a data thief, OnStar, or their competitors wanted to get a visualization of the locations described in a vehicle location report, it would be very easy using Google Earth. This creates even more privacy and security invasion concerns since the whereabouts of a customer's house, children's school and other private information could easily be discerned from their vehicle information.

Google Earth customers can also subscribe to enhanced versions of the program that allows access to extremely high resolution images of the globe (Google Earth Online). These advanced versions are making it even easier to accurately track a person's vehicle history and current whereabouts. The images on Google Earth have reached a level of such high quality that police are now using them to look for illegal marijuana fields. In Racine, Wisconsin, the police did just that to catch a man harvesting marijuana (Late Night). As the quality of Google Earth's images increases, the public's vulnerability to tracking through their vehicles increases along with it.

Conclusion

Vehicles are such a necessity in the lives of Americans that the related privacy issues affect nearly every American. If consumers do not stand up for their rights, companies and the government will be able to freely know anyone's whereabouts. The practice of tracking people without their consent is already becoming a reality with GPS navigation companies selling personal vehicle location information and employers tracking their employees every move. This problem is not limited solely to GPS navigation companies and employers, but with the decreasing prices for this technology, consumers are at risk of being tracked by one another. The GPS units described in this chapter offer convenience to both consumers and employers for a high price tag, but money is not the only cost. These technologies may soon carry the heavy cost of a complete loss of privacy.

Works Cited

"2007 OnStar-Equipped Vehicles." OnStar Vehicles Online. 2007. 15 Feb. 2007 <http://www.onstar.com/us_english/jsp/equip_vehicles/07_vehicles.jsp>.

Bohan, Suzanne. "GPS devices offer peace of mind, but at what price?" Oakland Tribune. 2006. WRITERFind. 20 February 2007 <http://www.findarticles.com/p/articles/mi_qn4176/is_20060904/ai_n16708035/pg_1>.

"Frequently Asked Questions." LoJack Hompage. 2007. FAQ. 23 February 2007. <http://www.lojack.com/faq>.

"General Motors Corporate Website." GM Online. 2007. GeneralMotors.com. 15 Feb. 2007. <http://www.GM.com>.

"GM Vehicle Showroom." GM Online. 15 Feb. 2007 <http://www.gmbuypower.com/index.jsp?&partnerId=900014>.

"Google Earth. Explore, Search, and Discover." Google Earth Online. 2007. Earth.Google.Com. 15 Feb. 2007 <http://earth.google.com>.

Joyce, Jim. "Conspiracy Goes Mainstream." CNBC. 2006. YouTube. 20 February 2007 <http://www.youtube.com/watch?v=bmCjoNNkUfg>.

Last Night in Little Rock. "A new GPS privacy issue, and Google Earth used to find marijuana patches." Crime In News, Talk Left Online. 2006. Talkleft.com. 15 Feb. 2007. <http://www.talkleft.com/story/2006/10/18/24911/289>.

Lemos, Robert. "Car spy pushes privacy limit." ZDNet News. 2006. Technology News. 20 February 2007 <http://news.zdnet.com/2100-9595_22-530115.html>.

McCullagh, Declan. "Snooping by satellite." CNET News.com. 2005. Staff Writer. 22 February 2007 <http://news.com.com/2100-1028_3-5533560.html>.

"Measuring Day-to-Day Variability in Travel Behavior Using GPS Data." U.S. Department of Transportation. 2006. Federal Highway Administration. 23 February 2007 <http://www.usa.gov/dot/highway/2033/gps/ad_152/index=2wm>.

Onley, Dawn. "Technology Gives Big Brother Capability." HR
Magazine. 2005. Vol.50, Iss. 7. 25 February 2007 <http://proquest
.umi.com/pqdweb?index=0&did=864066741&SrchMode=1&sid=3&
Fmt=3>.

"OnStar Privacy Statement." OnStar Online. 2007. OnStar.com. 15 Feb.
2007. <http://www.onstar.com/us_english/jsp/privacy_policy.jsp>.

"Recent Decision about GPS, Privacy, and the Fourth Amendment."
Berkeley Intellectual Property Weblog. 2007. Boalt Organization. 22
February 2007 <www.boalt.org/ biplog/archives/659>.

Schwart, John. "This Car Can Talk. What It Says May Cause Concern."
2003. The Newyork Times. 22 February 2007
<http://www.nytimes.com/2003/12/29/
technology/29car.html?ex=1388120400>.

Appendix A
GPS Vehicle Tracking Survey

The following is a survey to ascertain your knowledge of GPS Vehicle
Tracking capabilities. Please answer the following questions to the best
of your ability.

1. Which of the following GPS tracking companies have you heard
of (choose all that apply)
a. OnStar
b. Garmin
c. TomTom
d. Kenwood
e. MicroTech

2. Which of the following are GPS tracking systems capable of
(choose all that apply):
a.   knowing your speed
b.   knowing your location
c.   knowing whether you are wearing your seat belt
d.   recoding where you have been
e.   who is driving

3. For which of the following uses are GPS tracking systems
allowed to gather and distribute customers' information (choose
only one):
a.   Marketing research
b.   Give customer's driving records to government with no
     warrant
c.   Sell/Give to affiliates or anyone they do business with
d.   All of the above
e.   Only a & b

4. Under which of the following circumstances can someone track a
vehicle without the driver's knowledge?

A. If the tracker knows the driver
B. If the tracker owns the car
C. If the tracker is renting the car to the driver

5. Is it legal for your parents to track you without your knowledge if they are on the car's registered title?   Yes   No

6. Do you have a GPS navigation or tracking system in your car (that you are aware of)? Yes   No

7. If yes to 6, do you think that your driving habits are being tracked and stored?   Yes   No

8. How would you rank your knowledge of GPS navigation systems (1-10, with one be the lowest level of knowledge and 10 the highest). _____

20

Consequences of Camera Phones in Today's Society
Kelsey Good and Steven Moulton

Introduction

Every technological device that surrounds people today is continually evolving and advancing. Cell phones were once the size of a brick and nearly impossible to take anywhere but in the car. Today, some phones are so small you can fit them in the palm of your hand. With Bluetooth technology, the term 'hand held' is becoming obsolete because all you need is an earpiece to talk on your phone. In-phone camera technology is no different. The field is evolving along with the cell phones they are installed in, for the cameras to be better, faster, and clearer. Because the integration of camera phones into everyday life is so widespread, it is important to understand the history, technology, and future of camera phones. As with many other technologies before it, the camera phone has been use positively as well as to achieve negative aims.

History of Camera Phones

Camera phones are a relatively new invention. Philip Kahn invented the first camera phone in 1997 on the day his daughter was born. Using parts bought at Radio Shack, Kahn linked a digital camera to his phone so he was able to take pictures and send them over e-mail to his friends and family around the world. Today, the camera phone has evolved into an asset not even Kahn could have foreseen when he originally invented it. Modern cell phones are generation three phones, which means they have the capability to send and receive digital images, watch streaming video, access the Internet, and in some cases access Microsoft Office suite to write and send documents. Camera phones are heading towards more complex digital imaging with higher resolution and larger memory capacity. Phones will also be able to send and receive larger files at faster speeds, which means that video streaming on phones is moving towards television-like clarity and a faster connection. Because of the advancements of the cell phone camera over the years, many associate Kahn with a negative invention due to those who have misused it.

The Market for Camera Phones

The demand for cell phones in the U.S. is nothing compared to the rest of the world. In the U.S., the market has almost reached a saturation point. In the United Kingdom however, the amount of cell phone numbers recently surpassed the actual number of people ("Cell Phone Usage"). As a nation, Africa has one of the largest growth rates of new cell phone subscribers. Once considered a part of the world with no need for cell phone service coverage, the continent of Africa now has almost complete access to cell phone service. India currently has the biggest growth in a single market with six million new phones in January of 2007 alone (Gupta). With the globalization of cell phone use, the potential number of camera phones around the world is staggering. Legislation has already been created in countries where camera phones are more popular in countries that are technologically advanced, like South Korea. In South Korea a camera phone must make a clearly audible and distinct sound when a picture or video is taken. Camera phones are only gaining momentum and their presence in the market is increasing as popularity grows.

How Camera Phones Work

Camera phones are simple devices that do not take much demonstration or instruction to learn how to use. A small digital camera is mounted on the back or front of the phone along with an application on the phone that allows the user to take, store, and send pictures or videos directly from the phone itself. Once a picture or video is taken, it can be sent in the same way a text message is sent as long as the user on the receiving end has the appropriate software on their phone to view the picture. Internet enabled phones can also upload photos directly online to a user's online gallery or a website straight from the phone itself. As the technology grows more intricate and advanced, phones will be able to do more than ever. More recent versions offer the ability to watch music videos while listening to a song or even watch live TV from the screen on your phone. The only drawback to the increasing development of the technology and more advanced picture quality is the limited battery life. The use of the camera or video, and sending either of the two drains a phones battery and makes it difficult for a user to keep the phone charged over long periods of time.

Negative Uses of Camera Phones

Even though camera phones have made it easier to capture criminals, bring forward hazardous work environments, or even capture your European vacation, individuals are taking advantage of their features and also using them in a harmful way. It is important to look at how camera phones can negatively impact people and corporations through invasions of privacy, identity theft, and reputation attacks. It is also essential to examine and realize the actions being taken to minimize the impacts of these negative uses. In this chapter, the following areas will be covered: camera phones in the work place, as a means of sexual exploitation, as a tool to carry out identity theft, and to hurt one's reputation.

Camera Phones in the Work Place

Companies have been quick to realize the potential problems camera phones bring into the work place. This technology carries with it the risk of industrial espionage as well as privacy risks of both employees and visitors. To address these threats, some companies have placed limitations on camera phone possession and use.

With the emergence of the camera phone, companies have become concerned with the potential theft of secretive information. This is particularly important to companies that rely heavily on trade secrets for competitive advantage. Specifically, companies are exposed to product formulas, client lists, or marketing strategies potentially being photographed (Rupal). DaimlerChrysler, a Michigan based automobile producer, banned the use of cameras 35 years ago due to a proprietary leak. This policy was expanded five years ago to include camera phones. When asked about their ban on camera phones in the workplace, a spokesman from DaimlerChrysler said that "the nature of our business is proprietary and there are trade secrets we have to protect" (Rupal 1).

According to Kathryn Terrell, a human resource consultant from a Fort Collins, Colorado based firm, harassment is a much larger issue than the theft of trade secrets. "In my opinion, the bigger problem with camera phones is use by employees to impulsively take inappropriate photos" ("Cell Phone Usage Statistics"2). She is also a strong advocate of companies taking a hard line approach and adjusting policies to include camera phone abuse. In a survey of 400 human resource managers, only 7% of companies had written and implemented policies regarding camera phones, 15% were planning on implementing a policy in the next six months, and 77% lacked any written policy. Those without any policy in place are potentially liable for any harassment created by the use of camera phones within the workplace (Rupal).

Another issue companies may face from the use of camera phones in the workplace is employees' access to inappropriate photos. Since employers are unable to view what their employees are looking at on their phones, there is a risk they may be looking at and spreading pornography to other employees ("Should"). In the long run, this may be an obstruction to work performance and the attitude of the overall work environment.

In response to these inappropriate uses of camera phones in the workplace, companies are looking to ban the use of them. Already companies like DaimlerChrysler, Texas Instruments Inc., and Samsung do not allow recording devices (including camera phones) on company premises. Samsung, the pioneer of the camera phone, does not even allow cell phones at work because of the impending risk of the theft of confidential information and leaking of secretive technology to competitors ("Should"). Companies have the option of enacting a complete ban on camera phones, a ban in designated areas (such as technology sensitive areas and/or restrooms), or a ban restricting use during breaks. However, some argue that an all-inclusive ban may be ineffective since it is unenforceable and companies should instead focus on security where it matters the most (product development) and concentrate on training employees to spot problematic behavior (Rupal).

By banning the use of camera phones at work, you are potentially getting rid of any positive benefits created by their use. These may include their ability to facilitate accident investigations and document unsafe working conditions ("Should"). Thus, it is important to find a policy that fits best within the associated work environment.

Camera Phones and Sexual Exploitation

As camera phone technology advances, the picture quality has substantially increased while the overall size of the phone has decreased. This has made it easier to conceal the camera when taking pictures. Certain individuals have taken advantage of this by secretly taking photos and videos without the subject's knowledge and in locations that were once viewed as private.

Sexual predators have used cell phone technology as an advantage in taking both so-called "up-skirt" and "down-blouse" photos. An "up-skirt" photo is a picture that is taken pointed up someone's skirt without the knowledge of the subject. A "down-blousing" picture is a picture of a woman's breasts taken as she is bending over. After these shots have been taken, they are typically uploaded onto Internet voyeur sites (Collins). This is normally done without the subject ever knowing.

Most phones now have the ability to send photos or videos between other users and can automatically upload them onto the Internet, making the ability to catch one of these videos before it is made public near impossible. At a public high school in Delhi, India, a young man captured himself and his girlfriend having sex by using his video phone. He then proceeded to send the video to his friends. The video was eventually even sold on the Internet. In response to this occurrence, Delhi administration placed a ban on all mobile phones in schools (Nair).

The United States has taken action by enacting the Video Voyeurism Prevention Act, which prohibits the videotaping or photographing of anyone who is naked or partially naked in situations with "reasonable expectations of privacy." Some of these locations may include locker rooms, tanning salons, and changing rooms (U.S. Congress). Many countries have similar laws but they have not all been updated to include camera phones. In Scotland, a woman was changing in a locker room with her eight year old son at a local pool and was photographed on a camera phone. As in many locations where there is an instituted ban on photographs, Scotland's laws may not have been updated to include camera phones ("Menace"). This has led to an increase in litigation attempting to address these gaping loopholes.

The violations stated above occurred where reasonable privacy was expected, but similar infringements can occur while you are out in the public. In Japan, individuals have used infrared attachments on their cameras, which have allowed them to actually see through someone's clothing. While these individuals were later arrested, this is an illustration of how people are taking this technology to new dangerous levels ("Menace"). In Toronto, a man was using grocery stores as a location to snap pictures of his victims. He would appear to be browsing the bottom shelves and while crouching, he would use his camera phone to take "up-skirt" pictures of young girls (Brautigam). This man was only caught through security cameras in the grocery stores. In Boston, a cell phone salesman used a camera phone to snap a picture under a 17 year old's skirt as she was riding up an escalator at a local mall (Collins). In all of these examples, the subject never knew their picture was taken and still their privacy was being violated.

In response to the increase in using camera phones as a means for sexual exploitation, many states have taken initiative to make this a criminal act. California outlawed upskirting and downblousing after images that were taken at Disneyland showed up on the Internet (Collins). Other states like Ohio and Pennsylvania also increased their voyeurism laws to include these new offenses (Miller). This is undoubtedly a step in the right direction, but the problem is that the laws do not necessarily regulate the issue if the subject does not know their picture was taken.

Nick Ashley, a Toronto Police Detective said "cell phones are so common place in our culture now, people are quite used to seeing them in people's hands, it's not even something they give a second though to" (Brautigam A17). This is coupled by the fact that cameras are getting smaller while their picture quality increases, making it more and more difficult to know if your privacy was ever violated.

Identity Theft with Camera Phones

As identity theft becomes more prevalent in today's society, thieves are finding new means to gaining private information, which includes the use of camera phones. These phones are becoming more common place and the image quality is nearing those of digital cameras, making it easier for anyone to take an image from further away while still maintaining the same level of detail. This makes the everyday shopper exposed to bank theft by getting their credit card photographed, or to identity theft since licenses are occasionally displayed when making a purchase.

For example, a man was at a pizzeria and was paying for his order with a credit card. After the cashier ran the card, she set the card back down on the counter as it processed. During this time, the employee began playing with his cell phone. The man realized he had the same phone as the cashier and he heard a unique sound of a picture being taken. Only thereafter did the employee hand back the credit card. Moments later, he heard the sound of the camera storing data ("Camera Phones"). Later on that evening the man canceled his credit cards, but would he have known what took place if he owned a different camera phone? The typical shopper cannot tell that their credit card number is even stolen until charges show up on the monthly bank statement (Elphinstone).

In the *Pittsburg Post*, an article was written around the holiday season explaining methods in which to protect oneself from identity theft. One of the methods they suggest is to make sure to look over your shoulders when standing in line and verify that no one is taking photos of your credit cards or other forms of identification on their camera phone. By doing this, you are protecting important personal information and potential loss of identity or financial theft. (Elphinstone)

Camera Phones and Reputation

Another negative use of camera phones is utilizing these images to hurt another's reputation by posting them images for the public viewing. In a *USA Today* article by Maria Puente, she said "here in YouTube world whether you're a celebrity or a nobody, privacy can be a disappearing luxury thanks to technology in every pocket" (Puente D7). According to her, at any given moment a photo or video can surface on the Internet or in magazines with the potential to harm a person's reputation. A professor at the University of San Diego who does research in modern communications mentioned, "if the government is tracking calls, most people aren't going to feel the repercussions. They're more affected if a compromising photo gets on the Internet. That's personal invasion they can see" (Puente D7). These images and videos can impact the decisions of college admissions, employers, or friends. It is commonly said that people spend years working on building their reputation and yet have the ability to ruin it in seconds.

Recently, an *American Idol* semifinalist, Antonella Barba, was voted off after risqué photos of her appeared on the Internet. Most of these photos were for a calendar that was meant for her boyfriend, but later photos believed to be her participating in sexual acts surfaced again, which may have turned the heads of a few voters (Puente). Miss Nevada USA, Katie Rees, lost her crown after nude photos of her showed up on the Internet. Other celebrities such as Kate Moss (snorting cocaine), Lindsay Lohan, Britney Spears, and Paris Hilton (all three caught partying without underwear), have had their reputation hurt through the surfacing of these images on the Internet (Puente). These examples specifically target high profile subjects, but every individual is at risk when it comes to their image being uploaded onto the Internet.

Once these images make it onto the Internet, it is near impossible to get them removed. An attorney who specializes in technology issues at McGuireWoods LLP in Richmond, Virginia says that once a picture is "captured, the sky is the limit as to how far it can be distributed" (Kelley A1). The problem is that pictures taken in public belong to the individual who took the photo. Therefore, it is extremely difficult to get them removed from the Internet. ReputationDefender, an American company who will search the Internet for roughly $16 a month, will provide you a detailed listing of their results and for $30 they claim that they are able to get it removed from the Internet through legal threats (Wall). Even though companies may be able to get this reputation damaging material off of the Internet, the best way to prevent this from getting there in the first place is to not act inappropriately in public.

Impact

As camera phones become more prevalent in society, it is becoming much harder to avoid being photographed, especially as cameras continue to shrink in size. Countries and individual states are now attempting to pass litigation aimed at protecting the victim from this breach of privacy. In the meantime, it is important to know the potential misuses in order to protect oneself while in both public and private places, along with protecting any company secrets or preventing harassment in the workplace. Though the negative impacts of camera phones are important issues to keep in consideration, there have been positive outcomes to the invention. With bad also comes good, and weighing the two against one another is important when gauging not only the impact camera phones have had, but also the danger they may pose in the future.

Positive Uses of Camera Phones

The uses for camera phones are not limited to just negative ones; many good things have come from people using the device. Civilian crime fighting, documentation of current events, and significant personal events are all moments in time that can, and are being, documented by cell phone cameras.

Camera Phones in Crime Abatement

Civilian crime fighting is becoming more popular as cell phone cameras become more technologically advanced and provide clearer images with the capability to quickly transfer a large amount of memory. One of the most recent development in civilian crime fighting has taken place in Indiana and New York. Police departments in both states are developing a system in which civilians are able to send a picture taken with a cell phone to police dispatchers the same way 911 calls are currently made. "If you see a crime in progress or a dangerous building, you'll be able to transmit images to 911 or online to nyc.gov," the mayor of New York City, Michael Bloomberg recently explained in his State of the City address (Parez).

The problems that are inherent with this new system are being addressed by both states. The biggest of the many technological problems is the massive amounts of possible pictures being sent to the police department and subsequently slowing down the system. If the system becomes overhauled with pictures being received, it is possible the system's memory can fill up and no more pictures will be able to be sent in before the current pictures are looked at and dealt with. During this at-capacity-time, pictures of actual crimes taking place might not ever make it to the system. Instead, the pictures will be held back by superfluous pictures.

The second concern deals with the potential cost of not only the system itself, but also the manpower necessary to go through the pictures to discern whether or not an actual crime that necessitates follow-up has taken place. The respective police departments must go through each and every picture civilians send in just like 911 dispatchers must answer each and every call that comes into the station. In order to do this, dispatchers outside of the call center must be hired to go through a possible massive amount of pictures (Parez). With the solution of these problems, the 911 picture systems have the potential to increase the numbers of criminals caught in the act and convicted of their crimes.

Camera Phones and a New Form of Civilian Photojournalism

Since the mass acceptance of cameras with cell phones, civilian photojournalism has become a phenomenon that touches the lives of people around the world. Several institutions and agencies request pictures be sent over the Internet from any 'average Joe' that might have taken the photo with a camera phone. The horrific bombings of London subways and busses are an example of such a request. "London police are urging people who were near the scenes of Thursday's deadly bomb blast in the British capitol to send in any information they may have captured on their mobile phone" ("Police"). This information was not only sent to police departments in the area; civilians involved in or near the incident took pictures and video on their camera phones and sent them to news organizations around the world. Without these photos and video, the world might not have known exactly what happened in the subway tunnels that day.

Cell phone cameras are quickly becoming the best source for on-the-spot photojournalism simply because so many people carry a phone equipped with a camera with them during the day. With access to a phone at any point during a daily routine, there is no telling what events a person might be able to capture. For example, the world knew about the scheduled execution of Saddam Hussein days before it was supposed to take place. News organizations also knew there would be no camera equipment allowed at the execution. A guard present smuggled in a cell phone with a camera and took the only known footage of the execution. This video of the hanging is now available on several online video and news sites.

Vacationers in Southeast Asia documented some of the most moving and telling video of the destructive force of the tsunami that took place in December of 2004. Without this footage, there would not be photographic evidence of the real-time extent of the destructive force of the massive waves that killed so many and caused so much damage. Scientists are also able to study the footage of the waves in order to gauge the height and speed of the wave and equate it with the size of the underground plate-shift that caused the tsunami. Camera phones provide access to spur of the moment documentation of events important in the lives of many people around the world. Without them, society might not have access to certain moments in time that have been a major part of history.

Impact

Camera phones are changing the world by giving people the opportunity to share video and imaging information from the tips of their fingers at any time. This technology allows an expansion of the possibilities of crime fighting and access to images most never thought possible.

Future Research

As camera phones begin to play a major role in today's society, future research is necessary in order to dig deeper and unveil new and potentially more harmful capabilities. Further research needs to look specifically at how society copes with this technological change. To do this, interviews should be conducted with executives and human resource managers in both large and small businesses across all industries, lawyers that deal specifically with business and individual privacy suits, union representatives, and professors specializing in this field. Based on these interviews, one would be able to generate a better idea about whether camera phones have a positive or a negative impact on society. Also, this data would provide a wide variety of information regarding methods that can be used to protect reputations, privacy, identity, and company information.

Conclusion

Camera phones are a part of every day life. This is a fact, whether damaging or beneficial, insignificant or not. Because they are so prevalent in the every day lives of people all over the world, the importance of knowing both the dangers and the benefits of this invention is important. A camera phone can affect anyone, anywhere, whether or not they themselves own a phone equipped with a camera. Thus, privacy issues are relevant to almost everyone. Pictures and video taken by camera phones are accessible and free to anyone who chooses to watch them on the Web and, in some cases, on T.V. With the widespread reach of camera phones today, weighing the good and the bad brings an awareness of the issue and knowledge that as these technologies advance the related problems will evolve and advance as well. Camera phones look like they are here to stay and if they are to become an almost unavoidable and permanent feature in daily life it is important to understand what to be aware of and the necessary precautions to protect ones' privacy and identity.

Works Cited

Brautigam, Tara. "Man in court for cellphone photos of kids' bottoms." The Gazette 21 Sept. 2005: A17.

"Camera Phones & Credit Cards." Consumer Jungle. Feb 2007. 11 March 2007 <http://www.consumerjungle.org>

"Cell Phone Usage Statistics." CellNumbers.com. 12 March 2007 <http://www.cellnumbers.com/cell-phone-usage.aspx>

Collins, Monica. "Somebody's Watching You: Upskirting, Downblousing, Happy Slapping. As Camera Phones Proliferate, an Ugly Vocabulary is Born." Boston Globe 17 July 2005: 18.

Elphinstone, J.W. "Beware of Identity Thieves this Holiday Season." Pittsburgh Post – Gazette 20 Nov. 2006: E7.

Gupta, Shri. "Telecom Regulatory Authority of India: Press Release No. 22/2007." 15 Feb. 2007 <http://www.trai.gov.in/trai/upload/PressReleases/436/pr15feb07no22.pdf>

Kelley, Jeffrey. "Privacy fades away as the Internet puts your life in the spotlight." Richmond Times – Dispatch 4 Jan. 2007: A1.

"Menace of camera phones: Serious concerns raised about invasion of privacy." The Herald 14 Jan. 2005: 21.

Miller, Matt. "Man fined in case of mall 'upskirting'." The Patriot – News 22 Sept. 2005: B7.

Nair, Abhilash. "Mobile Phones and the Internet: Legal Issues in the Protection of Children." International Review of Law Computers & Technology July 2006: 177-185.

Perez, Luis. "City 911 to add video." Newsday.com 18 Jan. 2006. 12 March 2007 <http://www.newsday.com>

"Police appeal for phone footage." CNN.com 22 July 2005. 11 March 2007 <http://www.cnn.com>

Puente, Maria. "Hello to less Privacy: Camera phones lead to 'personal invasion'." USA Today 28 Feb 2007: D7.

Rupal, Parekh. "Proliferation of camera phones calls up a wide range of risks relating to the workplace." Business Insurance 23 May 2005.

"Should You Ban Camera Phones?" IOMA's Security Director's Report May 2004.

United State. Cong. "Video Voyeurism Prevention Act of 2003." Library of Congress. 25 Sept. 2003.

Wall, Matthew. "Someone out there doesn't like me." Sunday Times 26 Nov. 2006: 30.

21

Risky Business at Wireless Hot Spots

Travis Rabii and Kim Ward

Introduction

It has been a long week and the prospect of tucking yourself into bed has never seemed so inviting. You head up the stairs and notice your front door is not only unlocked, but propped open for anyone who happens to walk down your busy street; however, you continue on to bed instead of locking it up to keep safe. You are inviting anyone off the street to waltz right in and make themselves comfortable with the personal items in your private space. That is essentially what you are doing when you log on to any free wireless network. You are leaving your computer's front door unlocked and wide open.

The United States currently has the largest number of wireless networks offering free Internet access to a growing number of users. These free access points are becoming more readily available with each passing day. While a year ago it was common for public and private institutions and libraries to have networks set up for users, now businesses are capitalizing on the growing technological needs and desires of their typical consumer. Now more than ever, cafes, coffee shops, airports and even many restaurants offer free wireless to customers. Vice president for Gartner, a marketing research company,

Ken Dulaney predicts "100,000 hotspots within the next five years" will become available (Vaughan-Nichols 17).

Businesses are offering this incentive to customers, because free Wireless networks, also known as hot spots, are inexpensive to implement, and therefore, have become the ideal way to deliver wireless Internet access. Wireless networks have several advantages over wired networks. First, hotspots are substantially less expensive. Second, the hotspot user has the ability to move around without having to worry about maintaining a connection. This is especially beneficial to business employees on the road. For business use, the ability to roam reduces operational costs while increasing employee productivity. Lastly, hotspots cover a much larger physical area (Gruteser 11). But with all this ease and luxury comes risk.

Wireless networks are substantially riskier then wired networks. Wirelessworks operate like wired networks by using both access points and a mobile host. But unlike wired networks, Wireless networks send information via radio signals through a shared channel. Because the information is being sent through radio waves, other hosts can easily gather data being transmitted (Aura 6). This can be problematic when a victim is located in the vicinity of a hospital, law firm, or business, and the information being sent is data on patients or clients. By purchasing inexpensive hardware, a hacker can install an access point and access data that is transmitted on the frequency.

Public concern over privacy issues is steadily growing as more individuals become victims of identity theft. Internet users have expressed concerns for their privacy. "For example, according to one survey 94% of web user have denied a request for personal information and 40% have provided fake data" (Gruteser 12). Two forms of exposure are of biggest concern to users. First, users do not want to reveal names on anything which would allow someone to have a unique identification of the user. Second, users do not want personal information like salary, job title, age, sex, address, religious views, or political affiliation given to others (Aura 2).

The danger is not necessarily in the networks themselves, but rather in the individuals who use them to plant viruses and spy-ware or steal information. This leaves the question: Of what toll is this seemingly convenient and free service taking on consumers' privacy and the health of their computers?

Who?

The risks of free Wireless affect many different people even if they are not directly connected to a network. One example is the business owner whose reputation could be harmed if a customer's computer security was breached at their place of business. These proprietors are trying to provide the service as an incentive to visiting their shops, not to expose their customers to danger. Another group of victims could be the users of a computer who are unaware that the security of a pc had been compromised while at a free Wireless spot. For example, take the family that shares a laptop. If the mother is not aware her son had used free wireless at a coffee shop on the way home from school, where the computer has been implanted with spy-ware, why would she be concerned with accessing the family's bank accounts from the safety of their home? Another rising danger is business' users who work with trade secrets. If an employee unknowingly logs on to a peer-to-peer network, everything that is not properly protected on their computer is in danger of being stolen. That could include their employers' private data on recent deals, new products and strategies.

The need for wireless Internet access has also been seen by hospitals and clinics. Doctors can send information on a patient to the desired locations with amazing speed. If a wireless network is set up at a local hospital, then ideally, the radio signal would only be accessible to recipients within the building. However, radio signals can "leak" outside the building, thus allowing external hackers to use radio waves to receive the information being sent (NIST 6).

Naturally one would think the risks of free Wireless would cease when the user disconnects from the network, but unfortunately that is not the case. Once spy-ware is implanted on a computer, it is sometimes difficult to fully remove unless the user reformats the hard drive. Also, Peer-to-Peer networks do not disconnect completely; all the hacker has to do is get in a range close enough to another computer to link back up and have full access to documents. Anytime a user logs on to an illegitimate network, they can be affected by wireless risks.

What are the Risks Associated with Hot-Spots?

Despite the constant warnings relating to privacy issues, consumers easily forget the risks when they feel comfortable and secure at their local coffee shop. What people tend to overlook is who is sitting two tables away and what information that potential hacker can retrieve when they share the same network.

Four Types of Attacks on Wireless Networks

Wireless networks are vulnerable to four common types of attacks: jamming, active, passive, and man-in-the middle. Jamming attacks are when RF frequencies interfere with the operation of a wireless network. Jamming is a type of a Denial of Service (DoS) attack. It disables the use of the wireless network, usually due to another type of device that operates on the same Radio Frequency as the wireless network. This is not a large threat to wireless users, because while the attacker has to invest a lot of work into the attack, the damage is only a few minutes of lost communication.

There are two other types of interrelated attacks to be aware of in the computing world known as passive and active. Passive attacks are difficult to detect and occur frequently. They are not necessarily malicious in nature so they are not a large focus when it comes to security. However, passive attacks are important to mention because they are what allow active attacks. An active attack can range from unauthorized access, spoofing, Denial of Service (DoS), flooding, introduction of mal-ware, and/or theft of devices (Shimonski). In extreme cases, a hacker may use the information gathered in order to inflict physical harm to an individual.

One of the scariest types of attacks is known as a man-in the middle attack. With this attack, a hacker sets up an "ad-hoc" or "P2P" network outside the legitimate network. Ad hoc networks are set up within a larger framework, such as an airport, to lure users to connect to the internet. Because they are an alternative to the "infrastructure network," they are generally unprotected. Essentially, the hacker allows users to access the Internet through their computer, therefore, all of the user's information is available to them. Authentium, Inc. conducted a 3 day research study on ad hoc networks at the Chicago O'Hare Airport. The study "found more than 20 ad hoc networks each time, with 80% of them advertising free Wireless access." The company also found that many of the networks were displaying fake of misleading MAC addresses, a clear sign that they were "bent on mischief" (Gralla).

If a computer is configured to allow file-sharing, the hacker can access all of the files and data and also plant mal-ware on the computer. This is possible because even if a user is in a trustworthy place, this "Free Wireless" may pop up and appear to be a legitimate Internet source. These "men-in-the-middle" are able to breach user's security with as little as two pieces of knowledge about the wireless network. All they need is Server Set ID (SSID) and the rogue access point (AP). They use this information to set up an unauthorized access point. As wireless networks become common place, users are adjusting to logging on to a free network without authenticating or proper security checks. Because these hackers are not protected, any risks they expose themselves to can then be transmitted to the victim.

Why are People Willing to Expose Themselves?

The most common reason people expose themselves to free wireless risks is a lack of knowledge. Especially when in a trusted environment, security issues are not the first priority to many people. Also, businesses that might experience a high number of hackers would not be inclined to warn users because that might lead to a decline in business. Despite the constant warnings about privacy issues and identity theft, operating under the "It will never happen to me" notion allows users to connect and ignore the risks. Lastly, the convenience of being able to access email, account information, or even entertainment aspects of the Internet for free while outside the home weighs heavily on the benefit side. This is especially true when on the surface the cost to the consumer appears to be nothing, at least in the monetary aspect.

How do Attackers Operate?

During their time on the internet, a user of a wireless network frequently sends and receives data via radio waves. This data can be easily obtained by anyone with an access point, because it is being sent through radio waves. When data is obtained by attackers, it is analyzed to determine the approximate location of a Wireless user. Information on this location can be discovered in each layer of the network stack (Marco 14). Information like IP addresses does not give real world names of users or other personal information. However, it can be used to identify such things as MAC address or the Mobile home address. Also, IP addresses are set up to lead to a specific geographical location, like a university campus. This however is not applicable when firewalls and proxies are implemented. Access points at the physical and link layer can reveal the approximate location of a transmitter. Packets must be within a 50 to 100 meter range to be received by a transmitter. The Domain Name System (DNS) for routers usually includes broad location information like the names of cities. This means trace route based approaches can locate the proximity of a user's location (Gruteser 16).

The wireless network operators are the individuals assigned to maintain base stations of wireless networks. When acting as a router, they have access to "physical layer information" of packages sent through the router. Even when the package is intended for a different location, the operators may have the ability to eavesdrop on the information (Gruteser15). These risks are usually not relevant when the user and provider are bound by contractual agreements. But when the provider of a wireless network is unknown to the other party, such risks exist. Network layer and application layer information can only be obtained by parties within close proximity to a transmitter. This means this information can only be observed by a small number of network operators. One may draw the conclusion that these risks can be ignored because it pertains to a small population. But this risk increases dramatically when access points are densely populated like they are in major cities (Grutuser 17).

Ways to Protect

The first line of defense for Wireless users is an understanding of the risks associated with using a wireless provider. Users must understand that a privacy policy does not protect from having private information taken. Individuals within the service providing company can potentially obtain information the user would not want them to have (Grutuser 21).

Virtual Private Network (VPN) software allows for the messages being sent to be encrypted. Encryption means putting the communication between the two parties in code. By encrypting the communication, it becomes much more difficult for a hacker to eavesdrop. The University of Colorado at Boulder's ITS department offers free VPN software to all students and can be used even when a student is not on campus (http://www.colorado.edu/its/security/awarness/wireless).

Other encryption software, such as Wired Equivalent Privacy (WEP) and Wireless Protected Access (WPA), will also provide extra security. Even when encryption measures are being used, it is still recommended to use the latest in spy-ware and anti-virus software and implement firewalls. Another method of protection is to avoid sending messages which include sensitive information like social security numbers or bank account information unless using a VPN or Secure Socket Layer (SSL). The less time spent on a network, the less chance a user has of becoming a victim of a wireless hacker. Therefore, turning off the network router when it is not in use adds an additional layer of security. By setting up who is allowed to access a particular computer, a user increases privacy protection. MAC addresses are unique to each computer, so a user's computer will recognize frequent addresses and only allow those permitted. However, hackers have the potential to fake MAC addresses, so further security may be needed (http://www.colorado.edu/its/security/awarness/wireless/).

Different location sensing technologies range in their resolution. The more resolution this technology has, the more information is given on an individual's location. Therefore, having location sensing technology with a lower resolution will lead to less information on the location of a user (Gruteser 14). Proxy servers are intended to improve the performance of a computer's varied operations like access to the internet. They also provide some form of security to the user by hiding the user in a larger population. When the user is hidden in a large population, it is nearly impossible to locate and identify the user. Proxy servers also act as a means of security to the user, because a proxy hides the mobile nodes connected to a wireless network (Aura 7).

Research Methods

In this chapter, in order to research the vulnerabilities Wireless spots create, a variety of methods were used. First, it was essential to assess how aware wireless users were of some of the risks and whether or not they would be willing to prevent such risks. In order to measure this, a survey was conducted with wireless users ranging from ages 19-65. The survey was conducted via a web-based survey on SurveyMonkey.com. Next, the authors tried to find out why Boulder business owners offered these networks and if they knew about the risks. To do this, two Boulder businesses were surveyed who offer non-password protected wireless internet. Phillip Logue of the Brewing Market on Baseline and Broadway and Paul Cattin of Pekoe Sip House in North Boulder were both willing to speak on providing free wireless access. To learn the logistics of wireless networks and how hackers can infiltrate, numerous academic and technological articles were used. A personal interview was also conducted with Dr. Marco Gruteser, a former Ph.D. student from CU who focused on Wireless Location Privacy protection. The technology behind wireless networks was also studied.

Interviews with Proprietors that offer Free Wireless

Philip Louge of Brewing Market was completely aware of the security implications of a wireless network, but was hopeful that his customers and users of the network were as educated on security as he was. He also hoped the users were just accessing sites such as "Google" for school research and not personal accounts. When asked if he offered the wireless to draw in business, his initial answer was "yes" and that he wanted to serve the student population to the best of his ability. He said, "When our network goes down, so does our line." Paul Cattin of Pekoe Sip House expressed the same thoughts. He provided free internet, because he believes wireless is becoming available everywhere and it is a necessary option for customers to use in order to keep a competitive advantage.

These are prime examples of proprietors who are trying to keep customers happy. Lucky for them, thus far their networks have operated without security breaches. Hopefully, both of them will never have to experience any security breaches while their shops are in operation.

Survey Results

The survey conducted included 55 responses. The responses came from an age range of 18-50+. Fifty percent were ages 18-24 and 39% of respondents were 50+. The survey aimed to gauge respondent knowledge of wireless risks and to examine their familiarity with terms that are red-flags of danger. After preliminary knowledge and awareness questions, interest in protective software was measured.

Of the 55 surveyed, everyone used Internet for at least a half an hour per day. The majority, 55.6%, answered that they spent five plus hours online and the other large fraction, 22.2%, spent one to three hours. On average, of these hours only .81 were spent at free wireless hot spots. Only 42% spent any time at all at free wireless spots. A surprising finding was that respondent decisions were not affected by the price of the wireless access. When asked if they felt more secure if they had to pay a fee for the wireless access 33% respondents replied yes, 37% replied no, and 29% were undecided. That could be seen as a good sign for Internet knowledge across the board if people are concerned even when they are paying for wireless internet.

Importantly, seven out of 51 answered yes to accessing personal data at free wireless spots. That means over 13% of the sample log into personal accounts while on these possibly dangerous networks. Below is a chart depicting how secure people believe wireless networks to be. A score of one indicated feeling completely secure accessing all personal information while a score of 10 indicated not even feeling comfortable using the connection.

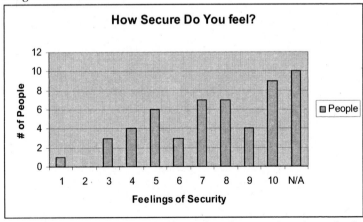

It is impressive and a good sign that the majority of people that answered this question were wary of free wireless networks. Also, when asked if they had ever been victims of identity theft or thought they could be, 66.7% replied yes demonstrating their awareness of security dangers. The most worrisome result discovered was the lack of knowledge of what peer-to-peer (P2P) networks or ad-hoc networks were. Of 54 people that answered the question, 30 were unaware of the meaning of these networks. That means that 55% of people would not even recognize the difference in connecting to a P2P network rather than an infrastructure one.

Research also sought to identify if people would be interested in software that would protect them and what attributes were important in the software. The first aspect was cost. Considering the research related to "free" Wireless networks, it is fitting that 41% would only use the software if it was free of cost. Only 3.8% were willing to pay more than $75.00 for the software.

Next, respondents were asked how important four specific characteristics were to using such software. The results are below:

	Very Important	Important	Somewhat Important	Not Important	Response Total
Affordability	51% (25)	35% (17)	12% (6)	2% (1)	49
Trial ability	37% (18)	31% (15)	18% (9)	14% (7)	49
Image	12% (6)	22% (11)	31% (15)	35% (17)	49
Relative Advantage	44% (22)	40% (20)	12% (6)	4% (2)	50

Once again, affordability is the main concern of respondents and relative advantage over other products. Thus, in order to impact the market, software designers and sellers need to make an affordable product that has a sufficient trial period and proves its advantages to the user. Looking back to cost analysis, 35.8% said they were willing to pay $10.00-$30.00 for software that would protect them.

Conclusion

After research into the increasing popularity of free wireless hot spots and the risks that come along with them, the most sensible solution is to educate not only the users, but also the business owners that are offering these networks. Awareness is increasing as security issues become more prevalent in society. It is important to encourage business owners to warn users of privacy threats or possibly have a disclaimer page when they log on to the free network. Although users may be turned off at first by seeing a warning page, they will realize it is to benefit their personal security. As wireless technology develops, new threats will materialize, but keeping consumers aware and educated is the most effective way to keep free wireless networks a viable place to access the internet.

Works Cited

Galla, Preston. "Dont Fall Victim to the "Fee WiFi Scam." <u>Computer World</u> (2007). 08 Feb. 2007.

Gruteser, Marco, and Dirk Grunwald. "A Methological Assessment of Locatio NPrivacy Risks in Wireless Hotspot Network." <u>University of Colorado Science Department</u>: 12. 08 Feb. 2007.

Gruteser, Marco, Bill Schilit, and Jason Hong. "Wireless Location and Privacy Protection." <u>Invisible Technology</u>. 08 Feb. 2007.

Shimonski Robert. "Wireless security". Microsoft Security (2004). 20 Jul. 2004

Vaughan-Nichols, Steven J. "The Challenges of WiFi Roaming." <u>Technology News</u>: 1-3. 08 Feb. 2007. "Wireless LAN Security." <u>Symantec</u> (2004). 09 Feb. 2007.

22

Citywide Wireless: Process, Implementation, Execution and Privacy Issues
Steve Monahan and Danielle Shea

We are committed to bring universal, affordable wireless broadband Internet access to all San Francisco's residents and businesses, and today we are one step closer to making good on that commitment. Internet access is the best way to connect to the new knowledge-based economy. Providing that access citywide is the first phase of our TechConnect strategy to reach out to all of our communities.

--Mayor Gavin Newsom,
San Francisco

Across the nation, in coffee shops and small Internet boutiques, there is a growing trend of Wireless Fidelity (WiFi) usage. The airways are becoming increasingly populated by Internet signals going to and from hotspots to computers. People are no longer required to be behind their desk plugged into an Ethernet cord to access the Internet. The public is now able to sit in a Starbucks and log onto any site on the World Wide Web using their wireless enabled laptop. This is a convenience to people who can afford to pay the subscription fee associated with many of these hotspots. Additionally, cell phone companies are offering media access cards that plug into the serial port of a laptop and allow for Internet access over cellular connections. Through these services, people are able to use their computers in more locations with greater ease of use.

The latest trend in accessibility is for local governments and cities to offer large-scale WiFi access programs sponsored by the municipality. These programs are agreements between tele-communication companies and city governments that are designed to provide affordable Internet access to every citizen that wishes to participate. This accomplishes both a political goal of abolishing the "technology divide" between the "haves" and the "have-nots" and a general improvement to the daily lives of the inhabitants of the cities involved with this advancement in technology.

Practical Considerations of Municipal Wireless
The Motivations Behind Citywide Networks

With technology reaching a point where large-scale networks are becoming feasible, many local governments are beginning to approach telecommunication companies and develop contracts with those providers to offer wireless Internet over the large areas of their city. Cities such as Orlando, Cupertinoand Anaheim have already implemented these large wireless networks in sections of their metropolitan area. Larger cities, such as San Francisco, Houston, and Philadelphia, are currently under negotiations with telecommunication companies or have already developed contracts for wireless networks that cover the entirety of their cities and are currently in the process of installation and implementation.

No matter where this process is taking place, there is a common political thread: affordable Internet. This new system for Internet access would provide a tremendous opportunity for many underprivileged citizens who, under previous circumstances would not be able to afford Internet. This initiative is known as bridging the "technology divide." Due to the increasing speed that the Internet and the corresponding technology behind it is progressing, there is an increasing "divide" or discrepancy between the underprivileged who cannot afford the technology of today and those who can.

The Internet is becoming an increasing asset to those who have access to it. Enabling anyone to get information on anything they desire. It increases the awareness of the social, political and global situations that face humans every day, and it allows for tremendous learning and personal growth potential. By providing the Internet to those who would not otherwise be able to afford it, cities are doing their best to eliminate the "technology divide" and give the underprivileged an opportunity to have access to all of the great benefits of this ever-expanding resource.

In addition to providing the many underprivileged people with access to Internet, this citywide access concept has an additional positive impact on the businesses and people who live and work in these locations. People would have access to Internet on their commute to work, be able to take their computer to any activity that they desired and have connectivity. Businesses could improve their efficiency by having their employees be able to access work no matter where they were, in traffic, at company events outside the office or from their home office, and all of this at a much more reasonable cost than with options that are currently available.

The Political and Business Processes of Establishing Citywide Networks

After the desire and concept of developing a citywide network, there comes the challenge of finding a method to make the concept a reality. There are multiple models under which a citywide network can be developed and executed. Although there are multiple variations and infinite possibilities for minor deviation from the following, the basic options available to a city wishing to develop a citywide network are: city-owned networks, single private owner, or multiple private owners. The following chart shows the different ownership and operation possibilities and the breakdown of how it works:

Table 1 - Municipal Wi-Fi business models

Who owns? / Who operates?	City	One private actor	Multiple others
City	Public utility	Hosted services	Public overlay
One Private actor	Wholesale	Franchise	Private overlay
Multiple others	Wholesale open platform	Common carrier	Organic mesh

Chart from Bar & Park

Under a city owned network, the original use for the network would be for specific city use (e.g. police authorities, firefighters, medical response units, city based utility operators and repair crews and other municipal employees). If the city decided to allow for public use, there would be several options. The first allows for the city to act as an Internet Service Provider (ISP) and manage the system itself. The second "...option is for the city to act as a wholesaler, reselling excess capacity in the network to a private operator, usually a telecom company or ISP" (Bar & Park 115). The final option would be for the city to act in a similar capacity to the previous example, but "...sell excess capacity to several ISP's, as an open platform" (Bar and Park 115). This last example would create a small market within the network with ISP's competing for subscribers at a certain price point.

A different ownership option for a citywide network is for a single private company to build, operate and maintain the physical network. With this type of ownership there are several options for the provision of the actual Internet service. The first is a city run ISP, with the city creating a telecom company and running through the municipality. No municipality has yet to consider this option as a viable opportunity.

The second possibility is for a private company to buy the rights to the provision of services for the network and then directly sell subscriptions to customers. This would be similar to municipal telecom lines being operated by a cable or phone provider. The third option "…is theoretically possible but so far not implemented in practice, [and] would see the private network owner function as a common carrier, making its WiFi network available to multiple ISPs" (Bar & Park 117).

The third ownership option for a citywide network would be for cities to promote the construction of multiple networks by different companies. This would result in multiple different types of businesses and organizations constructing their own physical networks, with the cities' consent, and then the Internet being provided by one of the following options. The first would be a common public overlay that offers citywide accessibility and the individual networks would pay to be a member. The second possibility is a common private provider of Internet service to all networks in the city. The individuals using the Internet (the public) would pay the ISP and then the ISP would pay the network based on volume of connection provided. The final option for the multiple network scenario would be multiple ISPs providing to multiple networks. This would be similar to the existing hotspot configuration, but on a larger scale, a network over an entire neighborhood, as opposed to just one retail outlet. This would also not provide the same continuity over the entire city that a single provider would allow for, thus, negating the effects of using this network on your commute or in different parts of the city.

With any of these different service provision options, the city plays a large role in ensuring that the original "technology divide" principals are made available. There needs to be an affordable option associated with all types of service so that the needs of underprivileged individual's could and would be provided for.

The Physical Implementation of a Citywide Network

The technology behind a massive citywide network is not as advanced as one would anticipate. Once an agreement on how the physical network is to be established between the city and its chosen method of deployment, the process of construction would be relatively uniform.

To begin, the chosen contractor would mount wireless base stations on municipally owned property such as light posts, buildings and street signs. These base stations are technologically similar to the existing wireless routers that many people have in their home, but much more powerful. Not only are these base stations able to send out much stronger signals than their home office counterparts, but they are also able to process hundreds more incoming and outgoing signals at any given time. This allows for fewer base stations handling a greater volume of traffic, and thus, fewer of the units are needed. Even though the base stations are more powerful than those available to the everyday consumer, there still needs to be thousands of units dispersed in a large city.

Unfortunately, there is drawback with these base stations; they can only process the signals they receive. Almost all laptop computers created today come equipped with a wireless connectivity device built into the system. In many of these enabled computers, the unit receives the signal, but does not have much "pushing" signal strength. This "pushing" signal strength is what the connectivity device needs to send requests for information to the wireless base station. In a small office or home environment, this lack of pushing power does not represent a problem, as the base station is only meters away. In a large city, this lack of "pushing" power poses more of an issue. With buildings made out of concrete and steel, the different components of equipment in buildings and in the vehicles on the roads, there are many obstacles for the signal to get through to reach the desired base station. In order for people to successfully communicate with their desired base station they would need to purchase an additional device called a "bridge" which boosts outgoing signals and would cost roughly $40 at a computer retailer. Anyone wishing to avoid timeouts and lag issues with their Internet will most likely need to purchase a bridge.

San Francisco, Earthlink, and Google: A Case Example

San Francisco, Earthlink and Google have recently entered into a contractual agreement for the provision of a citywide WiFi network. San Francisco asked for bids from a number of telecommunication companies and chose the proposal from Earthlink and Google. Under this agreement, Earthlink will provide the entire physical infrastructure associated with building, operating and maintaining the base stations and their connection to the ISP servers. "The Earthlink led consortium is expected to spend $8 million to $10 million to build the network in San Francisco" (Flynn).

There will be two options available to actually connect to the Internet through Earthlink's network, one provided by Earthlink and one provided by Google.

> From Google, at no cost, [people] will be able to connect to the Internet at the modest speed of 300 kilobits a second, about six times as fast as a dial-up connection but slower than cable service. The trade-off is that they will see a variety of on-screen advertising, through exactly what that will look like is part of the negotiations (Flynn).

The other option is "...for an estimated $20 a month, subscribers will be able to connect through Earthlink at roughly four times that speed [1.2 megabits per second] and see no advertising" (Flynn).

Earthlink is the ISP on other municipal wireless networks in Anaheim, Milpitas, and Philadelphia. This experience with other networks helped tip the scales in Earthlink's favor in the negotiations with San Francisco. This project is the first major implementation of Internet provision by Google. There are several groups that have stated concerns about the way that Google plans to provide free Internet over this new network. Due to the nature of how Google will create revenue through the free Internet, the usage of questionably invasive advertising, many people and groups are concerned with the privacy implications behind this service. Google would need to keep cookies on the computers of its subscribers to accurately pinpoint its advertising to the right type of consumer. It is also possible that Google would keep a record of websites visited by its subscribers within its own company database and reference the user's history to try and compile advertising to show to people as they surf the Web. This service has also been seen to company outsiders as a move by Google to "...move to expand well beyond search, into areas like local advertising and real estate listings" (Flynn). This has also been seen as a potential issue, as a conflict of interest on Google's part to maintain the privacy of their subscribers.

San Francisco has established a legal framework that is designed to protect the privacy of the individuals that subscribe to this service. The agreement between the City of San Francisco and Earthlink/Google has specific articles that protect the identity of subscribers, but that agreement is superceded by any need for the police to get information on you or by any authority acting under the provisions of the Patriot Act. There is nothing mentioned about the websites that the subscribers visit being logged and kept track of and nothing about to whom that consumer information can be sold.

Municipal Wireless Networks and the Implications on Privacy

There is no doubt about the benefits of a citywide WiFi network and providing that network at no cost to those who cannot afford or who wishes to not pay for the services. The connectivity possibilities of using the Internet on one's commute to work or away from the office, but still having the ability to access vital information on the go, is tremendous. Unfortunately, the amazing possibilities associated with citywide WiFi are overshadowed by cost that many people are unaware of. The cost of this free service in is often the loss of privacy.

Organizations Concerned with Privacy

There are several organizations that are leading a coalition to bring the potential privacy concerns with using public wireless networks. These organizations aim to inform people of what is happening behind the scenes in many of the companies that provide this new Internet accessibility frontier.

The American Civil Liberties Union (ACLU) is a group of concerned citizens of the United States that have come together to represent the civil rights of people who otherwise would have little to no representation in the government of this country. They are a nonprofit organization made of lobbyists and lawyers who fight for issues that they feel are underrepresented (American Civil Liberities Union).

The Electric Frontier Foundation (EFF) is a nonprofit organization that has dedicated its existence to defend the public's rights in the expanding and unpredictable technology sector. As technology progresses, there are increasingly more holes in the legal system that have no legal precedence, and thus, create opportunities for people to exploit those holes to their own advantage and often the disadvantage of people who are not protected by the law (Defending).

The Electric Privacy Information Center (EPIC) is a nonprofit organization that researches privacy issues in the face of new technologies as they present themselves to the public. They promote open government and raise awareness of potential privacy issues to the public (Electronic).

These three groups are spearheading an effort to ensure the privacy rights of the American public are protected in respect to citywide WiFi systems. The groups agree that the potential boons of these systems are great, but they want assurances from local governments and the companies that run the systems about the security of information that is communicated on and through their networks.

Due to the nature of how these citywide systems work, the ISP has many opportunities to collect private information on its customers. Even through a simple login name, a company is able to start a database of information on the user associated with that login. Every website that they connect to is recorded and stored on a database for later use by the company. There are no laws that prohibit companies from selling this information to anyone who desires to purchase it. In most circumstances, a login name is associated with a real name, a credit card, a phone number and a mailing address. With the sale of this information the private habits and consumer habits of the individual are exposed. The privacy of this individual is now in the hands of the highest bidder to do what they wish with it (Joint).

Many companies, including Google, say any information that is collected is kept on the database for a limited amount of time and then deleted. They also state that the information is retained for intra-company use only. Despite this information, people who work for these companies are still able to access this data and use it as they please, or smuggle data out to sell to a third party. There are also security issues with outside hackers breaking into the system and gaining large quantities of data on hundreds of thousands of people.

The previously mentioned groups want to ensure that there are not only limits on what information companies are able to track and record, but additionally add requirements to what security they enable to protect the data. Part of the proposed concept to limit privacy leakage and increase security, is to allow usage of the free services without needing a login. This enables people to use the Internet with anonymity, prohibiting linking Internet habits to individuals. Where they go and what they do on the Internet can still be recorded, but there would be no link to a name and no clues other than the ones deduced from the Internet habits to their gender, age or socioeconomic status (Privacy).

Other concerns are the linkage of credit cards, and the associated data with those cards, to individuals. The networks that require payment for usage would need to retain billing information on individuals to keep their subscription current. Through this data they can gain insight to how that person lives and interacts with the World Wide Web. This data could be sold to marketers who would then target their marketing profile to certain individuals. Those people would then be at the mercy of marketers who have their own quotas to meet in regards to what they see on the Internet and what information they receive in their e-mail. The advocacy groups believe that people should not be targeted for marketing based on what websites they visit. People have a right to choose for themselves what they want to see in their e-mail inbox and what advertising they see on a day to day basis (Joint).

It is important to consider that some information will need to be collected for certain activities. People who pay for premium service would need to maintain a profile with the ISP to ensure their continued access to what they paid for. Under the Patriot Act, any power that has the authorization necessary would be able to gain access to this data and use it in an investigation. Additionally, police agencies also have authority to use this data under special circumstances. Even if someone is investigated for another crime, their habits on the Internet coming to the attention of police agencies could lead to potential problems in the future. The ISP retaining this info is very dangerous in the hands of the wrong individuals.

Conclusions

Being that Municipal Wireless is such a new and growing trend within the United States, it is not surprising that there are still many issues that need to be worked through to make it a beneficial advancement in technology. As stated before, there are two main questions that need to be answered for citizens to feel secure on a Municipal WiFi network. "How will the network protect consumer privacy and how will the network protect information transmitted by users" (Joint)? Cities have attempted to answer these questions as thoroughly as possible but there are still issues to be worked out.

One of the largest concerns for those who doubt Municipal Wireless Systems stems from legal pressure. Agencies such as the ACLE, EFF and EPIC have asked how the ISP will deal with legal demands for user's personal information. There is no question that this issue will arise in lawsuits involving the Internet and its abuse by users. It has been stated that those "who have committed no wrong should be able to participate online without fear that someone who wishes to harass or embarrass them can file a frivolous lawsuit and thereby gain the power of the court's order to discover their identities" (Joint). From past cases, it has been noted that the service provider is the first person the courts will go to for information regarding Internet and its misuse. The users of Municipal WiFi need to be certain that the ISP protects their privacy. Protection begins with immediate notification of a court subpoena for user activity. The service provider also needs to be weary of giving out personal information to the courts in cases where it is unnecessary and unjust (Joint).

Another unanswered question regards the information transmitted by the users. In order for people to feel secure about using the WiFi system, they need to be certain that hackers cannot intercept information transmitted across the Internet. If users do not have this sense of security, then there is absolutely no point in Municipal WiFi because it will not benefit users who wish to access their bank accounts and medical records online.

Municipal WiFi is a technology that will benefit not only the underprivileged of our nation's cities who cannot afford Internet, but also will provide a convenience for the rest of the community.

Municipal WiFi is still a fairly new advancement that leaves many questions unanswered. There is no doubt cities will have to continually improve the technology and its security in order to protect the users' privacy. This is the way of the future, and it will be deployed more and more in the United States as well as internationally.

Works Cited

"A Privacy Analysis of the Six Proposals for San Francisco Municipal Broadband." Eric.ORG. 5 April 2006.
<http://www.epic.org/privacy/ internet/sfan4306.html>.

Bar, Francios and Park, Namkee. "Municipal WiFi Networks: The Goals, Practices, and Policy Implications of the U.S. Case. *First Transatlantic Telecom Forum.* 22 November, 2005.

Flynn, Laura. "Some Worries as San Francisco Goes Wireless." New York Times 10 April 2006.

"Joint Letter on San Francisco Wireless Internet Access." www.epic.org 19 October 2005. <http://www.epic.org/privacy/internet/sfws10.19. 05.html>.

American Civil Liberties Union. 15 March 2007. <www.ACLU.com>.

Defending Freedom in the Digital World. Electronic Frontier Foundation. 15 March 2007. < www.Eff.org. >.

Electronic Privacy Information Center. 15 March 2007.
<www.EPIC.org.>.